Custer in '76

G. A. Custer

Custer in '76

Walter Camp's
Notes on the
Custer
Fight

Edited by
Kenneth
Hammer

University of Oklahoma Press : Norman and London

Library of Congress Cataloging-in-Publication Data

Camp, Walter Mason, 1867–1925.
  Custer in '76 : Walter Camp's notes on the Custer fight / edited by
Kenneth Hammer.
      p.   cm.
  Originally published: Provo, Utah : Brigham Young University, c1976.
  Includes bibliographical references.
  ISBN 0-8061-2279-X
  1. Custer, George Armstrong, 1839–1876. 2. Little Big Horn, Battle of
the, 1876. I. Hammer, Kenneth M., 1918–   . II. Title.
E83.876.C16   1990
973.8'2—dc20
                                                                    89-70512
                                                                      CIP
  ISBN: 0-8061-2279-X

Contents

Illustrations

1976 —

Centennial
Year of the
Little Bighorn
River Fight

This
publication
was made possible
through grants from
the Custer Battlefield
Historical and Museum
Association, Inc.,
the Charles Redd Center
for Western Studies at
Brigham Young University,
and the UW—
Whitewater
Foundation.

Note to the reader:
The three sizes of typeface in the
text and in the footnotes of *Custer in '76*
were chosen as an aid to the
reader's comprehension: Words set
in larger roman typeface denote
material written by the editor, Kenneth
Hammer; those in small roman
typeface represent Walter Camp's words;
and passages in italics indicate direct
quotations by survivors of the
Custer battle interviewed by
Walter Camp.

Preface

Walter Camp wrote an incredible volume of notes on western Indian fights. It seems astonishing that this material has not been made generally available to western history students and historians until now, but because it was in private collections for over fifty years, it has only recently become accessible. A few of the notes written by Walter Camp were made available to Dr. Charles Kuhlman, who referred to these in his excellent study *Legend Into History: The Custer Mystery*. Other than Charles Kuhlman's reference, this is the first publication of the Camp notes.

The material Camp had collected was held by his widow Emeline for some years and was acquired from her by Brigadier General William Carey Brown of Denver, Colorado, in June 1933. He classified the books, papers, photographs, letters, and Camp's notes, then transferred them to Robert Spurrier Ellison, formerly chairman of the Historical Landmark Commission of Wyoming and an intense collector of Western Americana. Ellison died on August 16, 1945, and the following year most of his large collection was presented to the Lilly Library at Indiana University, including some of Walter Camp's notes. Additional material was given to the Lilly Library on March 13, 1967, including part of Walter Camp's notes, as a gift from the estate of Mrs. Robert Ellison. The Denver Public Library also acquired a small but valuable part of Camp's notes. Other material from Walter Camp's collection, including the bulk of his notes, was acquired by the Harold B. Lee Library at Brigham Young University in 1972.

From time to time new evidence comes to light to clear up some of the mystery of the Custer fight (or sometimes to add more to the mystery). It is hoped that the publication of these selected notes on the Little Bighorn River battle will bring new information to the buff and the historian. Camp's notes on other western battles such as Platte Bridge, Sand Creek, Washita River, Adobe Walls, and Buffalo Wallows are available at the Denver Public Library, the Lilly Library at Indiana University, and the Harold B. Lee Library at Brigham Young University.

Only minor typographical changes in Camp's notes have been made. Editing has been minimized. Redundant phrases have been omitted.

Thanks are due to A. Dean Larsen of the Harold B. Lee Library at Brigham Young University, without whose efforts this project would not have been realized; to Dr. Elfrieda Lang, Curator of Manuscripts at the Lilly Library, Indiana University; to McRay Magleby, designer, and Louise Hanson, editor, at Brigham Young University Press for their patience and generous assistance; and to R. Norvelle Wathen, Jr., of Louisville, Kentucky, for his magnificent aerial photographs.

Walter Mason Camp

Biography

Sites of Indian Fights

People Interviewed

Camp's Address

Camp's Preface

Walter Mason Camp, 1867-1925.

Walter Mason Camp

Walter Mason Camp was familiar with several Indian languages, including that of the Sioux. Thus it was not unusual to see a group of western Indians visiting his Chicago office to seek advice from their friend while on their way to see government officials in Washington. Walter Camp cherished his association with the American Indians and was a welcome visitor on their reservations. He was a student of Indian life, customs, and history.

Camp was born on April 21, 1867, at Camptown, Pennsylvania, the son of Treat Bosworth Camp and Hannah A. Brown Camp. His earliest paternal American ancestor was Nicholas Camp, who came from Essex County, England, with Reverend John Elliott in 1631 and settled in Massachusetts. Both his paternal and maternal ancestors served in the Revolutionary War. One of them, Israel Camp, was a private, and Israel's son, Job Camp, was a captain.

In Wyalusing, Pennsylvania, Walter received his early education and worked on farms and in the forests. In 1883, at sixteen, as a trackwalker for the Lehigh Valley Railroad, he acquired a working knowledge of telegraphy. Pennsylvania State College graduated him in 1891 as a civil engineer. In the years that followed he became a surveyor in Fresno, California, and a draftsman in San Francisco for the Southern Pacific Company; a construction engineer, then superintendent of operations for the Rainier Avenue Electric Railway in Seattle;

1

work-train foreman, surveyor, and section foreman for the Seattle Lake Shore and Eastern Railway; a graduate student and teacher of electrical and steam engineering at the University of Wisconsin at Madison; and superintendent of track construction for the Englewood and Chicago Railway. In 1897 he became engineering editor of the *Railway and Engineering Review* (later *The Railway Review*), a position he held for over twenty-five years. He became an authority on rail construction and maintenance, and his *Notes On Track* became a college textbook. One of his associates once said, "He was the best informed man I ever knew."[1]

In addition to his interest in railroads he had a cabin in the Michigan woods and a 240-acre dairy farm at Lake Village, Indiana, where he lived during his last years. But his interest in Indian life and customs and the Little Bighorn River battle dominated his life. He was a trailblazer in his zeal to record the facts of history from the people who had witnessed that history. His vacations for twenty summers were usually spent in research among Indians and in talking with people who had survived the Little Bighorn River fight. He personally visited over forty battlefields and interviewed almost 200 survivors of western battles. Through the persistent efforts of Walter Camp and General Anson Mills the exact site of the Slim Buttes fight was found and a marker erected.

His research was not limited to Custer's last stand but included the Washita River fight, Mackenzie's raid on Dull Knife's village, Baldwin's fight with Sitting Bull on Redwater Creek, the battle of Wolf Mountain, the Lamedeer fight, the Nez Perce campaign, the Cheyenne outbreak under Dull Knife in Nebraska, Baldwin's fight on the Little Porcupine, the Yellow Hand affair, the capture of Rain-In-The-Face, the death of Sitting Bull, and the Wounded Knee and White Clay Creek affairs.

---

1. *The Railway Review,* August 8, 1925, p. 197.

He was especially interested in the Little Bighorn River fight and the Sioux campaign of 1876. In seeking Elizabeth Custer's support for his studies he once wrote:

I have been twenty years studying the Battle of the Little Bighorn, at leisure and irregular intervals, and have visited the battlefield nine different years, sometimes staying more than a week at a time. As to the trail between the Yellowstone and the Little Bighorn, I have been over all of it five times, for the purpose of historical study, and I have been over the west end of it (between the divide and the Little Bighorn) eight times. I have interviewed more than sixty survivors of Maj. Reno's command, including eight officers, and more than 150 Indian survivors of this battle.[2]

Camp wrote an incredible number of notes in interviews with survivors. Curley, the Crow Indian scout who survived the Custer fight, said to Camp that he was the most painstaking person who had ever interviewed him. Camp cherished a dream of writing a book titled *History of the 7th U.S. Cavalry.* In later years he widened his view, intending to write a history of the Indian wars. In Washington, D.C., in January 1920 he addressed the Order of Indian Wars of the United States on "Some of the Indian Battles and Battlefields" and received the honor of being the first Honorary Companion of the Order of Indian Wars.

But time caught up with Walter Camp, and he never achieved his highest ambition. He last visited the West in 1920, and his health began to fail not long after that. He retired to his farm at Lake City but continued his editorial work for *The Railway Review.* He died at Kankakee, Illinois, on August 3, 1925, at the age of fifty-eight. It is hoped that the publication of this meager bit of his notes is in a small way a memorial to this dedicated student of the Little Bighorn fight.

---

2. Letter from Walter Camp, 7740 Union Avenue, Chicago, Illinois, October 31, 1917, to Mrs. E. B. Custer, 71 East 87th Street, New York City.

Sites of Indian Battles Visited by Walter Camp

Editor's Note:

Walter Camp by his own count visited at least forty-one western battle sites. This is an approximate listing of them. In Camp's notes are numerous accounts and interviews of many — but by no means all — of these fights.

Date	Engagement	Leader
Aug. 19, 1854	Grattan	Lieut. John Grattan
July 26, 1865	Red Buttes	Sgt. Amos Custard
July 26, 1865	Platte Bridge	Lieut. Caspar Collins
Aug. 29, 1865	Tongue River	Gen. Patrick Connor
Sept. 8–10, 1865	Powder River	Col. Nelson Cole
July 20, 1866	Powder River	Lieut. Napoleon Daniels
Dec. 6, 1866	Prairie Dog Creek	Col. Henry Carrington
Dec. 21, 1866	Fetterman	Capt. Wm. Fetterman
Aug. 1, 1867	Hayfield	Lieut. Sig. Sternberg
Aug. 2, 1867	Wagon Box	Capt. Jas. Powell
Sept. 17–25, 1868	Beecher Island	Maj. Geo. Forsyth
Nov. 28, 1868	Washita River	Lt. Col. Geo. Custer
Aug. 14, 1872	Baker's Battle	Maj. Eugene Baker
Aug. 11, 1873	Pease Bottom	Lt. Col. Geo. Custer
Apr. 1, 1874	Greenleaf Creek	Frank Grounds
Apr. 12, 1874	Reno Creek	Frank Grounds
Apr. 18, 1874	Lodgegrass Creek	Frank Grounds
June 27, 1874	Adobe Walls	Billy Dixon
Aug. 19, 1874	Adobe Walls	Lieut. Frank Baldwin
Sept. 9–11, 1874	Wagon Train	Capt. Wyllys Lyman
Winter 1875–76	Ft. Pease	Frederick Pease
Mar. 17, 1876	Powder River	Col. Joseph Reynolds
June 17, 1876	Rosebud	Gen. Geo. Crook
June 25–26, 1876	Little Bighorn	Lt. Col. Geo. Custer
July 7–9, 1876	Sibley Scout	Lieut. Fred. Sibley
Sept. 9, 1876	Slim Buttes	Capt. Anson Mills
Oct. 21, 1896	Cedar Creek	Col. Nelson Miles
Nov. 25–27, 1876	Dull Knife	Col. Ranald Mackenzie
Dec. 18, 1876	Redwater	Lieut. Frank Baldwin
Jan. 7–8, 1877	Wolf Mts.	Col. Nelson Miles
May 7, 1877	Lamedeer	Col. Nelson Miles
June 17, 1877	White Bird	Capt. David Perry
June 13, 1877	Cottonwood	Ben Norton
July 11–12, 1877	Clearwater	Gen. Otis Howard
Sep. 30–Oct. 4, 1877	Bear Paw	Col. Nelson Miles
Jan. 9–22, 1877	Cheyenne Outbreak	Capt. Henry Wessells
Mar. 5, 1880	Rosebud	Lieut. Samuel Miller
Mar. 9, 1880	Little Porcupine	Lieut. Frank Baldwin
Dec. 15, 1890	Sitting Bull	Capt. Edmond Fechet
Dec. 29, 1890	Wounded Knee	Col. James Forsyth
Dec. 30, 1890	Drexel Mission	Col. James Forsyth

Location	Indians	Organization
North Platte 9 miles below Ft. Laramie	Sioux	Det. 6th Inf.
5 miles northwest of Casper, Wyo.	Sioux-Cheyenne	Det. 11th Kans. Cav.
Near site of Casper, Wyo.	Sioux-Cheyenne	Det. 11 Ohio, 11 Kans.
Mouth of Wolf Creek, Mont.	Arapahoes	Powder River Exped.
East of site of Miles City, Mont.	Sioux	Powder River Exped.
Crazy Woman Fork, Johnson Co., Wyo.	Sioux	Det. 18th Inf.
Fort Phil Kearny, Wyo.	Sioux-Cheyenne	Det. 2nd Cav.
Near Fort Phil Kearny, Wyo.	Sioux	Det. 27th Inf., 2nd Cav.
Near Fort C. F. Smith, Mont.	Sioux-Cheyenne	Det. 27th Inf. and Civ.
Near Fort Phil Kearny, Wyo.	Sioux-Cheyenne	Det. 27th Inf.
Arickaree Fork Republican River, Colo.	Sioux-Cheyenne	Civilian Scouts
Near Antelope Hills, Oklahoma	Cheyenne	7th Cav.
Pryor's Fork Yellowstone River	Piegan	2nd Cav.
Yellowstone River, Mont.	Sioux	Det. 7th Cav.
Near Mouth Greenleaf Cr., Mont.	Sioux	Bozeman Exped.
South Fork Reno Creek, Mont.	Sioux	Bozeman Exped.
Lodgegrass Creek, Mont.	Sioux	Bozeman Exped.
Canadian River, Texas	Comanche-Kiowa	Civilians
Canadian River, Texas	Comanche-Kiowa	Det. 6th Cav.
Upper Washita River, Texas	Comanche-Kiowa	Det. 5th Inf.
Mouth of Bighorn River, Mont.	Sioux	Civilians
Near Mouth Little Powder Cr., Mont.	Cheyenne	Det. 2nd, 3rd Cav.
Rosebud Creek, Mont.	Cheyenne	Det. 2nd, 3rd Cav., others
Little Bighorn River, Mont.	Sioux-Cheyenne	7th Cav.
Bighorn Mountains, Wyo.	Sioux	Det. 2nd Cav.
Slim Buttes, Harding Co., Dakota	Sioux	2, 3, 5 Cav., 4, 9, 14 Inf.
Cedar Creek, Prairie Co., Mont.	Sioux	Det. 5th Inf.
Red Fork Powder River, Wyo.	Cheyenne	3, 4, 5 Cav. Det.
Redwater Creek Near Yellowstone River	Sioux	Det. 5th Inf.
Tongue River, Mont.	Sioux	Det. 5th, 22nd Inf.
Little Muddy or Lamedeer Cr., Mont.	Sioux-Cheyenne	Det. 2nd Cav., 5, 22 Inf.
White Bird Canyon, Idaho	Nez Perce	Det. 1st Cav.
Near Cottonwood, Idaho	Nez Perce	Civilians
South Fork, Clearwater River, Idaho	Nez Perce	Det. 1 Cav., 21 Inf., 4 Art.
Near Bear Paw Mts., Mont.	Nez Perce	Det. 2, 7 Cav., 5 Inf.
Fort Robinson, Nebraska	Cheyenne	Det. 3rd Cav.
Smith Creek, Mont.	Hostiles	Det. 5th Inf.
Little Porcupine Creek, Mont.	Hostiles	Det. 5th Inf.
Grand River, South Dakota	Sitting Bull	Det. 8 Cav., Police
Wounded Knee Creek, South Dakota	Sioux	2 Inf., 7 Cav., 1 Art.
White Clay Creek, South Dakota	Sioux	Det. 7, 9th Cav., 1 Art.

People Interviewed by Walter Camp

Name	Classification	Date of Interview	Main Subject
Jacob Adams	Private, Co. H, 7th Cavalry	Oct. 14, 1910	Little Bighorn River fight
Fred C. Ainsworth	Brig. Gen., U.S.A.	Jan. 25, 1914	Personnel records
Samuel Alcott	Private, Co. A, 7th Cavalry		Yellowstone Campaign
Tom Allen	Civilian participant		Bozeman expedition of 1874
Edwin H. Allison	Pioneer, writer	June 18, 1910	Surrender of Sitting Bull
Edward Ashley	Minister at Cheyenne Agency	July 10, 1914	Wounded Knee Creek affair
William J. Bailey	Private, 17th Infantry	Oct. 8, 1910	Little Bighorn River fight
Frank D. Baldwin	First Lieut., 5th Infantry	Jan. 20, 1913 & June 16, 18, 1919	Redwater fight, Nez Perce campaign
Albert Barnitz	Captain, 7th Cavalry	May 7, 1910 & Dec. 5, 1910	Washita River fight
James M. Bell	First Lieut., Co. D, 7th Cavalry		Little Bighorn River fight
Frank Berwald	Private, Co. C, 7th Cavalry		Little Bighorn River fight
Charles H. Bischoff	Private, Co. C, 7th Cavalry	Oct. 11, 1912	Little Bighorn River fight
Charles A. Booth	2nd Lieutenant, 7th Infantry		Little Bighorn River fight
Antoine Bouyer	Brother of Mitch Bouyer	Sept. 7, 1912	Mitch Bouyer
Margaret Bowman	Survivor	July 13, 1912	Killing of Bowman family
James P. Boyle	Private, Co. G, 7th Cavalry	Feb. 12, 1913	Little Bighorn River fight
David L. Brainerd	Co. L, 2nd Cavalry	Oct. 14, 1912	Death of Lamedeer
Montfort Bray	Montana landowner	Nov. 1911	Custer Campsite June 22
Latrobe Bromwell	Private, Co. E, 7th Cavalry		Little Bighorn River fight
Samuel Burkhardt, Jr.	2nd Lieut., 25th Infantry	Jan. 16, 1913	Custer battlefield
John Burkman	Private, Co. L, 7th Cavalry	Feb. 5, 1911	Little Bighorn River fight
F. G. Burnett	Pioneer	Sept. 18, 1913	
Andrew F. Burt	Captain, 27th Infantry	Jan. 29, 1914	Ft. C. F. Smith
Adam Carrier	Blackfoot Sioux	May 21, 1909	Little Bighorn River fight
Ben Clark	Scout, 7th Cavalry	Oct. 22, 1910	Washita River fight
George Colhoff	Private, Co. D, 5th U.S. Volunteers		
Mary C. Collins	Teacher, Standing Rock Reservation	June 15, 1913	Sitting Bull
Don A. Colvin	Participant	Feb. 20, 1914	Hayfield fight
Patrick Corcoran	Private, Co. K, 7th Cavalry		Little Bighorn River fight
John Crumb		Sept. 1, 1914	Platte Bridge affair
Alfred W. Dale	Hospital steward	Mar. 2, 1912	Finding dead soldier Aug. 1876 on Rosebud
George B. Davis	2nd Lieut., 5th Cavalry		
Dennis Duffy	Participant		Hayfield fight
Winfield S. Edgerly	2nd Lieut., Co. D, 7th Cavalry		Little Bighorn River fight
Mr. & Mrs. John Farnham	Pine Ridge Residents	July 1917	
Smith F. Foster	Private, Co. L, 8th Cavalry	Nov. 1920	Buffalo Wallow fight
Ernest A. Garlington	2nd Lieut., Co. H, 7th Cavalry	Oct. 18, 1912	Little Bighorn River fight
William Garnett	Indian Scout		Death of John Richard
Frederic F. Gerard	Interpreter, 7th Cavalry	Jan. 22, 1909, & Apr. 3, 1909	Little Bighorn River fight
Francis M. Gibson	First Lieut., Co. H, 7th Cavalry	Dec. 7, 1910	Little Bighorn River fight
George W. Glenn	Private, Co. H, 7th Cavalry	Jan. 22, 1914	Little Bighorn River fight
Edward S. Godfrey	First Lieut., Co. K, 7th Cavalry	Mar. 3, 1917 & Oct. 10, 1918	Little Bighorn River fight

Name	Classification	Date of Interview	Main Subject
Fred D. Grant	Aide to Gen. Sheridan	Apr. 19, 1910 & Mar. 22, 1910	Little Bighorn River fight
William J. Gregg	Private, Co. F, 7th Cavalry		Little Bighorn River fight
Edmond Guerrier	Indian Scout	Oct. 24, 1916	The Kidder affair
John E. Hammon	Corporal, Co. G, 7th Cavalry		Little Bighorn River fight
Richard P. Hanley	Sergeant, Co. C, 7th Cavalry	Oct. 4, 1910	Little Bighorn River fight
William G. Hardy	Trumpeter, Co. A, 7th Cavalry		Little Bighorn River fight
Luther R. Hare	2nd Lieut., Co. K, 7th Cavalry	Feb. 7, 1910	Little Bighorn River fight
Thomas W. Harrison	Sergeant, Co. D, 7th Cavalry		Little Bighorn River fight
George Herendeen	Scout, 7th Cavalry	Aug. 5, 1911	Little Bighorn River fight
William Heyn	1st Sergeant, Co. A, 7th Cavalry		Little Bighorn River fight
John Henely	1st Sergeant, Co. B, 7th Cavalry in 1875		7th Cavalry
Tom Hill	Indian Survivor	July 17, 1911	Nez Perce campaign
John Hunton	Pioneer	Jun. 10, 1918	Fort Laramie, Grattan fight
John Hurst	Participant	Oct. 6, 1912 & Sept. 11, 1916	Beecher Island fight
Charles K. Innes	Co. E, 27th Infantry	Jan. 1, 1916	Ft. Phil Kearny
Daniel A. Knipe	Sergeant, Co. C, 7th Cavalry	June 16, 17, 1908	Little Bighorn River fight
Fremont Kipp	Private, Co. D, 7th Cavalry		Little Bighorn River fight
Edward LeBain		Jan. 30, 1913	Nez Perce campaign
Jesse M. Lee	First Lieut., 9th Infantry	Oct. 27, 1912	Death of Crazy Horse
Thomas LeForge	Interpreter, 7th Infantry		Indian life
A. C. Leighton	Pioneer	Feb. 23, 1914	Hayfield fight
Max Littman	Participant		Wagon Box fight
Dennis Lynch	Private, Co. F, 7th Cavalry	Oct. 1908 & Feb. 8, 1909	Little Bighorn River fight
John Mahoney	Private, Co. C, 7th Cavalry		Little Bighorn River fight
Charles Martin	Lieutenant?	Oct. 14, 1912	Rosebud fight March 17. 1876
John Martin	Trumpeter, Co. H, 7th Cavalry	Oct. 24, 1908 & May 4, 1910	Little Bighorn River fight
Edward G. Mathey	First Lieut., Co. M, 7th Cavalry	Oct. 19, 1910	Little Bighorn River fight
Starr J. Maxwell	Idaho resident	Jan. 29, 1913	Nez Perce campaign
Thomas M. McDougall	Captain, Co. B, 7th Cavalry		Little Bighorn River fight
Hugh McGonigle	Private, Co. G, 7th Cavalry	Oct. 1908 & Feb. 7, 1909	Little Bighorn River fight
John McGuire	Private, Co. C, 7th Cavalry		Little Bighorn River fight
George Mizen	With Gen. Miles at Rapid City	Feb. 12, 1918	Wounded Knee Creek affair
William Moran	Private, Co. H, 7th Infantry		Sioux Campaign of 1876
Samuel Morris		Jan. 29, 1913	Nez Perce campaign
William E. Morris	Private, Co. M, 7th Cavalry		Little Bighorn River fight
Charles Morton	2nd Lieut., 3rd Cavalry	Jan. 27, 1914	Powder River fight
Luther H. North	Pawnee Scouts		Powder River Expedition
Thomas F. O'Neill	Private, Co. G, 7th Cavalry	Oct. 18, 1910 & Oct. 13, 1912 & Oct. 12, 1919	Little Bighorn River fight

7

Name	Classification	Date of Interview	Main Subject
Mary Owen	Resident, St. Joseph, Mo.	Aug. 30, 1919	Frank Grouard
James J. Peate	Guide, QMD, U.S.A. 1868	Jan. 18, 1913	Beecher Island fight
Tom Person	Montana resident	Aug. 25, 1917	Killing of Hoover boy
Henry Petring	Private, Co. G, 7th Cavalry		Little Bighorn River fight
Edwin H. Pickard	Private, Co. F, 7th Cavalry	Jan. 26, 1913	Nez Perce campaign
Edward Pigford	Private, Co. M, 7th Cavalry		Little Bighorn River fight
Baptiste Pourier	Scout	Aug. 1918	
Richard Pratt	First Lieut., 10th Cavalry	Jan. 25, 1914	Indian affairs
Bernard Prevo	Interpreter for Crow Indians	Feb. 23, 1911 & Sept. 28, 1913	Sioux campaign of 1876
William W. Robinson	2nd Lieut., Co. B, 7th Cavalry	Jan. 26, 1909	Rosebud fight March 17, 1876
Charles F. Roe	First Lieut., 2nd Cavalry	Dec. 8, 1910 & Nov. 11, 1912	Sioux campaign of 1876
Henry Romeyn	First Lieut., 5th Infantry	Oct. 14, 1912	Nez Perce campaign
J. G. Rowton	Idaho resident		Nez Perce campaign
Stanislas Roy	Sergeant, Co. A, 7th Cavalry	May 2, 1910 & Sept. 16, 1910	Little Bighorn River fight
Hugh L. Scott	2nd Lieut., Co. E, 7th Cavalry	Oct. 1915	Nez Perce campaign
Frederick E. Server	First Sergeant, Co. G, 2nd Cavalry	July 17, 1910	Sioux campaign of 1876
Louis Shangrau			
James M. Sipes	Barber aboard Far West	May 22, 1909	Little Bighorn River fight
John Sivertsen	Private, Co. M, 7th Cavalry		Little Bighorn River fight
Herbert J. Slocum	2nd Lieut., Co. F, 7th Cavalry	Jan. 23, 1920	10th Anniversary — LBH fight
Walter S. Sterland	Private, Co. M, 7th Cavalry	Feb. 5, 1913	Little Bighorn River fight
George Stover		Aug. 1918	
Charles W. Taylor	First, Lieut., 9th Cavalry	Feb. 6, 1912	Wounded Knee Creek affair
Peter Thompson	Private, Co. C, 7th Cavalry		Little Bighorn River fight
Richard E. Thompson	2nd Lieut., 6th Infantry	Feb. 14, 1911	Little Bighorn River fight
John G. Tritten	Saddler Sergeant, 7th Cavalry		Little Bighorn River fight
Charles A. Varnum	2nd Lieut., Co. A, 7th Cavalry	May, 1909 & Jan. 25, 1913	Little Bighorn River fight
Anna Vinatieri	Widow	Mar. 1, 1912	Felix Vinatieri, Band, 7th Cavalry
Mrs. H. H. Welsh	Indian survivor	May 21, 1909	Little Bighorn River fight
Jack Whipple		Jul. 6, 1910	Little Bighorn River fight
O. H. P. Wiggins	Pioneer	Jan. 20, 1913	Captivity of Mrs. Eubanks
Ferdinand Widmayer	Private, Co. M, 7th Cavalry	Oct. 7, 1910	Little Bighorn River fight
Charles A. Woodruff	2nd Lieut., 7th Infantry		Sioux campaign of 1876
George W. Wylie	Corporal, Co. D, 7th Cavalry	Oct. 16, 1910	Little Bighorn River fight
George S. Young	2nd Lieut., 7th Infantry	Jan. 26, 1913	Sioux campaign of 1876
Eli Zigler	Participant	Jan. 25, 1913	Beecher Island affair
Andrew Good Thunder	Indian survivor	Jul. 12, 13, 1912	Wounded Knee Creek affair
Ben Bear Lies Down		Jul. 23, 1914	
Black Bear	Indian survivor	Jul. 18, 1911	Little Bighorn River fight

Name	Classification	Date of Interview	Main Subject
Black Horse			Killing of Yellow Hand
Broken Foot	Daughter of Dull Knife	Aug. 26, 1918	Cheyenne outbreak of 1878
Clarence Three Stars		Aug. 1918	Indian Affairs
Curly	Crow Indian scout	Sept. 18, 1908 & Aug. 3, 4, 1909, Jul. 19, 1910, Sept. 30, 1913	Little Bighorn River fight
Daniel Blue Hair	Private, Troop L, 3rd Cavalry		
Foolish Elk	Indian survivor	Sept. 22, 1908	Little Bighorn River fight
Frank Goings	Pine Ridge Indian	Jun. 17, 1918	About Frank Grouard
Flying By	Indian survivor	May 21, 1907 & Jul. 27, 1912	Little Bighorn River fight
Goes Ahead	Det. of Indian scouts, 7th Cavalry	Aug. 5, 1909	Little Bighorn River fight
Goose	Det. of Indian scouts, 7th Cavalry	Jul. 26, 1911	Little Bighorn River fight
Hairy Moccasin	Det. of Indian scouts	Feb. 23, 1911 & Jul. 17, 1910	Little Bighorn River fight
He Dog	Indian scout	Jul. 13, 1910	Little Bighorn River fight
Hollow Horn Bear	Indian		Beecher Island affair
Hump Little Crow	Scout with Col. Miles	Jul. 13, 1912	Killing of Lamedeer
Joseph Horn Cloud	Pine Ridge Resident	Jul. 13, 1912	Wounded Knee Creek affair
Little Sioux	Det. of Indian Scouts, 7th Cavalry		Little Bighorn River fight
Little Wolf	Indian survivor	Aug. 26, 1918	Little Bighorn River fight
Mountain Chief	Blackfoot Indian	Mar. 5, 1916	Buffalo Hunting
No Feather	Indian survivor	Feb. 15, 1915	Nez Perce Campaign
No Flesh	Indian scout		Wounded Knee Creek affair
Red Bear	Det. of Indian scouts, 7th Cavalry	July 22, 1912	Little Bighorn River fight
Round Wooden Cloud	Det. of Indian scouts, 7th Cavalry	Aug. 2, 1910	Little Bighorn River fight
Running Wolf	Det. of Indian scouts, 7th Cavalry	Feb. 6, 1913	Little Bighorn River fight
Soldier	Det. of Indian scouts, 7th Cavalry		Little Bighorn River fight
Standing Bear	Indian survivor	Jul. 12, 1910	Little Bighorn River fight
Strike Two	Det. of Indian scouts, 7th Cavalry	Jul. 23, 1912	Little Bighorn River fight
Tall Bull	Indian survivor	Jul. 22, 1910	Little Bighorn River fight
Thunder Bear	Indian		Captivity of Mrs. Eubanks
Turtle Rib	Indian survivor	Sept. 22, 1908	Little Bighorn River fight
White Bull	Indian survivor		Little Bighorn River fight
White Man Runs Him	Det. of Indian scouts, 7th Cavalry	Aug. 5, 1909	Little Bighorn River fight
Yellow Bull	Indian survivor	Feb. 13, 17, 1915	Nez Perce campaign
Young Hawk	Det. of Indian scouts, 7th Cavalry	Aug. 7, 1910 & Jul. 22, 1912	Little Bighorn River fight

Address by
Walter Camp*

"Some of the Indian Battles and Battlefields"

I consider it much of a courtesy, as well as an opportunity, to again be a guest of the Order of Indian Wars at one of its annual banquets. Being requested to address you, I have to regret that I am not able to talk of any of the events of which I am to speak from experience, for I have never seen a "wild" Indian except in the "pacified" condition. To be invited into the atmosphere of a meeting like this is, indeed, a rare privilege for one who is only a student of western history instead of one of the makers of it, such as you veterans are.

Not having participated in any of the events of the frontier days of the West, the nearest approach I have been able to make to the realities of those times has been as a student and as a trail hunter. In days gone by you often followed hot on the trail of dragging lodge poles, only to be baffled when that trail split up and scattered in all directions. Of course, the trails that I have tried to follow in these later years were not discernible by scratched earth, nor by downtrodden grass, nor by pony droppings; but I have had to take for guidance official reports and maps, often roughly drawn, and the reminiscences of survivors; and, nearly always, there are local traditions as to the landmarks; and I can tell you truly that these various sources of information often diverge, and sometimes they mislead, or they may leave one in about as much of a perplexity as did the wily Indians their pursuers whenever they took it into their heads to split up and throw following troops off their track. And another source of difficulty is the extent to which settlers have gone in changing the names of streams and other geo-

---

*From *Proceedings of the Annual Meeting and Dinner of the Order of Indian Wars of the United States Held January 17, 1920.* Washington, D.C. 38 pp., 1920.

graphical features, for the names which were official in the day of your campaigns were usually the translated Indian names.

But there were any number of times when you did overtake them, or when they overtook you, or laid in wait for you; and you fought many engagements — a battle here, or a skirmish there; or, in the small hours of morning you "jumped" a village by some stream, in a valley or canyon; and in these days it is the problem of the historical investigator to hunt up and identify the sites where the more important of these events transpired. Some of these are well known; a very few of them are marked in some shape, and many of them have been lost as far as public knowledge is concerned. The sod over the graves of many of the soldiers killed in these Indian wars has remained unbroken save by the plow of the rancher, for, by necessity, identification marks had to be dispensed with to prevent exhumation by the foe. More than once did it happen that the final resting place of the brave soldier was, prudently, trampled under the hoofs of the animals ridden by the survivors, in order that all trace of burials might be obliterated. Thus, often has it occurred that identification of the resting places of the dead, as well as of the site of the engagement, was lost.

During frontier times the great highways across the plains and into the mountains were by way of the Arkansas, the Platte, and the Missouri rivers. The last named, only, was navigated, but in the wide valleys of the other two streams were the historic Santa Fe trail, following, generally, the course of the Arkansas until it reached the mountains; and along the Platte and its northern branch went the Overland trail, from which, well into the mountains, the Oregon trail branched off. Along both of these trails were numerous forts and supply depots, and many battles were fought right on the trails, particularly so in the case of the trail along the North Platte, but there were hundreds of engagements at long distances from lines of communication. As resourceful as was the Indian, he was, in the end, at a disadvantage when pursued by the indomitable men of the Regular Army under determined commanders. On good grazing the tough and hardy Indian pony was not easily to be overtaken, but when, in deep snows and the blasts of winter, he had to be put on forage of cottonwood bark, he stood a poor chance of getting away from the grain-fed, long-legged "American" horse and the Missouri mule. Even civilized war is hell, so we have been told by the best of authority, but war on Indians was certainly hell on horse flesh. In civilized warfare the contestants usually "dig in" or "hole up" for winter, but experience taught that the way to hit an Indian "under the belt" was to fight him in winter time; and the tactics of Custer and

11

Crook and Miles, not to mention others, were planned to that advantage.

The first severe blow struck the Indians after the Civil War was the destruction of the Cheyenne Chief Black Kettle and his camp on the Washita, November 27, 1868. This was a village of peaceable Indians, but no investigation could be made in advance of the attack, and the Indian custom of shedding the blood of the other race for the sake of revenge, without respect to who the individuals might be, was initiated here. The stroke did have the intended effect, as events afterward proved, and General Sheridan always insisted that Custer made no mistake. The site of that historic fight has not yet been marked. It is in Roger Mills County, Oklahoma, not far from the county seat town of Cheyenne. That part of the country is thickly settled and the land whereon the village stood is under cultivation.

Four years previous to this the unfortunate Black Kettle, while encamped on Sand Creek in Colorado, in obedience to the request of the governor of the territory that all peaceable Indians assemble at designated places, was attacked by Colorado militia, under Colonel Chivington, as you will remember. His village was destroyed; a large number of his people — women and children and old men — were massacred, and the survivors were scattered over the country. At the moment of attack the American flag was flying over the lodge of Black Kettle.

The site of that historic affair has not been marked. If it were possible we, as a nation, doubtless had rather the event could be forgotten. But while Black Kettle and his own band remained peaceable after this outrage, there were other Cheyennes, and Arapahoes, who did not forget it, and the toll of life exacted by them on defenseless settlers of Kansas and Nebraska during the next few years must have exceeded, by ten times, the number of Indians that Chivington and his men had laid low with shots and bayonets on Sand Creek.

Now, I shall not proceed chronologically in going over the list of battlefields which I have in mind, because to do so would keep me jumping all around the plains country, from one stream to another and from Texas to the Canadian border. But going forward now to 1868, in September, or a couple of months earlier than the battle of the Washita, with which I started, we have a very gallant and determined defense made by Lieutenant Colonel George A. Forsyth and his little command of fifty enlisted scouts on the Arickaree fork of the Republican in eastern Colorado. While these men were without military training, or largely so, they were plainsmen who had seen much service in that kind of country, and how efficiently they did their duty has gone down into history. The point is seventeen miles south of Wray, Colorado, on the Burlington Railroad, and it is marked by a splendid monument, the money for erecting it being appropriated jointly by the States of Colorado and Kansas. The site was not identified until 1898, or thirty years after the fight, when three of the survivors came out looking for it and actually passed it unawares. They would have given up the hunt as a failure had it not been, quite by accident, too, that a rancher who had settled there some twenty years previously had noticed horse bones and rope halters on what is commonly known as the "Island" (but actually it is not such), and directed them to a spot, which, after some reflection and exchange of recollections, they finally recognized as the scene of the battle.

In July of the year following, 1869, General Carr, then Major of the 5th U.S. Cavalry, with part of his regiment and some Pawnee Indian scouts, attacked the village of Tall Bull and his Cheyennes not far from where this fight of Forsyth's occurred, destroyed the camp, killed a number of Indians, and scattered the rest of them. Tall Bull was among the slain. The spot is on a divide between the Republican and the South Platte in eastern Colorado, and the place is not marked.

Before leaving the south let us go back to Oklahoma and Texas where in 1874 General Miles, with the 5th Infantry and part of the 6th Cavalry, and Colonel Mackenzie, with the 4th Cavalry, fought several engagements each in the fall of that year and greatly discouraged the Southern Cheyennes, Arapahoes, Kiowas and Comanches, who had left their reservations to resent the wholesale slaughter of buffaloes by white hunters, who were killing them solely for their hides. The fighting began with the famous battle of Adobe Walls in the latter part of June. The site of that fight is still far from a railroad and is not marked. There were two battles there — first, as already noted, by buffalo hunters, who defended themselves inside of store buildings for cover, with but small loss, while inflicting severe punishment upon the Indians; and later in the year a minor engagement was fought in the same vicinity by some of General Miles's scouts against a party of Indian raiders.

The site of the famous Buffalo Wallow fight, of September 12, between Indians and four soldiers and two civilians (Chapman and Dixon) has not been discovered. The site of Captain Wyllys Lyman's fight, while corralled with a wagon train and surrounded by a big band of Indians for three days, about the same time, is known but not marked. The rifle pits which he dug, with plenty of "45-70" empty cartridge shells lying about, are still clearly in evidence.

On August 30 and again in November, other troops of General

Miles fought important engagements farther south in the Panhandle of Texas, but I have been unable to get any information as to the exact locations of these events, and I therefore infer that they have not been marked. The points where Colonel Mackenzie fought his battles have been identified, so I am advised, but have not been marked.

Along the main Platte and the South Platte there were many engagements of a minor character, but a great deal of bloodshed, principally through attacks on ranches and wagon trains and small detachments that were doing escort duty. In December 1864 Indians attacked the stage station about a mile from Julesburg, where there was a post, and a relief party of soldiers of the 7th Iowa Cavalry who were sent out were cut off and about fifteen of them were killed. This was a running fight, and I do not think that any marker has been placed for it.

Below the forks of the Platte there were two noted posts: Forts McPherson and Kearny, and these were needed supply and refuge points on the old Overland trail. The first conflict with the Sioux was on the North Platte, some distance below the renowned Fort Laramie. Every one has heard of the Grattan "Massacre," where Lieutenant Grattan, with some twenty-eight or twenty-nine soldiers of the 6th Infantry from Fort Laramie, while trying to arrest some Indians, was attacked and all killed. He was in a big Indian village and showed poor discretion in the use of threatening and abusive language over a matter of no consequence and for which the Indians were hardly blamable at all. The place where this encounter occurred is not marked.

This fight took place in August 1854, and the next year General Harney went out to take revenge, and he got it by attacking a band of Sioux at Ash Hollow between the two Plattes in western Nebraska. Some eighty or more women and children were killed while trying to run away, and Harney made a reputation; but the revenge which the Indians took on emigrant trains and settlers, as usual, brought great hardship and terror upon the people of the frontier. Some ten years later in 1865 some 7th Iowa troops were attacked near the mouth of Horse Creek, farther up the North Platte, and an officer and one or two men were killed. These troops were escorting Indians on their way to some point near the forks of the Platte when the Sioux decided they did not want to go further and killed the officer, waded or swam the Platte, and escaped. The site is not marked.

This year was notorious for desperate fighting up in the vicinity of Platte Bridge, which was just above where the city of Casper now is. The city was named for Lieutenant Caspar Collins of the 11th Ohio Cavalry, who was killed in the battle of Platte Bridge in the latter part of July 1865. On the same day Sergeant Amos J. Custard, with some eighteen men, while escorting a wagon train, was surrounded, and all of the men with him were killed. This fight took place a few miles above the bridge, while Lieutenant Collins's battle began within a mile of the north end of the bridge and continued right up to the bridge. The site of neither battle is marked. From Deer Creek, below, to Red Buttes, above Platte Bridge, there were numerous engagements between small parties of soldiers and band of Indians, with considerable loss of life to the troops.

A few weeks later General Conner, with quite a force of California, Kansas, Nebraska, Missouri, and other volunteer troops of the Civil War organizations, left Fort Laramie for a campaign against the northern Indians. His command was in two columns, he, personally, conducting one part of it north or northwest to the Powder River country and thence over to the Tongue, while another large force started from Omaha and marched north, passing to the east of the Black Hills, thence northwest to the Little Missouri and on west to the lower Powder River. Conner's column struck an Arapahoe village on the Tongue, pretty well up toward the Bighorn mountains. He attacked and destroyed the camp and killed a few Indians, capturing some women, among whom was the wife of the leader, Black Bear. This fight was on the main Tongue River, and the site is not marked.

Conner's plan was to meet Colonel Cole, the commander of the eastern column, at or near the mouth of the Tongue on the Yellowstone. Cole followed down the Powder nearly to its confluence with the Yellowstone, when he was attacked by Sioux in large force and harassed continually for many days. For lack of grazing the horses fell off in flesh and, in a big snow storm during September, more than half of them died. Although both he and Conner had plenty of Indian scouts, they missed each other and failed to connect. Cole's command ran entirely out of supplies, nearly the whole force were set afoot, they wore out their shoe leather, and the expedition came near ending up in disaster.

On the march northward General Conner had built a supply station, which he named Fort Conner, on the west side of the Powder near the mouth of Dry Fork. Here, fortunately, he had left men and supplies, but the fact was unknown to Cole, and the men of the latter, very hungry and footsore, had made their way up the Powder to within two days' march of Fort Conner before they became aware that relief was nearer than Fort Laramie. A day or two later Conner, with a long wagon train and sixty days' supply of provisions, joined Cole at the fort.

Conner was much disappointed at the way things had turned out, and, greatly to his chagrin, here received dispatches directing him to march to Fort Laramie and hand over the command of the district to a Regular Army officer. This was done, the volunteer troops were sent east and mustered out of the service, and this was the last of Indian fighting by volunteer State troops on the plains.

Conner's losses in killed amounted to only one man, but a number with Cole's command were killed and buried, no one, at this day, knows where. Neither are the sites of his engagements known. Some of his artillery was rolled into deep water in the Powder and abandoned; and in recent years settlers have picked up rusty gun barrels and sabers on sand bars and at other places along the river, that are supposed to have been some of the abandoned property of this command.

During the next year, 1866, General Henry B. Carrington, with a battalion of the 18th U.S. Infantry, went out on the Bozeman trail on essentially the same route that had been traveled by Conner, and built three forts. The first of these was at the site of Fort Conner, which was only a ramshackle affair and tumbled down; so a new post was built and named Fort Reno. Carrington went on to the forks of the Pineys and built a fort which he named after himself, but later this was changed, by official order, to Fort Phil. Kearney. Still further on, at the point where the Bozeman trail (commonly known in those days as the Virginia City trail) crossed the Bighorn River, Fort C. F. Smith was built and garrisoned. These were among the historic army posts of the West, although garrisoned less than two years, being abandoned in the spring of 1868. The site of Fort Reno is marked only by debris, principally fallen chimneys of the buildings. It was filed on by a homesteader in 1918 and now is probably a plowed field, as the land is level and the soil fertile. Ten miles distant, on a main automobile route, a pretentious granite monument has been erected, with the simple inscription "Fort Reno." The site of Fort Phil. Kearney is a cultivated field and is not marked. The site of Fort C. F. Smith is still identified by portions of the adobe walls of some of the barracks.

During the less than two years that these three posts were occupied there was almost incessant fighting, and, on the whole, the troops suffered many losses from the Indians, who lay in wait to cut off detachments and to attack supply trains. A few days after Carrington had reached the Pineys, a party of officers and their families, with a small escort of soldiers, was attacked at the crossing of Crazy Woman Creek, and Lieutenant Napoleon H. Daniels was killed. On December 6 there was a skirmish some miles north of Fort Phil. Kearny, in which

Lieutenant H. S. Bingham was killed; and two weeks later the historic Fetterman disaster occurred, in which three commissioned officers (Fetterman, Brown and Grummond), seventy-six enlisted men, and two civilians were killed, no man getting away to tell the tale. The site of this battle has been marked by a well-constructed monument of granite boulders six feet in diameter and eighteen feet high.

Other soldiers and civilians had been surprised in the vicinity of the fort from time to time and killed. Wood for fuel had to be hauled from the mountain canyons about six or seven miles distant, and during the summer of 1867 the wood trains were attacked almost daily and compelled to corral and make a stand until reinforcements could be sent out from the post to drive off the Indians. On a high butte near the fort from the top of which they could overlook the whole country, a non-commissioned officer and squad of men were kept constantly on guard during day time to signal the fort whenever a wood train in the direction of the mountains or a supply train on the main trail was attacked by Indians. On the morning of August 2 the Indians appeared in large force, about 1,500 of them, as I have learned from their own accounts, with the intention of cutting off the wood trains in the mountains. Fortunately for the main train, it had proceeded nearly to the fort before the Indians showed up, but the guard for the wood camps and roads into the fort, consisting of part of Company C, 27th U.S. Infantry, commanded by Captain James Powell and Lieutenant John C. Jenness, had to leave their camp and take refuge, on short notice, within a corral of empty wagon boxes that had been used to hold cattle during night time. These two officers and twenty-five enlisted men (there were no civilians at this corral) made a most gallant defense for more than three hours until relief could be sent out from the fort. The Indians, who were very poorly armed, had planned to rush on the corral afoot, but greatly to their surprise, they, for the first time in fighting infantry, encountered breech-loading rifles. Lieutenant Jenness and two soldiers were killed and several others wounded.

The loss to the Indians in killed was surprisingly small, according to their own authentic accounts, and I want to say that I have generally found them to be reliable on such matters. Captain Powell estimated that he had killed as many as sixty of them, but the Indians report a much smaller number, although they say that more than a hundred of wounded had to be hauled off on travois. A significant fact which has a bearing on the number of Indians killed is that only one Indian body fell into the hands of the defenders, although it is a fact that many Indians had charged up within a hundred feet of the corral.

A clear-headed old man who survived this fight has told me that he never saw such poor shooting by soldiers in his many years of experience at Indian fighting. Anyhow, the shooting was sufficient to keep the Indians out of the corral, and the event has passed into history as one of the most hotly contested engagements with Indians that occurred in all the fighting of the plains, and such it undoubtedly was. It is commonly referred to as the "Wagon Box" fight.

A survivor of this battle, Max Littmann, who visited the place in 1916, pointed out a spot which seemed clear to him as the site of the battle; and an iron post, with an inscribed brass cap, has been planted there. However, another survivor came along three years later and disagreed with this location, and thus the matter stands. There are still five more survivors known to be living, and these, or some of them, ought to be consulted before proceeding with the erection of the monument that is now provided for. Contentions over such questions in the West often run to partisan extremes. When I first visited this locality nine years ago, I found five conjectural locations for the supposed site of the corral where this fight occurred, each clique of settlers being confident in their selection of the site, yet none of them had ever met a survivor of the battle.

The historic battle at Fort C. F. Smith occurred on August 1, 1867, when Lieutenant Sigismund Sternberg, with less than twenty enlisted men and a few civilians guarding haymakers about three miles from the fort, stood off more than a thousand Indians from about 9:00 a.m. to 5:00 p.m. The commander of the post, being aware of the fighting all that time, refused to allow a relief party to go out, although officers were eager to go, all day long; and, finally, as the shades of evening approached, he consented to their very urgent appeals. In this battle Lieutenant Sternberg and two men were killed, and no little loss was inflicted on the Indians. It was fully the equal of the "Wagon Box" fight in desperate defense, and the odds against the men in the corral of logs was about the same. There were fewer defenders than was the case at the "Wagon Boxes," and the fight lasted twice as long. As was the case at the "Wagon Box" also, not many of the Indians were armed with anything better than bow and arrows, or the result in both instances might have been different. The site of this battle is known, but it has not been marked.

The Fort Laramie treaty of 1868 gave to the Sioux and Northern Cheyennes all the country between the North Platte and the Yellowstone, and from the Bighorn mountains to a line east of the Black Hills, for a perpetual hunting ground; or, in the language of the treaty, "as long as grass grows and water flows." However, the "license" with which the whites regarded this poetic agreement amounted to virtual rejection of it almost from the start, and conflicts with these northern Indians kept up. The Indians, also, seeing that the treaty rights were not being respected by the whites, overran the boundary lines and committed depredations both south of the North Platte and north of the Yellowstone. While large Indian populations under Red Cloud and Spotted Tail had settled down on reservations, there were bands of discontented Sioux under Crazy Horse and Sitting Bull and Cheyennes under several leaders who had no use for the reservations except for occasional trade, and they preferred to roam the wilderness unhindered and to live on the buffalo in the way of their forefathers.

The surveys of the Northern Pacific Railway in 1872 and 1873 had to be conducted under strong escorts of soldiers, and attacks were frequent. These attacks occurred at points all the way across North Dakota and along the Yellowstone. What is known as "Baker's Battleground," where Major Eugene M. Baker, of the 2nd U.S. Cavalry, had a minor engagement, is a few miles east of the present town of Billings and is marked in temporary fashion. General Stanley, whose command included nearly all of the 7th U.S. Cavalry under General Custer and infantry besides, had two engagements with the Sioux in August 1873, Custer being personally engaged in both of these. One of the fights occurred on the north side of the Yellowstone, a few miles west of where Fort Keogh is now, and the other, a week later (August 11), was on the same side of the river, on what later came to be known as Pease Bottom. Both of these sites have been identified and temporarily marked. Custer once made an effort to cross his men over in bull boats to fight the Sioux on the south side of the Yellowstone. The next day, however, the Sioux crossed by swimming their ponies over and attacked him on his own side, near the mouth of the Bighorn. In this fight Custer had a horse wounded and his orderly was killed. Lieutenant Charles Braden was severely wounded.

The next year, 1874, a party of mining prospectors, organized at Bozeman, invaded the Indian country south of the Yellowstone and had several hard fights with the bands of Sitting Bull and Crazy Horse. From the standpoint of the invaders, this expedition was successful. Although followed by large numbers of Sioux for more than a month, they went just where they pleased, with plenty of supplies hauled by horse and ox teams, and they treated the foe with contempt. In two of the battles the bodies of Indians, both alive and dead, fell into their hands and were treated in just the way Indians would have done had the situation been reversed. Invariably these men "dug in" every night, and the rifle pits in each of nine locations are still very well preserved, and some of these have been marked by wooden signboards. The manner in which they picked their ground for a fortified camp in each place would, I think, be a worthy study for the military historian. Their entire route up the Rosebud was traversed by General Custer two years later on the campaign from which he never returned.

During this same year, 1874, General Custer made an exploration of the Black Hills, and his official reports, together with those of the geologists and newspaper correspondents who went with him, led the whole East to believe that the Hills were full of gold "from the grass roots down," as the current rumors expressed it. In spite of military forces on all the roads to turn people back and the destruction of outfits and wagon trains in some instances, no less than eleven thousand miners, according to creditable estimates, had gotten into the Black Hills by the fall of 1875. This violation of the treaty soon brought matters to a head with the Indians, for by the spring of 1876, Sioux from all of the Missouri River agencies and from the Red Cloud and Spotted Tail agencies in northern Nebraska had gone out and joined the hostiles under Sitting Bull and Crazy Horse.

This brings us to the heavy fighting of the year 1876, the history of which has been much written, and I need not go into the details of the plans for the campaigns nor follow all the movements of the troops that were marched and countermarched over the plains and through the mountains that year. If there be some here who did not participate in those campaigns, however, let me say that the Sioux and Cheyennes who went out to fight that year carried firearms almost to a man; and not a few of them carried repeating rifles of the Winchester pattern, which were just then coming into favor with big game hunters all over the country. No longer did Army officers idly boast that they would not hesitate to undertake to "ride through the whole Sioux nation" with a few companies of veteran soldiers, as some of them had in times past been quoted as saying.

The first clash came on St. Patrick's day on the Powder, just a few miles north of the Montana line. Here Colonel Reynolds, who, according to his own statement, had never seen an Indian village before, with detachments of the 2nd and 3rd Cavalry attacked and captured a camp of 104 lodges, but sans Indians, who ran off far enough to get their families out of harm's way and then returned and hung about the camp sharpshooting while the soldiers were trying to burn it. One Indian was killed, and four soldiers — some dead and some alive but wounded — fell into the hands of the Indians. Before the destruction of the camp was complete, Reynolds ordered the thing abandoned and marched off. He drove off with him a large herd of captured Indian horses, but nearly all of these were recovered by the Indians that night. The site of this fight has been well identified but not marked, although government headstones for the four soldiers who perished there have, through the kind offices of General Mills and Major Lemly, been shipped out to Wyoming at the nearest railroad point and will be placed on the battlefield next summer.

Three months later, June 17, General Crook, commanding in person, met the whole congregation of the Sioux and the Cheyennes at the head forks of the Rosebud in an all-day fight. Crook's forces here amounted to 1,028 men, all told, and for an hour or two the way the conflict would turn seemed uncertain. He lost nine men killed on the field and more than thirty wounded, and had fired away so much ammunition that, thinking discretion the better part of valor, retired back to the foot of the Bighorn mountains, whence he had come. Could Crook have pressed on at this time there might never have been any Little Bighorn to record in history, for on the day of this fight Custer was still on the Yellowstone; and the point where Custer did strike the Indians eight days later, to his utter defeat and annihilation, is only forty miles from where Crook fought identically the same Indians on June 17.

The battle of the Rosebud extended all the way from the bend of the creek, where Tom Penson's ranch now is, to the forks, a distance of about 2¾ miles. It has not been marked, but government headstones for the men killed there, nine in all, have been shipped to the nearest railroad point and will be set up on the battlefield. The remains of these men now lie scattered about the fields, where some of them have been upturned by the plow, and along a side hill, where, supposedly, they were dug up by Indians soon after the battle.

As for the battle of the Little Bighorn, you know that the site has been marked by a monument on which are inscribed the names of the men killed with both Custer and Reno, 263 in all, of whom 207 were killed with General Custer. This was a battle in three fights, the one in which Custer fell and where the monument stands being known as the engagement on Custer ridge. The sites of Reno's fight in the river bottom, where he lost twenty-nine men killed, and on the bluffs where he lost twenty-seven more killed and some sixty wounded, have not been marked but should be. Leaving Custer's part of this fight out of consideration entirely, these two fights under Major Reno were about the hottest affairs of the kind, where the troops got out of it still in shape to fight on, that the historian will find opportunity to study. There were "heaps" of Indians there and, as they say, they had "heaps of guns"; they were not handicapped for lack of firearms as they were in the fighting soon after the Civil War.

After the battle of the Little Bighorn, the Indians pulled straight for the Bighorn mountains. Soon after, General Crook's forces were reinforced by the addition of the 5th Cavalry, under Merritt and Carr, and the Indians led him a long chase. He followed their trail down the Rosebud to within a day's march of the Yellowstone, where he was joined by General Terry and some 1,100 men. The combined forces, about 2,500 men, struck across to the Tongue, on the Indian trail, which was not hard to find, as the Indians had burned up the grass behind them. From the Tongue the trail led to the Powder, during the rainiest August ever known in that country, and beast and man plodded on with great difficulty. Still, the trail led on toward the Little Missouri, and, at length, the buffalo being all chased out of the country and the grass very poor or gone entirely, both commanders thought best to hunt for supplies.

General Terry pulled straight for Fort Abraham Lincoln on the Missouri, but Crook elected to make a bee line for the Black Hills, where he would, if he could reach them, be back in his own department and likely be able to find supplies in the mining camps. Crook had about 1,500 men, and his movement to the Black Hills has gone down in history as the "starvation march." Although his outfit was far more experienced in Indian fighting, yet he was in much the same fix as had been Colonel Cole with his 1,400 volunteer soldiers on the Powder eleven years before. More than 400 horses played out and had to be killed, the majority of the men were afoot, either without horses or leading them, the rations were exhausted and the men were living on horse flesh, wild plums, and bullberries. Seeing that he would never get to his destination with all of his force unless unusual measures were taken, he dispatched Captain Anson Mills ahead with the pick of the horses and 150 picked men to go to the Hills and return to meet him with supplies of food.

But this march was not to be without glory, for Mills, plodding on through rain and fog, ran into an Indian camp in broad daylight, sought cover, and the next morning fell upon them while they slept, or just missed doing so. He got the camp of thirty-seven lodges with the herd of fat horses and held on. Without anticipating any such result, a long-sought object was here attained, for, much by accident they had "found Indians" — more than enough for Mills — and enough to put up considerable of a fight against all of Crook's command. Mills had found the camp at the foot of Slim Buttes, on the east side; and just through a gap, but eight miles distant, was the whole outfit of Sioux and Cheyennes that Crook had been following all the way from the Bighorns.

When the Indians had heard from the refugees from the captured village what had happened, they got up onto their horses and rushed through the Buttes, but, very fortunately for Mills, Crook arrived simultaneously with his whole force, and there was skirmishing and fighting all over a township of open country the rest of that day. Thus, Slim Buttes became a historic affair, and King and Bourke and Finerty have written classic accounts of it.

In this battle three men were killed, an officer lost a leg, and many were wounded. On the Indian side the loss in killed was more, and there were a few prisoners, whom Crook turned loose unharmed when he marched away the next morning. The site of this battle was lost for more than forty years; but it has been found, and a monument will be placed on the site of the village next summer. The remains of the men killed and buried there were taken up by the Indians, and they lie there on top of ground until this day. Government headstones have been sent to be set where these remains will be reburied.

With the exception of small parties of agency Indians who sneaked back to their reservations from time to time, the great mass of the Sioux and Cheyennes who were out fighting in 1876 remained out all the following winter. Crook planned to hit them in their winter quarters, and he found the Cheyennes, under Dull Knife, on the Red Fork of the Powder, up in the foothills of the Bighorn mountains. There Colonel Mackenzie surprised them in the late days of November 1876 and won the most decisive victory of troops over the Indians of that year, destroying their camp and driving the whole population out into bitter winter weather. In this battle Lieutenant John A. McKinney was killed. The site is well identified, but not marked.

Up north, on the Yellowstone, General Miles, with the 5th Infantry and some of the 2nd Cavalry, operating from Fort Keogh cantonment, kept up the same tactics. After the middle of December a portion of his command, under Captain Baldwin, with foot soldiers wading through deep snow, attacked Sitting Bull's Indians twice, on the Missouri and on Redwater Creek and on the latter occasion destroyed their village. The sites of these events have not been marked. Three weeks later, or in January 1877, General Miles met the forces of

Crazy Horse on Tongue River, about ninety miles from the cantonment, shelled them out with artillery and pursued them some distance
up the stream. The site of this engagement is known, but not marked.
In the following May, General Miles surprised and captured the camp
of Lame Deer, a Minneconjou Sioux chief, on what is now known as
Lame Deer Creek, near Lame Deer agency of the Northern Cheyenne
reservation. By mistake, Lame Deer, who was trying to give up peace-
ably, was menacingly driven to self-defense, was killed and the camp
was destroyed. The site is pointed out by Cheyennes who were
present, but it is not marked.

Except for occasional raids that were made by Sitting Bull's band
that had run over the line into Canada, there was now a lull in the
fighting with the Sioux, but, after outrageous treatment, the Nez Perces,
hitherto a peaceable lot of Indians, took to war, or, rather, were driven
into it, and they led General Howard far from his base. The heaviest
of the fighting was with Captain David Perry of the 1st Cavalry in
White Bird canyon in June 1877 on the Clearwater in Idaho; at Big
Hole, on the other side of the Bitter Root mountains; at Canyon Creek,
north of the Yellowstone; and on Snake Creek, not far from the Canadian line, commonly known as the battle of Bear's Paw mountain.
Here the remnant of the Nez Perces, under Joseph, after White Bird
and his band had gotten away, surrendered. The site is well identified,
but not marked. At Big Hole, where three officers were killed and
several more wounded, including General Gibbon, the commanding
officer, a granite monument marks the site of the battle. The sites of
the battles in White Bird canyon and on the Clearwater have not been
marked.

In 1878 the Bannocks went to war, and there was some fighting in
Idaho, but without large casualties on either side. The windup came
when a number of Indians who had sought asylum east of the mountains were caught by General Miles, with an escort on a pleasure trip,
in their camp on Clark's Fork and routed, losing their lodges. In this
fight a veteran officer, Captain Andrew S. Bennett of the 5th Infantry,
was killed. The site has not been marked, and the settlers, so I have
learned by correspondence, do not agree as to the exact site.

As to the wars with the Apaches, I am not able to give you any
information other than what I have gained from reading the books and
magazines. I will conclude, therefore, by jumping ahead twelve years
to the culminating event of the Ghost Dance war, if it may be called a
war, the battle of Wounded Knee. Anyhow, a good many troops were
called into the fuss, and it fell to the lot of the organization that became

so famous for Indian fighting, the 7th Cavalry, to fight the last of the hard battles of the Indian wars. I will not go into the details of the engagement any more than to say that neither side was expecting a fight, the Indians having surrendered the day before and had camped with the troops over night. The blunder that started the firing was committed by one of the Sioux, so they admit themselves. The site of this battle is marked by a marble monument erected by Joseph Horn Cloud, a son of one of the Indians who was slain there, and the inscription is in the Sioux language. The names of the forty-seven heads of families who were killed there are included in this inscription, and the battle is designated the "Big Foot Massacre." The monument in memory of the soldiers who were killed there has been erected at the old home of the 7th Cavalry, Fort Riley, Kansas.

I will take occasion in closing to pay deserved tribute to the distinguished toastmaster of the evening, General Godfrey. I began with the battle of the Washita in 1868, and he was there and is now the only surviving officer who participated in that engagement. I told you about the Little Bighorn, and he was there, commanding a company. I have told you of Bear's Paw, and he was there, shot off his horse, desperately wounded. I finished with Wounded Knee, and, behold, he was there. He participated in every one of the four historic battles that made this regiment so famous in Indian campaigns, and these four stand out conspicuously among the illustrious events of the plains.

Camp's Preface to the Interviews[1]

On the afternoon of June 25, 1876, the 7th U.S. Cavalry, commanded by Lieut. Col. Geo. A. Custer, was following the trail of a large body of Indians westward into the valley of the Little Bighorn River in the . . . territory of Montana. Without certain knowledge of the location of the Indian camp, the regiment, numbering 617 officers and men, with about 53 Indian and civilian scouts and packers additional,[2] had been divided into four parts, or battalions, about noon of that day. Two of these battalions together, comprising 53 percent of the regimental strength, were in the advance and were marching close together, up to a point within 5 miles of the village. Here informal and hasty reports from some of the scouts, and incorrect deductions by Custer from his own observations, led to the wrong conclusion that the Indians were fleeing before them. Without any attempt at investigation Custer hurried forward the battalion of Maj. Reno, comprising 20 percent of the regimental strength, with the scouts additional, to overtake the Indians and bring them to battle, with assurance that he (Reno) would be supported. Reno did exactly as he was ordered, by proceeding some 4½ miles and bringing the Indians to battle, in the valley, supposing all the while that Custer would be at his back to support. In this Custer failed to keep his agreement and Reno at once found more Indians than he could handle, and, after fighting for 20 minutes or less, fell back, without attempting to cover his retreat, thereby suffering heavy loss.

---

1. Walter Camp field notes, folder 107, BYU Library. Camp's preface was intended for his projected book. (Camp's notes here and in following interviews are reproduced almost verbatim with very little editing in order to preserve their authenticity and flavor. — Ed.)

2. In Walter Camp's notes the numbers here are missing. Numbers have been added. — Ed.

We will now go back to Custer. Instead of keeping within support-
ing distance of Reno he had changed his mind and marched his battalion, comprising 33 percent of the regimental strength, on a diverg-
ing route. After proceeding 3 miles he suddenly came into view of the
valley and saw the village, all standing and no Indians running away.
Here, for the first time, he became aware of his mistaken impressions
of the situation.

At this point the two battalions were more than one mile apart
within full view of each other but with nearly impassable ground and
a river between them. Reno was in the valley and Custer on high
bluffs to the eastward, and as yet, neither had engaged the Indians.
Custer continued three miles farther, with a view to attack the village
on the flank, and had passed out of sight of Reno's division before
Reno's battle began. Custer may have heard, but he never saw, Reno's
fight or any part of it.

Custer proceeded within menacing distance of the large village on
the opposite side of the stream and about 1½ miles farther down the
valley than Reno's advance but did not attack it, at least he did not
attack with determination. The Indians swarmed out to meet him,
and, between 15 and 30 minutes after Reno had retreated, the battalion
of Custer became engaged, fell back from the river and still farther
down the valley, to a high ridge. The Indians who had gone out to
meet Reno had now returned and joined in the fight against Custer.
On this ridge all of Custer's battalion were surrounded and killed with
the exception of one Crow scout, who escaped from the ridge early
in the battle. This fight from the time it started — down near the
river, lasted between one and two hours.

About the time Custer's fight began, or a little before, the third
division of the regiment, comprising 20 percent of its strength and commanded by Benteen, joined Reno at a point on the bluffs east of the
river, to which Reno had retreated. Here both battalions, entirely
ignorant of Custer's plans or movements but hearing his firing, remained two hours, undecided what to do. Meantime these two battalions were joined by the fourth, comprising the pack train and its
escort, and bringing up the remaining 27 percent of the regiment. As
no one in particular was exercising command, one captain, out of
impatience, had advanced a mile or more with his troop in the direction of Custer, going within full view of about half of Custer's battlefield 2 or 2½ miles distant in an air line. Custer's resistance had now
ended and the officers of this troop saw, through their glasses but without understanding at the time what they saw, the Indians killing

Custer's wounded. In about a half hour three more troops joined this one in advance, but were soon attacked by the victorious Indians leaving the scene of the Custer fight and fell back 1½ miles to favorable ground where a stand was made. Here the Indians attacked savagely and in great force. The fighting lasted the remainder of the day and all the next, with further losses, in addition to those of Reno's first fight and that of Custer, of about 27 men killed and 45 wounded. On the evening of the second day the Indians took down their village and left the valley, in advance of the approach of a column of cavalry and infantry under generals Terry and Gibbon, and during the forenoon of the third day the remnant of the 7th Cavalry was relieved by this force.

Such, very briefly, are the general facts concerning the eventful battle of the Little Big Horn. It was no massacre; there was no ambush, no trap set for the white troops to enter. It was a battle in three fights, fair and simple. The Indians had met Custer's detachments in detail and defeated them, all within sight of their village.

The haphazard plan, or absence of plan, of this battle, with the commanding officer killed, was the source of many misunderstandings over the responsibility for the general result, and in the years that have passed the battle has been fought over many times in print. . . .

Maps

The Military Division
of the Missouri

Routes of the Three Columns
in the Sioux Expedition of 1876

Custer's Movements from
June 21 to June 25, 1876

Reno's Retreat from the Valley Fight

Aerial View of Weir Point

Aerial View of Reno's Route
from the Valley Fight

Walter Camp's Map
of the Battleground

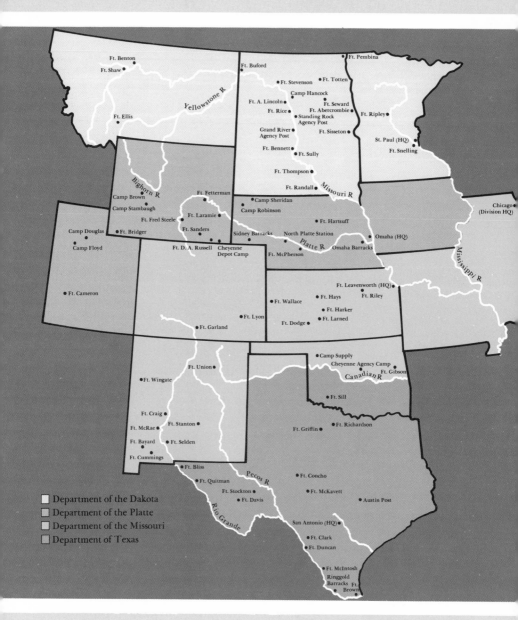

Department of the Dakota
Department of the Platte
Department of the Missouri
Department of Texas

In 1870 the Military Division of the Missouri was commanded by Lieut. Gen. Philip H. Sheridan in Chicago. About seventy-five posts, camps, and stations in the four departments of the Military Division were garrisoned by less than 20,000 officers and men. In the vast area of the Military Division there were ninety-nine Indian tribes comprising almost 200,000 Indians.

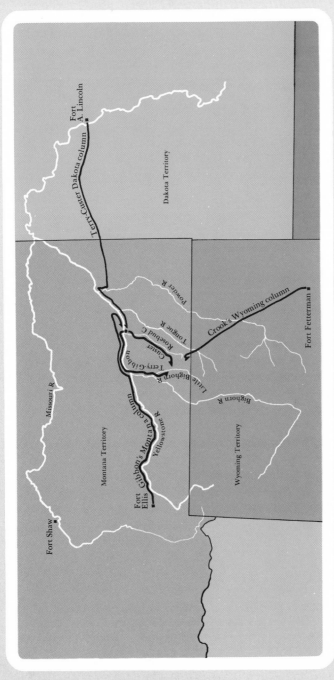

Routes of the three columns in the Sioux expedition of 1876. General Sheridan had planned to converge the three columns in the Yellowstone River country, but Crook's Wyoming column was brought to a standstill by the Northern Cheyennes on June 17. On June 21 Gen. Alfred Terry, who led the Dakota column, and Col. John Gibbon, leader of the Montana column, held a conference aboard the supply steamer Far West. Those attending included Lieut. Col. George A. Custer and Maj. James S. Brisbin. They planned that Custer would follow an Indian trail up the Rosebud and seek an encounter with the hostiles. In the meantime, Terry would accompany Gibbon up the Yellowstone and Bighorn rivers to support Custer on the Little Bighorn.

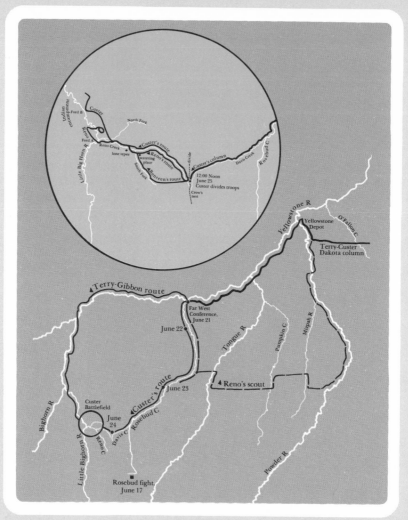

In mid-June Maj. Marcus Reno made a reconnaissance from the Powder River
to the Rosebud in search of the hostiles. He located a wide trail leading up the
Rosebud. After the conference on the Far West on June 21, Custer moved up
the Rosebud ten miles and went into camp. The next day he marched thirty-
three miles and camped on the Rosebud. On June 23 he rode twenty-eight
miles and went into camp about 9:00 p.m. but broke camp about 12:30 a.m. to
move toward the divide between the Rosebud and the Little Bighorn. General
Terry and Colonel Gibbon, in the meantime, had moved up the Yellowstone
and Bighorn rivers. Crossing the divide at noon on June 25, Custer divided his
regiment into four columns. Capt. Fred Benteen, with Companies D, H, and K,
moved south toward the Little Bighorn. The other three columns followed
down Reno Creek toward the Little Bighorn.

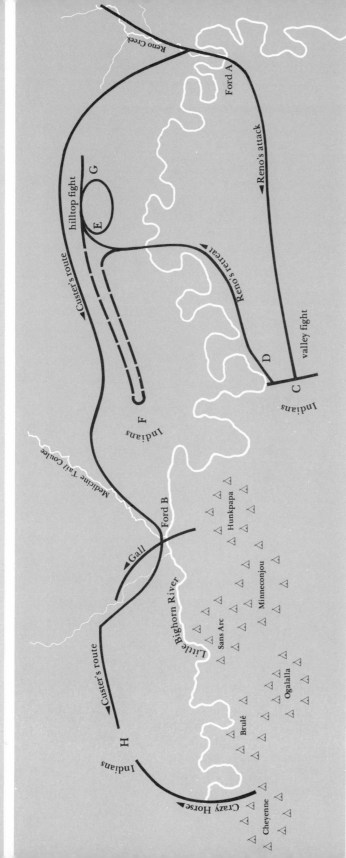

Major Marcus Reno was directed to attack the south end of the village. Custer turned right to attack from the north. Reno was soon on the defensive, finally retreating from the valley fight and crossing the Little Bighorn. He joined with Benteen and the packtrain on a bluff and attempted a reconnaissance to locate Custer, who had gone down Medicine Tail Coulee to an encounter with the hostiles at Ford B. From there Custer was forced north to Custer Ridge, where his companies were annihilated.

Custer Ridge

Route to Custer Ridge

Custer's route toward Ford B

Medicine Tail Coulee

Ford B

Indian encampment

Weir Point

Route

© 1975 R. N. Wathen, Jr.

In the foreground is Weir Point where Reno's companies were forced back in their attempt to join Custer, who was then on Custer ridge some four miles to the north.

Benteen joins
from south

Reno-Benteen hilltop fight

Route to Weir Point and return

Route of Reno's companies from the valley fight. They crossed the Little Bighorn in the foreground about 4:00 p.m. on June 25 and struggled up the bluffs to the hilltop. Here they were joined by Captain Benteen's companies and the pack train. From the hilltop they made an unsuccessful attempt to reach Custer, who was then about four miles to the north. The companies were forced back to the hilltop site where the fight continued into the next day. General Terry and Colonel Gibbon came up on June 27 and relieved Major Reno's companies.

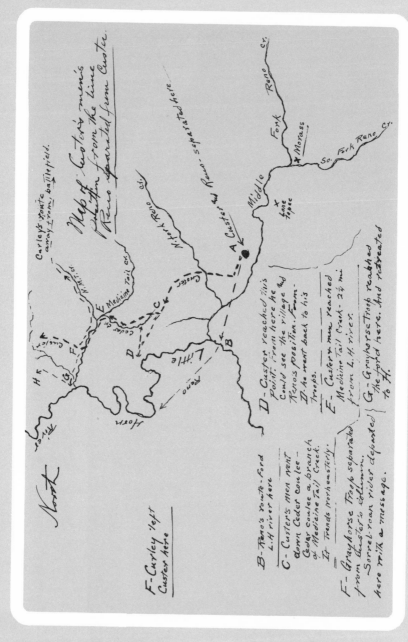

North

Map of Custer's men's position from the time Reno separated from Custer.

Curley's route — away from battlefield.

F — Curley left Custer here.

Reno Cr.

Fork

Middle

So. Fork Reno Cr.

Morass

Lone Tepee

A Custer and Reno separated here

N. Fork Reno cr.

Medicine Tail cr.

Custer

Cedar

E Medicine Tail cr.

N. Mills cr.

Custer

Little

Horn

River

Reno

B — Reno's route — Ford L.H. river here.

C — Custer's men went down Cedar Coulee — Coulee a branch of Medicine Tail Creek. It trends northeasterly.

D — Custer reached this Point. From here he could see the village and Reno's position. From IT he went back to his Troops.

E — Custer's men reached Medicine Tail Creek - 2½ mi. from L.H. river.

F — Grayhorse Troop separated from Custer's column. Sorrel-roan river deported here with a message.

G — Grayhorse Troop reached the ford here. And retreated to H.

Walter Camp's map, referred to in his interviews. The letter designations do not refer to the traditional Ford A and Ford B but are points of reference that Camp used in his interviews.

Photographs

The Battlefield

Commanding Officers

Indian Chiefs

Officers

Scouts

Previously Unpublished
Photographs

The Battlefield Monument
1876 and 1886

The Battlefield

View of the battlefield, 1975.

Commanding Officers

Brig. Gen. Alfred H. Terry, from the De-partment of Dakota at St. Paul, was in command of the Sioux expedition of 1876.

Col. George Crook, from the Depart-ment of the Platte at Omaha, was in com-mand of the Wyoming column.

Col. John Gibbon, 7th Infantry, was in command of the Montana column from Fort Shaw.

Lieut. Col. George A. Custer was in com-mand of the 7th Cavalry in the march of the Dakota column from Fort A. Lincoln.

Sitting Bull, prominent leader of the Hunkpapa Sioux, fled to Canada after the Little Bighorn River fight and did not return to the States until 1881.

Two Moon, a minor Cheyenne chief, whose role in the Little Bighorn River fight was probably colored in later years.

Rain In The Face, a prominent Sioux, was in the fight. A legendary account credits him with cutting out and eating the heart of Tom Custer.

Gall was a hostile Sioux and a leader in the Little Bighorn River fight. He continued as a leader of his people on the reservation and died in December 1894.

Officers

Capt. Thomas H. French was with Company M in the valley and hilltop fights. The next year he fought against the Nez Perce at Canyon Creek.

Lieut. George D. Wallace was with Company G in the valley and hilltop fights. He was killed in 1890 in the affair at Wounded Knee Creek.

Capt. George W. Yates, commanding Company F, was killed with Custer. The post at Standing Rock Agency was named Fort Yates in honor of his galantry in the Civil War.

Charles A. Reynolds, a scout for the 7th Cavalry, was killed in the valley fight, where a monument marks the site today.

Capt. Frederick W. Benteen, with Companies D, H, and K, joined forces with Reno in the hilltop fight and displayed outstanding gallantry.

Maj. Marcus A. Reno, 7th Cavalry, commanded Companies A, G, and M in the valley fight and the regiment in the hilltop fight.

Capt. Thomas M. McDougall was with Company B, guarding the pack train, and joined with Reno in the hilltop fight.

Capt. Thomas B. Weir was with Company D in the hilltop fight. As revealed in the Camp interviews, he began the movement toward Weir Point in an attempt to reach Custer.

Curley, who enlisted in the Detachment of Indian Scouts, 7th Infantry, was assigned to the 7th Cavalry because of his knowledge of the Yellowstone Valley.

White Man Runs Him, a Crow Indian scout, was in the hilltop fight briefly but withdrew and returned to his home at Crow Agency.

Hairy Moccasin was enlisted in the 7th Infantry along with Curley and the other Crow scouts. He and White Man Runs Him withdrew from the hilltop fight.

Goes Ahead, a Crow scout, was interviewed by Walter Camp. He was with White Man Runs Him in the withdrawal from the hilltop fight.

White Swan (Strikes Enemy) was wounded in the right hand in the valley fight. In 1904 he was buried in the Custer Battlefield National Cemetery.

Young Hawk, a leader in the Detachment of Indian Scouts, was in the valley and hilltop fights. He had been in the Black Hills expedition in 1874.

Sioux (Little Sioux), a nephew of Bloody Knife, was with Strike Bear in the capture of the Sioux ponies.

Strike Bear (Red Star), a Ree scout, crossed the river with the Reno column, captured some Sioux ponies, and drove them to Yellowstone Depot.

Daniel Ryan, corporal, Company C. Killed at the Little Bighorn.

William Cross and family. Quartermaster scout.

Charles Windolph, private, Company H.

William A. Hardy, trumpeter, Company A.

William Heyn, first sergeant, Company A.   *Thomas Harrison, sergeant, Company D.*

George Herendeen, quartermaster scout.   *John Sivertsen, private, Company M.*

The monument erected in 1877 on Custer ridge. Bones were gathered from the battlefield and buried at this site. Photo by Stanley Morrow.

The present battle monument was cut from Vermont granite and shipped by rail to Bismarck, Dakota, the end of the railroad, and by steamboat to Fort Custer, Montana, thence by sled and oxen to the site where it was erected in 1886.

Interviews With 7th Cavalry Officers

Winfield S. Edgerly

Charles A. Varnum

Luther R. Hare

Thomas M. McDougall

Edward S. Godfrey

Edward G. Mathey

Francis M. Gibson

Charles C. DeRudio

Interview with Winfield S. Edgerly[1]

On Reno's scout up Powder and across to Rosebud he had Officer Lowe[2] and 20th Inf. with battery 2 Gatlings along. These were abandoned once on the trip because of rough country but later recovered and this may have had some influence with Custer not to take them along. . . . When Custer advised against taking them along Lowe wept (or almost cried).

Edgerly says when regiment left mouth of Rosebud no one expected the Indians would make a stand anywhere and fight. Custer said he would find them if he had to follow them out and back to the reservation. Nobody thought that any hard fighting would take place. He thinks Custer's plans all right considering the amount of information Custer had as to numbers of Indians. Custer's idea was that Indians would scatter and run in all directions. Hence he sent Benteen to southwest. Reno was to charge from south and when Custer saw Knipe's 60 to 75 Indians he undoubtedly thought they were about to scatter to the east. Hence his plan all along was to have his troops disposed to head them off in all directions. If they would go north Gibbon would get them.

---

1. Walter Camp field notes, folders 103 and 108, BYU Library. Winfield Scott Edgerly was second lieutenant in Company D, 7th Cavalry. He was born in Farmington, New Hampshire, May 29, 1846, and graduated from the Military Academy on July 1, 1866. He served with the 7th Cavalry from 1870 through the Wounded Knee Creek affair in 1890. He was promoted to brigadier general in 1905 and retired in 1909. He died September 27, 1927, and was buried in the National Cemetery at Arlington, Virginia. More biographical information is found in the *Annual Report of the Association of the Graduates Of The . . . Military Academy . . . 1931.*

2. William Hale Lowe, Jr., second lieutenant in the 20th Infantry, Fort Snelling, Minnesota, was detailed by General Alfred Terry to accompany the Dakota column of the Sioux expedition with two rapid-fire Gatling guns.

In regard to Gatlings said it was the feeling with many of the officers that would have a hard ride and did not wish to be encumbered with artillery. Said Custer told him on night of June 21 that there was much hard riding ahead to overtake the Indians and that once he got after them he would follow them until they got back to reservation.

Herndon[3] was not sent to scout Tullock's creek because it was on west side of divide between Rosebud and Little Bighorn and as soon as Custer got over divide the scouts had approximately located the village in another direction than that of Tullock's creek.

After Custer and scouts came down from Crows Nest told officers that Sioux scouts had been discovered and running toward village and he had decided that would press on and attack village then instead of waiting until next morning as had planned. Indians would probably not stand against whole regiment of cavalry and he expected to find them trying to get away.[4]

Divided reg. into four battalions, Benteen, Reno, Keogh and Yates and had McDougall rear guard for pack train. He took Keogh and Yates with him.

Gibson and party went to tops of several hills and reported no Indians and then having gone 5 or 6 miles from where regiment divided, Benteen swung back to right and followed Custer's trail. Edgerly says one reason Benteen kept so close to Gibson and six men was that Gibson had to go to top of several hills enroute to see if any Indians on other side and in this way Benteen by keeping to the lower ground kept gaining on him. Edgerly does not think Benteen's side trip on a.m. of 25th was Custer's effort to create an appearance of complying with Terry's order, but Custer's own idea not to allow any Indians to escape in that direction.

After Martin came up with message, Edgerly heard him telling the boys that Reno had attacked village and was killing Indians and squaws right and left.

After Benteen read the message handed him by Martin he was heard to remark: "Well! If he wants me in a hurry, how does he expect

---

3. George Herendeen. He was employed by General Terry on June 21 to accompany the 7th Cavalry up Rosebud Creek and to scout the Tullock's forks region and report the results to Terry.

4. Edgerly says that from interviews he has had with Indians he learned that Indians early got information that Custer was crossing divide, but from precedent expected him to attack at daylight next morning. Were not anticipating that he would show up in middle of the day. Hence their ponies were still out grazing and generally unprepared.

(Walter Camp field notes, folder 103, BYU Library.)

that I can bring the packs? If I am going to be of service to him I think I had better not wait for the packs. . . ."

Edgerly says Cooke and Keogh went to ford with Reno and he had been told by officers with Reno that they actually crossed. As Keogh was in charge of squadron of Custer's battalion (and Yates the other) it was not so necessary that he be with his co.[5] Think both of these went to river to be in first of fight with Reno, expecting Custer to come right along on Reno trail. Edgerly thinks Custer really intended to follow Reno into village but that when he got near the river he changed his mind. He thinks Knipe's account probably an explanation of Custer changing his mind.

Martin had said that Reno had attacked village and driving away Indians and killing right and left and when got down near river saw horsemen scampering toward bluffs[6] and thought must be Indians Reno was driving out of village, but Half Yellow Face beckoned to come up toward right and went up there, and Reno's men were coming up bluff, some wounded and crying for water. Few Sioux then around behind rocks and bluff firing on Reno's command. Skirmish line formed and these Indians soon driven away.

Heard heavy firing in direction of Custer and clouds of dust over in village and Indians riding back and forth.[7] Edgerly says that after Benteen met Reno on bluff they could hear firing in direction of Custer very plainly and Weir said: "Edgerly will you go down with the troop if I will?" Edgerly said yes and Weir said, "Well, I will go and get permission" and when Weir returned and started off alone Edgerly supposed he had the permission. It had been the habit of Weir to permit Edgerly handle the troop in his place a good deal, and Edgerly

---

5. Edgerly says officers in Reno's battalion told him that Cooke and Keogh actually went to the ford with Reno's column wishing to get into the fight as Reno was to attack first. Keogh having command of a squadron of Custer's column was probably allowed to go by Custer, as he was not so much needed by his company.

(Ibid.)

6. Edgerly says Benteen's battalion went nearly down to Ford A — near enough to see Reno's men retreating to the bluffs.

(Ibid.)

7. Weir now asked Edgerly if he did not think right to go to Custer's assistance and if he would go if D Troop went alone if he could get permission and Edgerly said he would and Edgerly heard First Sergeant also express himself likewise. Weir went over toward Reno and came back with an orderly and started off and Edgerly supposing Weir had permission followed with the troop. Weir afterward told Edgerly that did not have permission and that he did not ask for any.

(Ibid.)

followed on with the troop from force of habit.[8] Edgerly says that Weir started off without orders and that he (Edgerly) followed with the troop under the mistaken impression that Weir had permission. After they got out ahead Lieut. Hare came out with instructions from Reno to open up communication with Custer if they could. Hare returned to Reno and then M, K and H came out. Troops M, K and H followed D Troop out, but probably not until after Hare got back after delivering order to Weir to try to open up communication with Custer. Thinks they must have followed within ½ hour of time D left. Thinks no more of the troops followed, or if they did they did not advance very far.

When Weir and Edgerly went out from Reno did they not see Custer's trail. Does not recall seeing it anywhere. Edgerly says he does not think they could have relieved Custer in any way by going toward him after Benteen met Reno, but, so far as they had any information at that time there was no reason why they should not have tried it.

Edgerly soon turned to right into a little valley *which must have been the one followed by Custer and his men, or nearly parallel to it.* . . . Weir standing on high point signaled that Indians were coming and he therefore turned back and circled over to left and crossed his track and swung . . . ahead to high ground in front of Weir — he was on second Reno Peak (farthest north). French's troop came up next them. Godfrey, then Benteen. Weir personally never got as far ahead as Edgerly.

He moved ahead along ridge, dismounted men and began to return fire of Indians. Edgerly says he went to a point which I locate as one of the two Reno peaks farthest north. Another peak in direction of Ford B (as he remembers) but somewhat lower than the one he was on was occupied by Indians who began firing. Edgerly said that when looked over toward Custer battlefield saw Indians shooting as though at objects on the ground, and one part of hill on Custer battlefield was black with Indians and squaws standing there. Firing out here lasted about ½ hour when were ordered back to Reno's position.

Edgerly says that when retreated from the advance there were not many Indians in their front, but became more numerous as retreated back. Edgerly says when he was ordered to fall back there were not many Indians in his front and he obeyed reluctantly. Says the 7 troops

---

8. A typescript copy of a letter to Captain Edward S. Godfrey from Captain Edgerly January 17, 1886, Fort Keogh, Montana, concerning the advance to the high point on June 25 is in the Manuscript Room, New York Public Library.

could have gone farther but thinks if they had got down into the hollow as far as Dry Creek or beyond, with the pack train, they would probably all been wiped out.

Vincent Charlie was hit in hips and when he fell struck his head and head began to bleed. Edgerly told him to get into ravine out of danger for awhile. Vincent Charlie was the man wounded that Edgerly had to leave when out in advance. Edgerly says that in the advance toward Custer and fighting getting back to Reno hill only one man killed and only one horse lost. Vincent Charlie was killed and body when afterward found had a stick rammed down the throat.

Edgerly says that when he fell back had trouble to get up on his horse and that there were Indians within 15 feet of him firing at him and his orderly. This was from the most advanced point. His horse kept swinging around away from him, and his orderly had to ride around to that side to stop the movement of Edgerly's horse. All this time the Indians were firing at them at close range and the orderly, an old veteran, kept smiling. Finally Edgerly mounted and they got out of there in a hurry. Afterward Edgerly inquired of the orderly why he smiled or what he saw to laugh at and orderly replied the bad marksmanship of the Indians so close to them.

Retreated back and found other troops already formed in line on Reno hill where remained until morning of 27th. 1st Sergeant Winney of K Troop was killed just at dusk on 25th. He raised up and was hit and cried out. When they went to see what was matter he was dead.

Benteen charged just before heaviest firing stopped and just before 10 a.m. June 26, and Benteen came right over and advised Reno that Indians were massing in front of the line (over toward the north) and advised charging them, which they did right away at Benteen's command. Edgerly thought Indians were then getting short of ammunition and had resolved on something desperate. This was very probable, for the fighting after this was desultory and scattering on Indian side and they naturally would not desire to expend all their ammunition. This is probably what saved Reno's 7 companies and why Indians soon left valley as Terry approached.

Edgerly says that after Benteen charged and drove Indians off on south he came over and told Reno that Indians were massing off to north of him and would be into his lines from that direction if he did not charge them. Accordingly Benteen took station on highest point and gave order for the charge. Whole line on ridge on north side of hospital issued from their pits and charged Indians and drove them off. Just before charge all Indians seemed to be firing at Benteen but he was perfectly cool and did not change color.

Horses killed on Reno hill Edgerly did not recall definitely but says there must have been as many as 50. On morning of 27th horses very thirsty and they were taken directly down bluffs to water. They would sit on haunches and slide at steepest places. Their rush for the river when got near to it was very pathetic.

Edgerly says that Genl. Custer, Tom Custer and Cook lay at highest point of ridge. Only a few dead on top of ridge. From this I take it that ridge has been leveled up where monument now is. Edgerly says that but few of the men on the Custer battlefield were scalped. Perhaps one reason was that most of the men had had their hair cut short before starting on the expedition. Calhoun was not mutilated. Crittenden had numerous arrows sticking in his body. Edgerly says Calhoun's men lay in remarkably good line, with the officers in their proper positions for a cooly planned resistance. Edgerly says Serg. Bustard found near Keogh. Serg. Varden found near Keogh. I Troop Trumpeter also near Keogh. Edgerly says one of the shots that went through Comanche struck Keogh's leg, breaking his leg. Edgerly says Vic was horse killed. Dandy was with pack train.

What means of identifying officers left when they were buried and discuss how markers may now be mixed? *Small stake driven with man's name written on it.*

Edgerly says one of E Troop's gray horses was found wounded at the river near Custer battlefield, and appeared to be much frightened and very shy but followed the troops at a distance all way to crossing of the Yellowstone.

Edgerly's estimate of Indians was 4000 warriors. He bases this on no. of tepees in village and what he saw when Indians went off on evening of 26th. Says Hare, who had seen large droves of cattle and horses in Texas remarked that there must be more than 20,000 animals in the column when Indians left the village. Dead Indians left in village — 11. Edgerly says were 6 in one tepee and 5 in other. He saw them. They were finely dressed and ornamented and tied standing up to a vertical pole in each case.[9]

---

9. Edgerly's lengthy statement at Fort Yates, Dakota, was published in the *Leavenworth Weekly Times* (Kansas) 18 August 1881, as "An Account of the Custer Battle" and is reprinted in William A. Graham's *The Custer Myth* (Harrisburg, Pa.: The Stackpole Co., 1953), pp. 219–21, as "Edgerly's Statement Made 18 August 1881 at Fort Yates."

Interview with Charles A. Varnum, May 1909[1]

Wagon train struck the Powder above its mouth and then swung back and circled around to clear bad ground. It did not go beyond Powder. Along the Rosebud valley there had been a series of camps or villages. The ground had been scratched up by travois [Indian trailing platforms] and had been overrun in all directions.[2] The Indians had been drying lots of meat, and all the buffalo had left the country.

On divide [between Rosebud Creek and Little Bighorn River] there is a ridge running east and west at right angles to main divide. This spur ridge runs toward Rosebud, and Custer came along south of

---

1. Walter Camp field notes, folder 65, BYU Library. Charles Varnum was a second lieutenant in Company A and was commanding the Detachment of Indian Scouts on June 25. He was born on June 21, 1849, graduated from the Military Academy on June 14, 1872, and was appointed second lieutenant in Company A, 7th Cavalry. He was in the Yellowstone expedition in 1873, the Black Hills expedition in 1874, and the Sioux campaign in 1876. In 1877 he fought Chief Joseph in the Nez Perce campaign. In the Wounded Knee and White Clay Creek affairs he fought the Sioux and was awarded the Medal of Honor for most distinguished gallantry at White Clay Creek. He was retired for disability on October 31, 1907, and died on February 26, 1936, the last surviving officer of the Little Bighorn River fight.

2. We quote here from a letter written by Charles Varnum on April 14, 1909, from Boise, Idaho, to Walter Camp:

With my scouts I acted as advance guard up the Rosebud and my instructions were, particularly, not to let any trail get away from us without letting Custer know of it. On June 24th after marching about 20 miles the command halted and I was sent for and came back to the head of the column. Custer told me that Godfrey had reported that a trail of a part of the Indians had gone up a branch stream to our left about ten miles back and Custer was rather angry that I had let anything get away from me. I told him of the thoroughness of my work at the front where I had the two Jacksons and Cross & Fred Gerard scattered with my Indians across the whole front and I did not believe the report. After discussion Lieut. Hare was ordered to report to me as an assistant and I changed horses and went back the ten

this ridge. The 7 Sioux were going eastward along this ridge.[3] There were two lodges at the lone tepee — one standing up and another had been broken down.

miles with some of my Rees and found where quite a party had gone up a stream with their travois to find a suitable crossing and ... had worked back to the main trail. I rejoined the command ... and then resumed my place in advance Hare taking the right front and I the left. We made about ten miles more and went into camp.... Custer came over to the Scout camp and had a long talk with the Crows. (Half Yellow Face was still out to the front somewhere so there were only five Crows present.) After a while he called me in and told me that the Crows reported that between us and the Little Big Horn was a high hill with a sort of Crow nest in the top where the Crows watched the Sioux when they were on that river and the Crows were on a horse stealing trip. That their camp could be made out in the clear light of the morning when the daylight broke. The Indian trail we were following led in that direction and the Crows believed their camp was on the Little Big Horn. Custer said that the Crows were going on at once and he wanted an intelligent white man to go with them and take some Rees for messengers & Boyer as interpreter and send him back word what we discovered. I said that meant me, but he said it was a tough mean job, but I insisted that that was my place, only I would like to take Charley Reynolds with me, for some one to talk to. He told me to do so and to start about 9 o'clock and he would move with the command at eleven and in the morning he would be bivouaced under the base of the hill I was on and he would expect to get word from me there. I left as directed taking Boyer, Charlie Reynolds, five Crows (Half Yellow Face, being still away) and eight or ten Rees. The Crows were our guides. Except that we stopped two or three times in the dense undergrowth along a stream to let the Crows smoke cigarettes we were on the go till about 2.30 or 3 a.m. on the 25th, and as day light broke I found myself in a peculiar hollow like old Crow nest at West Point, near the summit of a high ridge in the divide between the Rosebud and Little Big Horn. This latter stream was in plain sight about ten miles off. A timbered tributary led down to the Rosebud and up which we had evidently come during the night. Another led down to the Little Big Horn. On this were the two lodges that you know of and which I understand were filled with dead bodies of Indians, probably from Crooks fight of the 17th. ....I crawled up [the hill] & watched the valley till the sun rose. All I could see was the two lodges. The Crows tried to make me see smoke from villages behind the bluffs on the Little Big Horn & gave me a cheap spy glass but I could see nothing. They said there was an immense pony herd out grazing & told me to look for worms crawling on the grass & I could make out the herd; but I could not see worms or ponies either. My eyes were somewhat inflamed from loss of sleep & hard riding in dust & hot sun & were not in the best of condition, but I had excellent eyesight & tried hard to see but failed. About 5 o'clock I sent the Rees back with a note to Custer telling him what the Crows reported, viz a tremendous village on the Little Big Horn. I do not remember the wording of my note but I was told when the command arrived that Custer got it.

(In Walter Camp Collection, box 7, folder 15. BYU Library.)

3. The following is a continuation of Varnum's letter to Camp:

After sending off the Rees we saw one Indian riding a pony & leading another at the end of a long lariat & some distance behind, an Indian boy on a pony. They were evidently hunting stray stock and were perhaps a mile off toward the Little Big Horn and riding parallel to the ridge we were on. There was a gap in the range to our right and the Crows thought they would cross there & soon discover Custer. By this time smoke could be seen in a ravine towards the Rosebud showing where Custer was. The Crows were mad that he lighted fires. Boyer said that White Swan, who seemed to be a sort of leader, wanted us to try & cut him off & kill them where they crossed the range so they would not discover the troops. Boyer, Reynolds & two Crows with myself started off dismounted to do so. After, perhaps, a half mile of hard work through very broken country, where we could see nothing I heard a call like a crow cawing from the hill and we halted. Our two Crows repeated the immitation but you could easily see they were talking or signaling and we started back. I asked Boyer what was the matter but he did not know. On our return we learned that the Sioux had changed their course away from the pass but soon after our return they changed again and crossed the ridge. We could see them

60

Varnum and his orderly Strode[4] had passed these, some distance over to the left, and gone on over toward the southwest to a point on high ground from which he could overlook the valley of the Little Bighorn, then turned back and after some time met Custer's column.

Roy's account of position of skirmish line opposite point of timber and troops leaving from south side of timber is correct. M was on left, A in center and G next the timber. G had been sent into timber. Moylan had sent alternate files into timber to get ammunition from horses. (This he would naturally do before all in belts were fired away).

Varnum left the timber late and before reached river overtook head of column, which was being led by Reno and Moylan, whom he did not at first notice, but upon making some remark about ought not to be retreating so disorderly, Reno made some reply to the effect that he was in command. Varnum saw Hodgson fall on east side of stream. Where Dr. DeWolf and his orderly were going up, a number of others had started, but when it was seen that Indians over to the left and higher up the hill were firing on them, someone yelled for them to get down into ravine to right. As De Wolf looked around he was hit and fell.

Varnum says it was longer than 10 min. after Reno got up that

as they went down the trail towards the command and could then see a long trail of dust showing Custer was moving but we could not see the column. Before it came in sight the Sioux stopped suddenly, got together & then as suddenly disappeared, one to the right & one to the left, so we knew that the Sioux had discovered our approach. About this time ... [Six or seven Sioux] rode in single file along the crest of a ridge forming a divide of the stream running into the Rosebud and in the direction of that stream. That they would soon discover Custer's command we knew and watched them accordingly. The crest where we were was higher than they were and as they rode along the crest, reflected against the sky their ponies looked as big as elephants. They rode leisurely but soon, all of a sudden, they disappeared and soon afterward one black spot took their place. They had evidently ran off to alarm their camp, leaving one man to watch the column. The command came in vision about this time and we watched it approach the gap where it halted. I rode down towards the column & soon met the Genl. He said, "Well you've had a night of it." I said yes, but I was still able to sit up & notice things. Tom Custer & Calhoun then came up to us & Custer was angry at their leaving the column & ordered them back. I told the Genl. all I had seen, as we rode back towards the Crow nest hill and we climbed the hill together. Custer listened to Boyer while he gazed long & hard at the valley. He then said "Well I've got about as good eyes as anybody & I can't see any village Indians or anything else," or words to that effect. Boyer said, "Well General, if you don't find more Indians in that valley than you ever saw together you can hang me" Custer sprang to his feet saying, "It would do a damned sight of good to hang you, wouldn't it" and he & I went down the hill together. I recall his remark particularly because the word damn, was the nearest to swearing I ever heard him come, and I never heard him use that but once before and that was in an Indian fight on the Yellowstone August 4th 1873. We rejoined the command and he sent for the officers to assemble and I hunted for water & grub, as I had had none since about 8 o'clock the night before.

4. Private Elijah T. Strode was orderly for Lieutenant Varnum and was wounded in the right ankle in the valley fight on June 25. He was taken to Fort A. Lincoln on the steamer _Far West._

Benteen came along. . . . He thinks must have been 20 min., and 4:00 p.m. or later when pack train arrived and 5:30 p.m. or later when the three companies moved down to support Weir. Varnum was out ahead with these advance companies and said they were not hard pressed when they began to fall back, but by time got back to corral the high hill over to the north was black with Indians. (Says in this advance all the cos. actually had started, including pack train.)

Benteen was really the only officer looking out for the whole command and he handled things well and fought very gallantly. Varnum acted as a sort of adjutant for Benteen, going forth and back between him and the hospital. Benteen the only man he ever saw who would not dodge when bullets flying — seemed to pay no heed to them whatever.

The Indians would get up as close as they could under cover and then fire rapidly for some time. While this was going on the soldiers would lie down close to ground and keep quiet. As soon as the firing would close there would be a general "ki-yi" all around, and the Indians would get ready to charge, whereupon the soldiers would rise to their knees and fire as hotly as they could to hold the Indians back. As man after man was killed or wounded it began to look as though defeat was gradually coming on, and even Benteen expressed some doubts about being able to hold out. French reinforced Benteen by extending H co.'s line further south along the hill. The charge from Reno's side was toward the northwest.

On morning of June 26 so worn out that Siebelder[5] carried me asleep down into hospital and covered me up. Varnum was slightly wounded in both legs on June 26.

Benteen dug no intrenchments until after noon on June 26 and then only the U-shaped trench. There was no long trench extending south but some boxes of hardtack had been carried up and used for protection along this line. There was a full circular intrenchment on bluff just above river when McDougall dug trench night of June 26. Hodgson grave was near this, just up the bluff.

On night of June 26 saw all four of Gerard, Bill Jackson, Tom O'Neil and DeRudio come in. *When DeRudio called out, after being challenged, I ran up the bluff, off the bench and stumbled over the body of a dead Indian which had been scalped. Some of horses were taken down and watered night of June 26 and all taken down morning of June 27.*

---

5. Private Anton Siebelder of Company A.

About 7:00 p.m. on June 26 Varnum offered to leave the lines if he could get a nervy man to go with him. McDermott was not inclined to go. Accordingly a Co. G man offered to go out with the Indian scouts and Reno wrote messages for them to carry. Half Yellow Face wanted them to mention in the message that he had captured some ponies and killed a stated number of Sioux. Varnum supposed they had gone, but after dark found that they did not make the attempt. Neither Indian nor white man got out of the lines on either June 25 or 26. Varnum is positive about this.

When dead were buried, Varnum and some scouts were posted on high ground east of Custer battlefield to watch for Indians. This was done by Reno to punish Varnum for adding some additional matter to the notes which Reno had tried to send out of lines on June 26. Varnum was thus not permitted to see any of his friends who had been killed with Custer. Calhoun was identified by filling in his teeth.

Varnum does not think there was any possible chance for Reno and Benteen to rescue Custer. Thinks Custer made a mistake in dividing his command. Had whole command stuck together, thinks would have driven the Indians out of the village and destroyed all the property in it. Does not think Reno could have held the timber.

In 1877 Reno was courtmartialed and suspended from service two years without pay for taking liberties with J. M. Bell's wife, and in 1880 he was again courtmartialed and dismissed for looking into the open window of the daughter of Col. Sturgis. . . .

Varnum was in the battles of Canyon Creek and Bear Paw Mountains against the Nez Perces in 1877 and in battle of Wounded Knee and White Clay Creek in 1890. [At] Wounded Knee Varnum was standing with Whitside when fight started. The first sergeant was pulling cartridges from belts of Indians and filled a hat. Varnum had his pipe shot out of his mouth when firing began. Varnum granted medal for "Most Distinguished gallantry in action at White Clay Creek S.D. December 30, 1890." This was fight with Brules at the Mission.

Custer was a young officer and was hated by Benteen and other of the old Civil War colonels for the discipline maintained. While Custer was a spectacular man in some respects, he nevertheless was wide awake, full of push and withal, a very efficient officer. These qualities caused jealousy and hatred on the part of some. He had great endurance and energy and in all his military service he was always the leader. Benteen and Reno always hated him. Custer knew this but was considerate of them and was always ready to do them favors. Custer's worst moral failing was the gambling habit to which he was passionately attached.

Interview with Luther Hare, February 7, 1910[1]

Camped on Rosebud about 5:00 p.m. June 24. Marched again at 11:00 p.m. and does not know how far from camp to point where turned up Davis Creek. Did not know how left Rosebud until next morning. Marched until some time before daylight and then went into camp and lay there until between 8 and 9. Before this Custer had been out ahead with scouts viewing valley of Little Bighorn. Marched again between 8 and 9 and went up nearly to divide and halted. Lay concealed less than ½ mile east of divide for more than an hour. This was between 10:00 a.m. and noon. During this halt Custer again went to Crows Nest to look at Indians.

After Custer had come down from Crows Nest he heard Mitch Bouyer say to him: "General I have been with these Indians for 30 years and this is the largest village I have ever known of," evidently judging from the signs of the trail.

After leaving the divide Varnum pulled out with the Rees, and Hare took the Crows. Custer told Hare to keep a lookout and send back a report as soon as he should discover any Indians. Hare pulled

---

1. Walter Camp field notes, folder 16, BYU Library. Luther Rector Hare was born on August 24, 1851, at Noblesville, Indiana, and entered the Military Academy on September 1, 1870. He graduated June 17, 1874, and was appointed second lieutenant in the 7th Cavalry. He was engaged in the Sioux expedition in 1876 and was on duty with the Detachment of Indian Scouts under Lieutenant Charles Varnum on June 25. In 1877 he was engaged in the Nez Perce campaign against Chief Joseph. He continued to serve on frontier duty and was in the affair at Wounded Knee Creek in 1890. During the Spanish-American war he fought in the Philippine Islands and was retired for disability in 1903. He died at the age of seventy-eight at Walter Reed Hospital on December 22, 1929, and was buried in the National Cemetery, Arlington, Virginia. More biographical information is found in the *Annual Report of the Association of Graduates of the . . . Military Academy . . . 1931*. See also Frederic Remington, "A Gallant American Officer" *Colliers Weekly,* 7 April 1900.

out and after going some distance looked back and saw Custer coming right behind him with the command so he (Hare) increased his gait, but before he got to lone tepee was overtaken by Sergt. Major Sharrow in a great rush with Custer's compliments and said he (Custer) had as yet heard nothing from Hare. Hare sent back his compliments and said he would report Indians as soon as he could get sight of any of them. Hare says Custer seemed to be very impatient, as above account shows. (Custer's sending two or three men after Benteen, in same manner after Benteen had struck out, illustrates the same thing.)

Before got to lone tepee Varnum's scouts had come over to Hare, and Varnum and his orderly had gone on ahead toward the river. Varnum returned and met Hare just before got to lone tepee. At lone tepee Hare heard Cooke tell Reno to go on in pursuit of the Indians and Custer would follow right behind and support him. Thinks Custer may have later repeated the order verbally. Before this Custer had ordered the scouts ahead but they refused to go and Custer ordered them to be dismounted and their horses taken from them.[2] Gerard explained matters to the Rees and so they rode out ahead of Reno and reached Ford A about $\frac{1}{2}$ mile ahead of them.

At the ford the scouts watered and pulled out just as Reno and his battalion came up. Reno stopped here and took plenty of time to water. Was here 10 or 15 min., says Hare. Hare says it is not true that Reno did not give his men time to water.

While Reno was watering, Hare went on down valley with the scouts, and about $\frac{1}{2}$ way (1 mile) down to skirmish line some of the Rees took after a herd of Sioux ponies. An Indian with these ponies turned and fired on the Rees but they chased him and captured some of the ponies and ran them off. The remainder of the Rees went on down and went into timber after Reno and his men did and that they forded the river a long way farther downstream than Reno's men did. He thinks about half way between timber and where Reno retreated across. Says he remembers seeing the Rees after he got to top of hill on retreat. Says they were up there while Reno was advancing down river toward Custer. He does not know why 2 Crows went with Reno and 4 with Custer. Did not know that Cooke and Keogh went to Ford A with Reno. Did not remember seeing Billy Cross in valley fight, but had no distinct recollection of him anywhere.

---

2. About the tumult of Rees when ordered ahead. Rees did not want to go alone. Wanted soldiers right with them. All this was result of misunderstanding on their part.

(Walter Camp field notes, folder 94, BYU Library.)

65

In valley fight there was a coulee 300 or 400 yds. in advance of the skirmish line (this has all been cut away by erosion of the river) and the Indians were pouring out of it as if concealed there and waiting for the soldiers.

In timber he did not hear any order to retreat. Clear brought his horse and said the command was leaving. When he started, A and M had gone quite some time and G had left just ahead of him, but he caught up to M. Co. M had taken away off to right, on a line straight for Ford A, and French had become separated from his co. and 3 or 4 Indians after him, but his co. turned to left and forded where rest did. Clear was killed just after leaving timber.

While going up bluffs on retreat he saw some Sioux going up ahead of them. He saw the Indians fire who killed Dr. DeWolf. Just before got to top of bluffs he saw a mounted Sioux going north along bluffs just below top of same.

Reno made him acting adjt. Benteen came up about 10 min. after Reno got to top of bluffs, and about 10 min. after this Reno sent Hare to packs. Hare's horse had been shot through jaws at roots of tongue, so that tongue hanging out of mouth and he traded horses with Godfrey and started for packs. Heard no firing in direction of Custer before he started.

He met packs north of north fork of Sundance Creek.[3] A mile or not much more from Reno, but out of sight of Reno. Returned right away — was gone from Reno about 20 minutes. Just as he got back he heard firing in direction of Custer and was told that previous firing down there was heard while he had been gone. Just as he got back he looked and saw Co. D advancing toward Custer. They were some distance out but still in sight. Thinks other 6 cos. did not advance until at least a full hour after Reno retreated up [bluffs].

Reno sent him to go to Weir and tell Weir to connect with Custer. He found Edgerly out ahead but says Edgerly did not hold his advanced position more than 10 min. M, K and H cos. were strung out along bluffs behind Co. D parallel with river but no co. quite up to Co. D. Says he (Hare) did not order any co. back on his own authority.

---

3. Hare met pack train about half way between right branch of Benteen Creek and Reno Hill.

(Camp MSS, Field Notes, Walter Mason Camp, box 2, folder 8, Lilly Library.)

Sundance Creek has also been called Ash Creek, Benteen Creek, and Reno Creek. — Ed.

Says Benteen and Reno were discussing matters. (They were standing about ½ mile in rear of Co. D) and Benteen suggested to Reno that they fall back as they were in a poor place for defense. Benteen remarked that Indians could pass around them to the east and also by river flat at the west and would soon be in their rear if did not fall back. This was probably why Reno decided to fall back. Hare does not remember who gave the order to fall back.[4]

While out in the advance with Co. D the Indians were thick over on Custer ridge and were firing and at that moment Hare thought Custer was fighting them. In falling back Hare was with Co. K. Weir and French were covering retreat, but before men were formed on Reno hill these two companies came tearing along and passed Co. K., which dismounted at the point where Reno retreated up the bluffs (500 yards north of Reno hill) and held the Indians in check. Hare thinks this move of Godfrey a clever one, as otherwise the Indians would have followed the men right into the corral. On the hill the companies were in order from right to left — A D G K M B.

On evening of June 25 De Witt Winney was killed. Julius Helmer (whom Capt. Hale had sent out to the regt. to make 1st sergeant as soon as he [Hale] would return. Hale was then on recruiting service) was shot through the bowels and died in great agony, begging of his comrades to kill him to put him out of misery.

After sun went down there was a long twilight, when could not see well to take aim. Soldiers finally ceased firing and so did Indians, but the latter all of a sudden started up again.

He went up on Benteen's line in p.m. June 26 to see about men going for water and he and Benteen walked around. The Indians were shooting a hail of bullets at them. He asked Benteen if he desired to draw the Indian fire and Benteen smiled and said: "If they are going to get you they will get you somewhere else if not here." (This was after they had charged. The Indians all around and the firing had slackened.) Says Benteen was superintending the men going for water on June 26. Says there must have been more than the 12 Roy speaks of who went for water, for they went at several different times and Roy might not have known of others going. Says Mike Madden was an intemperate fellow whom no one had much respect for, and when he

4. Reno says Hare, on his own responsibility, using Reno's name, ordered troops to fall back from advance, after seeing large no. of Indians approaching. Hare says that in this Reno was mistaken. Says he did no such thing.

(Walter Camp field notes, folder 16, BYU Library.)

volunteered to go for water everyone was much surprised.

Varnum (this was probably Benteen as Martin says) had heel of boot shot off. A bullet ticked Benteen's thumb. Hare says McDougall slightly wounded. French went up and helped Benteen in his second charge and then remained with Benteen. After his own charge Benteen could see Indians concentrating in front of other 4 cos., D, G, K and B, and then went over and told Reno that he (Benteen) had just run them out of his own front and he (Reno) had better charge and drive them out of his (Reno's) front.

On Custer ridge he saw the dead horses near Custer. The talk at the time was that these had been shot down by the soldiers for barricades but it did not impress him that such was the fact. Says he buried men near Calhoun. He says Calhoun and Crittenden's bodies lay near together. An arrow had been shot into Crittenden's eye. Tom Custer was horribly mutilated but his heart was not cut out. He does not recall any scalped in group with Custer except Cooke, one of whose side burns had been cut off. Thinks 7th Inf. buried Reno's men in valley. . . .

Hare has no doubt about the correctness of the Indian claim that they lost only 47 killed outright. He says many of the soldiers were raw and not trained to shooting.

Says Cansby, Brown and Stein were left at Powder river. He is not certain where Tritten was. He remembers particularly about Stein being left at Powder but does not recall the reason why.

Hare says had plenty of ammunition. Each troop had a mule packed with (2 boxes) 2000 rounds and headquarters had another, making 13 mules and 26 boxes or 26000 rounds besides what men carried in belts and saddles, which was 100 rounds each.

Interview with
Thomas M. McDougall[1]

Says Co. B and himself along on Reno's scout. Says Co. I and Keogh along on Reno's scout.

McDougall says in letter February 26, 1909, that shortly after [he] passed the burning tepee, eight or ten Indians passed with about 15 ponies. Ask if he meant 15 besides the ones they rode. *Yes.* Also when and where did he see the remainder of the Rees? *Did not see them.* What the scout said when he passed McDougall, the scout being among Rees: "*Whole Sioux nation over there in valley and I am going back to Powder River cantonment.*"

Hare[2] met pack train about ½ mile east of Reno hill. Did packs follow right on Custer's trail all way to bluffs? *Turned to left a little before got to bluffs and joined Reno.* Says he saw and talked with Boston Custer when he came back to the pack train. [Ask] McDougall as to what time he came up to Reno (about 4:00 p.m.) and particularly whether Custer's trail passed near by where Reno afterward fortified. *Don't know.* In the court of inquiry Reno admits that it did, or says

---

1. Walter Camp field notes, folder 24, BYU Library. Thomas M. McDougall was Captain of Company B and was with the pack train on June 25. He was born on May 21, 1845, at Fort Crawford, Prairie du Chien, Wisconsin, and at the age of eighteen was appointed second lieutenant in the 10th Louisiana Volunteers of African Descent, and served during the Civil War. He was assigned to the 7th Cavalry on December 30, 1870, and was engaged in some notable campaigns in the following years. He was retired for disability on July 22, 1890, and resided in Wellesville, New York. He died July 3, 1909, and was buried in the National Cemetery, Arlington, Virginia. His letter dated May 18, 1909, Wellesville, New York, to Edward S. Godfrey concerning the aftermath of the Little Bighorn River fight is in the Manuscript Room, New York Public Library.

2. Lieutenant Luther R. Hare had been on duty with the Detachment of Indian Scouts, and after the retreat from the valley fight, Benteen ordered him to ride to the pack train and hurry it up to Reno hill.

his attention was called to it but that he personally did not see it.

When got within sight of Reno hill the top of it was covered by men and he did not know whether they were Indians or white men. He was now moving with one platoon ahead of packs and one in rear. He now put ammunition packs together and gave orders that in event of attack the head platoon should deploy and try to stand them off, and if unsuccessful the details of enlisted men with the ammunition packs should immediately lead the animals in a circle, shoot them down and then lie behind them and fight as long as they could. They could live on mule meat for a few days.

Says that as soon as he got up he reported that packs were up, but Reno apparently paid no attention, as he replied that "Bennie (Lieut. Hodgson) is lying right over there." Weir had gone when packs got up.

McDougall says that when he arrived with pack train all was quiet with Reno's and Benteen's men and one would not have imagined that a battle had been fought. No line had yet been formed and so he (McDougall) immediately threw out a skirmish line. Says that if the Indians had appeared suddenly at this time and attacked they could have annihilated the whole 7 cos.

On Reno hill what talk of trying to join Custer when McDougall came up and afterward. Right away he heard firing and asked Godfrey if he heard it. Godfrey, who was deaf, said he believed he did. Mc-Dougall then said: *I think we ought to be down there with him,* and went up to where Reno and Benteen stood talking and expressed to them the same opinion. Reno did not appear to regard the seriousness of the situation.

How long did he remain on Reno hill before whole command of Reno started to find Custer? *One and a half hours.* Had D troop gone out when packs came up? *Yes, but were still in sight.* How long after he came up did Reno attempt to open up communication with Custer? Reno said (at court of inquiry) that he did as soon as Mc-Dougall got all of his packs up. *Waited some time after this.*

McDougall says all 7 cos. went out, Moylan with Co. A being the last to start. Moylan had the wounded. On the advance Benteen's men were by file along ridge parallel with river. The pack train merely got started before it was ordered to fall back. The rear then became the head of the columns. Moylan was having difficulty getting along with the wounded, and just as they were ordered to fall back McDougall had offered to let Moylan have one of his platoons to assist with the wounded.

Finally when the column started to fall back he (being on very good terms with Benteen) quietly remarked to him that if not careful there would be a second Ft. Phil Kearney affair. He then said quietly to Benteen that Reno was doing nothing to put the command on the defensive and that he (Benteen) being the senior capt., had better take charge and run the thing. . . . Benteen grinned and did as was suggested. After selecting the hill for his own line (Co. H) he came over and helped to form the line on the other side.

McDougall says he thinks the reason why Benteen did not assert himself before this, namely, when it appeared to everyone that all should go to support of Custer, was that Benteen hesitated to go on and join Custer, having come up with Reno, who might set up the technical claim that he was the commanding officer of both battalions. Reno and Benteen had not been on friendly terms and Benteen would not wish to stir up trouble. When, however, he saw that Reno was thoroughly incompetent to handle the situation he did finally take hold and practically, if not formally, command the whole situation. He kept watch of Reno, going frequently to where Reno was lying, and when he saw the need of action anywhere about the lines he either suggested what should be done or else positively ordered it done. Benteen always came over smiling, inspiring the other officers and men with confidence.

Locate 5 cos. at Reno hill besides Benteen and Moylan. Just as I have them on map. On Reno Hill Benteen had on his line all men who could be spared from the details with the pack train. As fast as horses or mules were killed they were rolled over on their backs and other horses were tied to the legs of the dead ones, thus releasing the horse holders to go up and assist men on the line.

Corroborates statement that bullet went through French's hat. McDougall says Varnum wounded twice in legs. At a safe distance away the hills were black with Indians looking on while warriors were as thick as could get within firing range. From Benteen's line could see black heads sticking up all around.

Dorn[3] killed while waking McDougall up. On June 26 many of the Indians were wearing the clothing and hats of Custer's dead soldiers. One Indian in particular was riding forth and back parading a guidon [a small flag, unit marker]. This he kept up a long time, until finally the boys tumbled him off his horse. Beating of tom toms behind Indian lines and then they would charge. Says the hottest fire against his position was from direction of north or from along edge of bluff.

---

3. Private Richard B. Dorn of Company B.

Says that at times the Indians would shoot showers of arrows trying to drive soldiers out by plunging fire. . . .

Benteen had a hard line to hold, and when he (McDougall) and French saw Benteen's men being picked off rapidly and carried down to the hospital they discussed between them a plan of facing some of their men the other way to resist the Indians should they carry Benteen's line. Says that when French and his co. went up to reinforce Benteen on June 26 he got there just about in time, and by their combined charge they cleared the front of Benteen's line of Indians and drove them away. After this the Indians began to mass in front of the line on north side of hospital and Benteen, quick to see it, came over and very gallantly superintended the charge from that side. In this Co. B took part with the others. When Benteen came over . . . the whole north side charged but Co. B charged straight ahead.

About 19 men volunteering to go for water and only 12 permitted to go at one time. Says thinks so. Says that when water parties would go down he had his Co. fire into fringe of timber on opposite side of river to drive Indians out and protect men going for water.

When position was changed on night of June 26 Cos. A. and B went down on bench just above river, B on south side and A on north side of gully running straight down from H Co.'s line. There Hodgson was buried. Men who recovered Hodgson's body on night of June 26 were Criswell, Private Ryan and Saddler Bailey, all of B troop.[4]

Keogh had with him picture of McDougall's sister which was recovered years after the battle from Indians with a spot of blood on it. Also Keogh's watch was recovered at same time.

There were few or no dead cavalry horses between top of ridge and deep ravine where Co. E men were found. Says there were only a few bodies between deep gully and where Genl. Custer lay. Is sure there were less than a dozen and might not have been more than ½ dozen. In his letter of 5/18 he says he found most of E troop *in the ravine.* Does he mean in the deep gully? Were there as many as 28? *Yes. All the bodies in the deep gully were buried in the gully — none was carried out. Homeyer was in there and Hughes.*[5]

---

4. Private Harry Criswell, Private Stephen L. Ryan, and Saddler John E. Bailey.

5. Frederick Hohmeyer was first sergeant of Company E and Sergeant Robert H. Hughes was from Company K.

Just where did he find Comanche?[6] On which side of the river and how near deep gully where it meets river? *Village side opposite mouth of deep gully. Saw only 5 or 6 dead Indian ponies on Custer battlefield.* Says Maj. Ball of 2nd cavalry told him that on scout up Little Bighorn he found many dead Indians.

On the night march to the steamer Mike Madden[7] was dumped out of the litter and fell into a cactus bush.

---

6. We quote here from a letter written by E. G. Mathey on April 13, 1910, from Denver, Colorado, to Walter Camp:

At the time I was riding Comanche, the horse belonged to the Government and if Col. Keogh ever bought the horse I never heard of it and I believe the horse belonged to the U.S. at the time Col. Keogh was killed. Comanche was received, with other horses, when the 7th Cav. was in camp, near Fort Dodge, Kansas, preparing for the Washita Campaign. I think it was sometime during September or October 1868, the horse was four (4) years old that spring so that he was about 12 years old when Col. Keogh was killed....

(In Walter Camp Collection, folder 12, box 7, BYU Library.)

7. Saddler Michael P. Madden had been wounded in the right leg in the first water party. Dr. Henry Porter amputated his leg on the battlefield. Madden was being carried to the steamer *Far West.*

When dumped into the cactus bush the language used by Madden is said to have left no doubt that a considerable spark of vitality was still present with the wounded man.

(Camp MSS, field notes, Unclassified Miscellaneous IX, Lilly Library.)

Interview with
Edward S. Godfrey[1]

When leaving the mouth of Rosebud on June 22 all battalion formation was abolished and each captain made responsible for condition of his co., as to grazing and watering horses.

On morning of June 25 when Sergt. Curtis of Co. F came in and reported the case of hardtack matter, Keogh heard it and immediately came up and began to discuss it and suggested that the matter be reported to Custer who then was up on the divide. Presently Custer came in and it was told him. He had officers call sounded.

Custer now told of Sioux scouts having discovered the command from in front, so that the concealment of the regiment any longer was useless. Said he had intended to lie back and make all arrangements to attack the village the next morning, but under the circumstances he had decided to go on and attack at once. He now ordered that each troop commander inspect his co. and equipment and detail men for the packs, and the first to report would be given the advance and the last

---

1. Walter Camp field notes, folders 36 and 37, BYU Library. Edward Settle Godfrey was born on October 9, 1843, in Kalida, Ohio. He served in the Civil War and entered the Military Academy on July 1, 1863. He graduated on June 17, 1867, and was appointed second lieutenant, Company G, 7th Cavalry. He was promoted to first lieutenant the following year and was in the fight against Black Kettle's Cheyenne village on the Washita River on November 27, 1868. He took part in the Yellowstone expedition in 1873 and the Black Hills expedition in 1874. He was stationed in Louisiana and Mississippi until 1876 when he was engaged in the Sioux campaign. He was in the Nez Perce campaign in 1877 and received the Medal of Honor for his gallantry on September 30, 1877, when he "led his command into action when he was severely wounded." He also participated in the Wounded Knee Creek affair in 1890. He was promoted to brigadier general in 1907 and retired the same year. He died on April 1, 1932, at Cookstown, New Jersey.

would escort the packs. Benteen walked off and almost immediately came back and reported his co. all right without having made the inspection (Benteen testified to same effect at Court of Inquiry) McDougall was the last to report and he was given the packs to escort for that day June 25.

Benteen being ahead, Cooke came up after passing divide and gave Benteen his orders to make scout to the left, and said he would also have Cos. D. and K. Reason for sending Benteen off to left was that Custer expected to find Indians scattered along the river and did not know whether he would find them down stream or up stream from the point he would strike the river at.

When Benteen had watered his horses at the morass he waited there some time — in fact so long that some of his officers began to get uneasy, especially as they were hearing firing (which must have been Reno's). Capt. Weir, especially, became impatient and wanted to go. One officer inquired of another: "I wonder what the old man (Benteen) is keeping us here so long for?" Some one suggested that he was probably giving the men a chance to fill their canteens. Finally this uneasy feeling among the subordinate officers became known to Benteen, in some manner, and Weir said they "ought to be over there" (where the fighting was going on) and, being at the head of the column, started out with his co. Benteen, seeing this, immediately ordered the column to advance. At this time the pack train was coming up and the leading mules had reached the water and, being very thirsty, plunged in.

Some time after passing the lone tepee Sergt. Knipe met Benteen, and as he passed, some one asked him what was going on up ahead and Knipe said "they are licking the stuffing out of them" etc. When they came to point where Custer's trail separated from that of Reno there was some discussion as to which one should be followed. The debate was settled by Weir starting off on the left-hand trail, following on after Reno, while the other two companies followed the right-hand trail. Benteen, with his orderly, took a mid-position between the two trails and went on ahead. Between water hole and river Benteen and men went at a gallop most of the time. The average speed was fast.[2]

_____

2. Godfrey was confused in his statement about Weir's movement, for in another interview Camp recorded that "Godfrey says that when Benteen came to where Reno's and Custer's trails parted, Benteen was undecided what was best to do. They were hearing firing to the right and Weir took that trail and Benteen and Godfrey took left trail or Reno's and followed it close enough to river to see Reno's retreat through the trees along river. Weir took the right and he was ahead of the other two troops." Camp Mss Field Notes, Walter Mason Camp, Unclassified envelope 130, Lilly Library, Indiana University.

The sound of the firing now grew nearer (probably Reno in retreat), and at one time pistols were drawn in expectation of meeting Indians who might be coming that way. Godfrey does not recollect exactly where Trumpeter Martin came up with the message, but says it was a good distance from point where they met Knipe. Martin must therefore have come up after the battalion of Benteen split up on the two trails.

When got nearer Godfrey says met an Indian driving some ponies and he thinks it was Half Yellow Face. (It might have been one of the Rees.) He asked him where the soldiers were and the Indian pointed to the right and the column bore off that way. Godfrey does not think Benteen got to Ford A and thinks Benteen could not have seen Reno's retreat until he (Benteen) got to the ridge, and Benteen must have been some distance ahead of his command.

A little incident which happened while waiting on the bluff before setting out toward Custer. Some Indians were grouped together away over in the valley (afterward thought to be around McIntosh's body), and Godfrey held a carbine at an angle of about 45 deg. and shot. The Indians immediately scattered, and the bullet probably struck close to them and gave them the impression that the soldiers had got the range of them.

In the advance toward Custer, Co. D went out first, then M, K and H. These men were at intervals along the high ridge and two high peaks, in a line approximately north and south, M behind D and K behind M. Benteen did not remain there long, but went back and joined Reno, who was coming up with the rest of the troops. Here Godfrey's impression was that a stand would be made, putting the packs in the hollow behind the surrounding hills, to the west, north and east.

He was soon surprised, however, by Hare riding up and saying that the commanding officer (Reno) had ordered that they fall back. Directly M troop came galloping up and went past and next Co. D went past without Edgerly, who was having difficulty in mounting his horse. After those two troops had passed, Godfrey said to Hare: *Look here, hell's to pay,* for the Indians were coming in swarms along the ridge which the troops had just left. (There were no Indians in the coulee to the east, so Godfrey says. By this I mean the coulee down which Custer marched.) Godfrey, after passing the long ridge some distance dismounted his men, forming a skirmish line at right angles to the river and began to hold the Indians in check, at the same time sending the lead horses on back on the line of retreat. (This corroborates what others have said, namely that Godfrey's

76

covering of retreat was near where stand was made.)

On Custer battlefield Godfrey buried "Boss" Custer,[3] who lay down on side hill some distance below the General.

Night of June 26 Godfrey's Co. K was on a prolongation of the line to the right along a ridge or spur extending down toward the Little Bighorn. When Bradley of Gibbon's command came up on June 27 he came up along this ridge. (He must mean to right of line facing the river.)

Tom Custer lay on his face up on top of the ridge with arrows shot in his back and head and back of head all smashed in. Godfrey at first thought it was Tom Custer by the shape of his body, and when he was rolled over and stretched out one of his arms they found "T.W.C." tattooed on his arm. Says there were but few bodies between this ridge and the deep ravine.

Godfrey saw the cavalry horse near Yellowstone in August 1876. Bridle gone. Heard about carbine being found with it but did not see it. Horse was shot in the head. Grain sack was on the saddle.

---

3. Boston Custer was a civilian guide employed by the 7th Cavalry Quartermaster. He was a brother of George and Thomas Custer.

Interview with Edward G. Mathey, October 19, 1910[1]

Remembers that about the time Hare met him to get ammunition some others met the pack train, one of whom he thinks was a half-breed. (This could hardly have been Cross.) Has a faint recollection of one or two others besides the half-breed. Is positive that Yates with Co. F was escort to the pack train on June 24. Says Keogh and French both may have been rear guard besides, but Yates was the escort. He talked with Yates several times that day.

After column left the divide on June 25 and had gone some distance, Cooke came back with orders from Custer for Mathey to keep the mules off the trail, as they were raising too much dust. Mathey did this. Cooke rode back a second time to the packs and Mathey asked him if he (Mathey) was doing any better by keeping the mules off the trail and Cooke said "yes." This was the last that Mathey saw of Cooke.

Mathey says that on the night of June 24 Custer asked him to report which company's packs were giving the most trouble. Mathey said that he remarked that he did not like to make comparisons, seeing that all were doing the best they could, but if required to do so he

---

1. Walter Camp field notes, folder 63, BYU Library. Edward Gustave Mathey was born on October 27, 1837, in France. He enlisted in the 17th Indiana Volunteer Infantry in June 1861 and was appointed second lieutenant in that regiment in May 1862. He resigned in August 1862 and was appointed second lieutenant in the 81st Indiana Volunteer Infantry. He served with his regiment in the Civil War. Mustered out of service as a major in 1865, he was appointed second lieutenant in the 7th Cavalry in 1867 and promoted to first lieutenant in 1870. He was in the Sioux campaign in 1876, and from June 22 he commanded the pack train accompanying the 7th Cavalry. He was in the Nez Perce campaign in 1877. He retired as a Major for disability in 1896 and was later promoted to lieutenant colonel. He died on July 17, 1915, in Denver, Colorado.

would have to name the packs of Companies G and H. McIntosh took the criticism good naturedly, but it made Benteen angry.

Mathey says that he buried Mark Kellogg's body on June 29. Says it was the last one buried. Says it lay near a ravine and between Custer and the river. Says it had been overlooked or not seen and that he was sent to bury it after all other burying had been done. It strikes me (WMC) that some one else told me of Kellogg's body being found between Custer and the river. . . .

Interview with
Francis M. Gibson,
December 7, 1910[1]

Capt. Gibson says Benteen told him to keep going until he could see the valley of the Little Bighorn, (Although I do not find where Benteen himself speaks of giving such orders), and that he (Gibson) thought that he did so. He now thinks however that he only went far enough to look down on the valley of the south fork of Sundance Creek,[2] which has cottonwood along it and Gibson might not have expected to find water as there was none in sight in Rosebud at a distance.

On way to river did not see any fleeing Rees. Gibson met the 3 Crows before got to Reno on hill. They pointed out the direction where Reno's men were. Says that Benteen got to point where Reno retreated up before Reno got up out of bottom.

When came to point where Custer's trail parted from Reno's Benteen said: "Here we have the two horns of a dilemma." Gibson advised taking the right-hand trail and says that Co. H, at least, took it. He does

1. Walter Camp field notes, folder 45, BYU Library. Francis M. Gibson was first lieutenant in Captain Benteen's Company H. He was on temporary duty with Company G in the hilltop fight. Gibson was appointed second lieutenant in the 7th Cavalry on October 5, 1867, and was in the Yellowstone expedition in 1873, the Black Hills expedition in 1874, and the Nez Perce campaign in 1877. He retired for disability on December 3, 1891. Gibson's letter to his wife, dated July 4, 1876, giving an account of the fight is in Katherine Gibson Fougera's *With Custer's Cavalry*, 1940, 1942, Caxton Printers, Caldwell, Idaho. A typescript from Gibson to E. S. Godfrey dated August 9, 1908, Gloucester, Mass., narrating Benteen's march to the left and his understanding of Custer's reason for ordering the movement is in the Manuscript Room, New York Public Library and the Dustin Collection, Custer Battlefield National Monument. The Gibson-Fougera Collection is in the Custer Battlefield National Monument Museum and consists of papers, photographs and relics.

2. Also Ash Creek, Benteen Creek and Reno Creek (see fn. 3 in interview with Luther Hare).

not remember Co. D taking the left, but sure that H took to right. Does not recall about Benteen personally taking to center between two trails.

Gibson thinks Weir went as far ahead as Co. D did. When Benteen got up ahead with Co. H and it was seen that Indians were coming over from Custer ridge to meet them Benteen said: "This is a hell of a place to fight Indians. I am going to see Reno and propose that we go back to where we lay before starting out here."

At daylight that morning, at Benteen's suggestion, a number of trumpeters were collected to blow reveille, so as to notify all concerned, including the Indians, that there were still some men left on the hill.

Gibson says that Benteen came up from seeing Reno and said: "Well, it is getting pretty hot." Benteen said: "We have got to charge them" and did so, and after that were not troubled so much from that direction. Benteen's charge was about 9:00 a.m.

Indian was killed near Benteen's line on hill just before the charge took place. Gibson says there was only one charge and that some of French's men were with Co. H on that charge. On Reno hill Benteen's fingers were grazed by a bullet.

Interview with
Charles DeRudio,
February 2, 1910[1]

DeRudio says his family was the Italian nobility, and he showed me parchment records of the family dated 1680. He was in 79th New York regiment in Civil War and in 1864 was put in command in some colored regiment. For a number of years after joining 7th Cav. he was a 2nd Lieut. in Co. H, with Benteen.

In summer of 1870 he was in command of Co. K and escorted a colony of settlers. These settlers had about 150 armed men and when they heard of Indian troubles were on the point of turning back, when

---

1. In Item No. 11, The Robert S. Ellison Collection, Denver Public Library, Denver, Colorado. Charles [Carlo] Camilus DeRudio was born in Belluno, Venetia Province, Italy, on August 26, 1832. He arrived in New York in 1864 and entered military service as a private, 79th Highlanders, New York Volunteers, serving with the regiment about two months in 1864. He was commissioned second lieutenant, Company D, 2nd U.S. Colored Infantry on October 17, 1864, and was honorably mustered out of service on January 5, 1866. He was appointed second lieutenant, 2nd Infantry, on August 31, 1867, and was assigned to the 7th Cavalry July 14, 1869. He was promoted to first lieutenant on December 15, 1875. During the Little Bighorn River fight he was on duty with Company A and was engaged in the valley fight. In the ensuing retreat to the hilltop he was missing, but he later rejoined the command on the hilltop. He was promoted to captain on December 17, 1882, and he retired at San Diego, California, on August 26, 1896. He died on November 1, 1910, in Pasadena.

"My Personal Story" (about DeRudio by Brisbin) was first published in the *New York Herald* July 30, 1876, and reprinted in the *Chicago Times,* August 2, 1876, and the *Frontier and Midland Magazine,* January 1934, 14:2 155–59, Montana State University, Missoula. "Major DeRudio, A Man With a Charmed Life" was published in the Washington (D.C.) *Star,* October 16, 1910. Melville Stone's "Charles DeRudio (Carlo DiRudio) 1st Lt. 7th US Cavalry" in *Colliers Weekly,* May 15, 1920, has biographical material not found elsewhere.

DeRudio advised them to go on. He would protect them until they could get their houses built, and then they could easily defend themselves, as the Indian warfare in Kansas was then by small parties of thieving Indians. Their object was principally to steal stock and did not attempt to kill except where they found the whites defenseless or unprepared to fight.

These settlers went on and after a few days a man came riding back in great haste and reported that the Indians had run off a number of horses and cattle. DeRudio got after them promptly and, after a chase of about 60 miles got all of the stock back. That fall a memorial signed by 115 settlers of Solomon Valley, Kansas, tendered their thanks to 2nd Lieutenant DeRudio for standing off Indian attacks so effectively that only one settler was killed during that time. The memorial mentions that Company G was stationed at the forks of the Solomon.

After some time in 1870, at Ellsworth, Kansas, Company G presented DeRudio with a gold mounted saber, which he showed me. When Custer heard of this he called DeRudio to him and advised that the acceptance of the saber on the part of DeRudio was unprecedented in Regular Army, was in disobedience of regulations and was prejudicial to good discipline. He rather scolded DeRudio for accepting it.

DeRudio says that in spring of 1876 he was promoted to First Lieut. and being in Company E, he should have been put in command of it, as was customary. However, Custer put A. E. Smith in command. Smith belonged to Company A, and Custer had DeRudio and Smith change places. Smith was a favorite of Custer, and for this DeRudio never quite forgave Custer. DeRudio did not enjoy serving in Co. A under Moylan, and, being appointed adjt. of Benteen's squadron, he thus was not attached to Co. A for some time. When Custer got to the Rosebud he broke up the squadron organization and DeRudio went back to Company A.

At five p.m. on June 24 Custer camped on the Rosebud at a place where the stream is very crooked and at 11:00 p.m. broke camp and started on. During the night Custer sent DeRudio back to instruct Keogh, who was rear guard, to get the pack train along faster and close up. Trumpeter Hardy was ordered to go with DeRudio and these two rode back 10 miles and found Keogh still in the Rosebud with sixteen mules stuck in the mud. The rest of the packs were scattered all along the trail for several miles. Hardy had a gray horse, and DeRudio was constantly in dread that they might be discovered by any Indians who might be loitering along the trail. However, they got back and found Keogh cursing the mules and the packers, and then he and Hardy returned to the front and had difficulty in locating Custer. On the way they encountered a band of whooping Indians and at first supposed they were being taken in by Sioux, but the party proved to be Tom Custer and some scouts who mistook DeRudio and Hardy for Sioux.

In the morning of June 25 Custer came back and said he had been up ahead with scouts, but his glasses were not strong enough to discover anything. DeRudio had the strongest glasses in the regiment, which had been presented to him by an Austrian optician, and Cooke came to DeRudio and asked if he would lend them to Custer. DeRudio did not like to do this, but consented, and Custer took them and went ahead again. When he returned he said he had seen some cloud-like objects which the scouts said were pony herds. Custer had these glasses when he was killed. After crossing divide, Company A was in the advance. Soon after this DeRudio saw a freshly killed buffalo at the side of the trail and after inspection concluded that the buffalo had been killed that morning.

After passing lone tepee, DeRudio stopped somewhere to fill his canteen and did not catch up with the command until it reached the river. Here he found Reno and Gerard sitting on horses in the river, Reno drinking from a bottle of whisky. DeRudio was the first man to ford the river, and as his horse surged ahead he splashed water on Reno, who said: "What are you trying to do? Drown me before I am killed?"

DeRudio corroborates Gerard's story about Ford A. Says it was at foot of bluffs which came to a break here and said there was a little hill on river bank on east side (Says there were two fords — one where Reno crossed and another a short distance down the river. Recrossed the one at the end of the bluffs, just north of a cut bank.) Said timber on west side was 200 yards wide. At Ford A Reno's battalion watered horses and when men got clear of timber formed the companies and went forward down the valley. Does not think the delay here was long, but some little time before all who were watering horses got up and together. The column then left — fronted into line with Company A on right, G in center and M on left. The Indian scouts were ahead and to left going down the valley. Does not remember seeing them capture Sioux ponies.

Says on skirmish line, A was on right, G in center and M on left. This disagrees with Moylan. The fact that DeRudio saw Sergeant White and took his gun leads me to think that A was in center and next to M. Says fight on skirmish line did not last over 10 minutes if it did that long. Does not remember sending from skirmish line for ammunition. On skirmish line he found Sergeant White wounded and took his gun and fired two shots at Indians over on hills to west. Saw the bullets strike short of Indians, but could hear Indians' bullets whistling over his head, showing that Indians had superior guns.

He took a squad of men and went into timber to go to north side of it to river bank to watch against Indians coming in from that direction across river. After he went in, Co. G sent into timber also. In the timber was a cleared place of 2 or 3 acres where there had been some lodges but had been taken away. In the timber was the dry gravelly bed of a creek or wash from river in high water.

He took his small party and went over to river bank and presently Trumpeter McVeigh came in leading DeRudio's horse and said: "Here Lieut., is your horse." DeRudio said: "I do not want my horse," but McVeigh said: "They are leaving the timber, Lieut." but as DeRudio had heard no bugle calls he doubted McVeigh's statement. As McVeigh spoke, the party of men with DeRudio started to break and leave him and DeRudio tried to halt them calling to one of the men to get a guidon, but the man said: "To hell with the guidon, don't you see the Indians are coming in?" DeRudio looked and saw a party of Indians coming into the timber and the men with him all fled.

He picked up the guidon and mounted and held the guidon across his lap and started out, but some Indians fired at him and he jumped down and kept quiet for a while. When he got to open plain he saw Reno and nearly the whole battalion in full retreat and some of men already across river climbing the bluffs. Charley Reynolds was kneeling on one knee firing at Indians and probably fired half dozen shots before Indians got him. He was just outside of timber. His horse had evidently been killed.

DeRudio now led his horse to edge of timber and decided to ride through Indians and overtake command. Most of the Indians were in pursuit of command and he thought he could probably ride through without being noticed by the whole bunch. He was just trying to mount his frightened and trembling horse and had his foot in stirrup when a buck jumped out of the brush and fired and then began to yell, frightening both DeRudio and the horse, and the horse broke away. He thinks the horse was struck by the Indian's shot. This was on top of bank on south edge of timber.

DeRudio dodged back into timber, and as he did so, the Indians at a distance ceased firing and set up a peculiar cry. Wondering what this could mean DeRudio looked out and saw the Indians pointing to bluffs and Benteen's battalion was in full view. DeRudio says this is what saved Reno's battalion from entire destruction. The appearance of Benteen checked the pursuit after Reno.

DeRudio says Reno should have held to the timber. Says there they would have had reasonable shelter, and Indians would never have come into the brush to fight, and Reno could easily have stood them off and held a thousand of them there who went down to fight Custer.

DeRudio now retired into timber and found Tom O'Neill, Gerard, and Bill Jackson hid in a low place. They called to him and he joined them and remained a while, but later began to think he had better look for some way to escape and so crawled up bank at south edge of timber to look out. While here an Indian rode up and dismounted and entered the brush within a few feet of him and cut a switch. De-Rudio drew his revolver to shoot the Indian in case he should be discovered, but did not desire to fire unless he would be compelled to do so. The Indian did not discover him and so he let him depart unmolested. DeRudio now crawled into a hollow place in the bank where a cottonwood stump had rotted and secreted himself, but soon three shots rang out quite close to him and looking up he saw the smoke from the shots. He was now much alarmed and thought he had better move, and looking out he saw squaws chanting and cutting up one of the sergeants who had been killed or wounded on the plain. Soon after this he saw Indians carrying a dead or wounded Indian back toward village and in a little while the Indians set fire to grass, for what purpose he did not know.

On a.m. of June 26 the Indian whom DeRudio mistook for Tom Custer was riding Tom Custer's horse which DeRudio easily recognized.

On morning of June 27, Gibbon came up the valley, and Bradley, who was with the flankers on the left, discovered the dead on Custer ridge. Later in the day, when Benteen was saddling up to go over to Custer battlefield, DeRudio asked to go along and Benteen told him he could take Sergeant Pahl's horse, as Pahl had been wounded. Bradley went along to guide Benteen. They followed the trail of the five companies to the river down Medicine Tail coulee. The whole command of five companies had gone nearly to the river, and two shod horses had gone quite to the river bank and the tracks seemed to indicate that they had shied around quickly in some blue clay as if turned suddenly by their riders. Says Custer's trail was in column of fours part of way but in one or two narrow places had changed to column of twos. The first dead man was near Ford B and about 150 yards from river. Says this man was not Sergt. Butler. He was neither stripped nor scalped.

On battlefield he counted 214 dead, Bradley counted 214 and Benteen 212. Does not recollect appearance of dead around Keogh.

Custer lay on top of a conical knoll. Five or six horses lay as if they had been led there and shot down for a barricade, as empty shells lay behind them. These horses were all sorrels from Company C. No one in the group where Custer lay was scalped. DeRudio is positive about this. Lieut. Riley lay near Custer and his body was shot full of arrows. Cooke's sideburn had been scalped from one side of his face and his thighs were cut open in several places.

Does not remember any enlisted men being identified and is not sure about Company E men, but saw a heap of men in a gully and says the dead horses nearest the river were gray ones belonging to Company E. Nowlan found Sturgis' shirt in village and it had a bullet hole, showing that Sturgis had been shot through the body. Dr. Lord's surgical case was found in village.

DeRudio says he was the only man in the regiment who carried a saber in the Little Bighorn expedition. He had done this on previous expeditions, and the soldiers had often joked him about it. Says Custer did not have a sword or saber on this expedition and was not in the habit of carrying one on campaigns.

John S. Hiley. After the battle a board of survey was appointed to take inventory of the property of the men killed and DeRudio was the recorder of this board. Hiley's trunk was opened and in it was found among other things, a faro bank, Hiley being a great gambler. In the trunk also was a letter from Hiley's mother, showing her to be lady of the nobility of Scotland. In this letter she informed him that the matter of some trouble he had gotten into in his native country was soon to be settled up and he could then return home without molestation. DeRudio wrote to this woman, who replied with a request that Hiley's effects be sent to her. He referred her to the Adjt. General at Washington and to him she made application thru the British ambassador and the effects were turned over to ambassador by order of Adj. General. Says Hiley's name was Forbes. DeRudio says the effects of soldiers killed that were not claimed were put up and sold and brought about $5500 (fifty-five hundred dollars).

DeRudio says the story published in fall of 1876 in *New York Herald* and other papers as coming from him was written by Major Brisbin. DeRudio had given Brisbin a statement of the facts with a promise from Brisbin that they were not to be published, but Brisbin violated the agreement. Says Brisbin colored up the story considerably and that the article is not accurate in some of the details.[2] Says there was a coulee full of Indians 300 or 400 yards ahead of skirmish line. This must be where bend of river is now.

———

2. The following is an extract from a letter dated December 20, 1922, to an unidentified correspondent from Walter Camp, a copy of which is in the editor's possession:

DeRudio personally did not write any newspaper stories in 1876, '77 or '78. There is a story written in the first person under the name of Lieut. De-Rudio, but it was written by Major Brisbin, of the 2nd Cavalry. DeRudio told me this himself, and cautioned me not to take all of it seriously, saying that Brisbin "colored" it a good deal. The same story published in Helena paper in July, 1876, that you refer to was published or reprinted in a Louisville paper in 1878, also in the New York Herald, *I think in 1876, and Brisbin got paid for them all. He made a good deal of money as a newspaper correspondent, and was the author of a number of books.*

Interviews with 7th Cavalrymen

Daniel Knipe
John Martin
Thomas F. O'Neill
Stanislas Roy
Roman Rutten
Jacob Adams
John McGuire
Richard P. Hanley
George W. Wylie
William E. Morris
Henry Petring
George W. Glenn
Dennis Lynch
John Sivertsen
Edward D. Pigford
Ferdinand Widmayer
John Foley
James Wilber
Patrick Corcoran
Hugh McGonigle

Daniel A. Knipe's Account of Custer Fight given to me on June 16 & 17, 1908[1]

The regiment had a battery of 2 Rodman and 2 Gatling guns (5 barrels each . . .), but Custer, wishing not be be encumbered, decided not to take these [and] sent these over to Gibbons command before starting from mouth of Rosebud. . . . Left mouth of Rosebud June 22 soon after noon. Still on Rosebud night of 23rd on main Indian trail. All day 24th on Rosebud. About 30 Ree scouts; Charley Reynolds, scout; Curley, Crow scout; Isaiah (colored scout and Sioux interpreter); Mitch Bouyer, scout; Bloody Knife, scout; there may have been more scouts. Went into camp on night 24th but when Crow scouts came back with information about 9 . . . hurriedly packed up at 10:00 p.m. *I went at trot and gallop all night long.*

On morning 25th unsaddled in ravine on west slope of divide between Rosebud and Little Bighorn and made coffee etc. Here Sergeant Curtis and detail of F troop about 8:00 a.m. went back after box hard bread lost off pack train during night and found 2 Indians helping themselves. He brought it back and Custer immediately ordered to mount and go ahead. Up to this time he had intended lying concealed all day but when he knew that he had been discovered by Indians he would wait no longer.

Between 10:00 and 11:00 a.m. Custer and 2 scouts returned from

---

1. Camp MSS, field notes, box 2, folder 8, Daniel A. Knipe, Lilly Library.

In his story Knipe says that his name is Kanipe, but it is commonly spelled Knipe. He was enlisted as Knipe. Knipe was born on April 15, 1853, near Marion, North Carolina, the son of Jacob and Isabella Mosteller Knipe. He enlisted on August 7, 1872, in Lincolnton, North Carolina, and was in the Yellowstone expedition in 1873 and the Black Hills expedition in 1874. He married the widow of First Sergeant Edwin Bobo on April 12, 1877, and was discharged from the 7th Cavalry in August of that year. He died on July 18, 1926, at Marion, North Carolina. His story is in *Contributions to Montana Historical Society,* vol. 4.

reconnoiter and to where regiment was standing and there divided regiment.[2] Custer took C, E, F, I, and L. C to Tom Custer, E to Lieut. Smith, I to Keogh, F to Yates, L to Calhoun. Reno 3 companies: G to McIntosh, 1st Lieut.; M to Capt. French; A to Moylan. Capt. Benteen: H to Benteen, D to Weir, K to Godfrey, Lieut. McDougall B Co. with pack train. Custer with 5 cos. followed trail Reno on left and Benteen on far left.[3] All went forward at trot and gallop in column of twos and struck Indian camp and lone tepee,[4] and Custer ordered it set afire and just then Reno and whole command came in sight and came over and Reno and Custer rode together for some distance.[5]

Reno followed Benteen Creek down on main trail and forded Little Big Horn about noon. At this time Sergeant Knipe of Co. C saw Indians up on bluff some distance beyond where Reno later fortified.[6] A little beyond this Tom Custer verbally gave Sergeant Knipe

---

2. Was Kanipe the one who told of throwing away small sacks of oats as the regiment passed the divide? *Yes.* Had these been taken along as a precaution against running short of feed? Says yes not compelled to do so but each man who wanted to did so, carried perhaps 2 gallons apiece in small sacks. This was west of divide, after regiment was divided. *This feed we got off the boat Far West at mouth of Rosebud.*

(Camp MSS, field notes, box 2, folder 8, Daniel A. Knipe, Lilly Library.)

3. We quote here from a letter written by Daniel A. Knipe on July 20, 1908, at Marion, N.C., to Walter Camp:

Custer with his five companies followed Reno's trail, on after him, some distance down Benteen's Creek; seeing about fifty or a hundred Indians up on the bluff to the right of Little Big Horn he turned square to the right, increasing our speed, and General Custer did not leave his five companies. He rode right in front of them all the time. The command never halted, nor did Custer ever leave his five companies from the place up on the divide where he divided his regiment until after I got my orders to go back; and when the command got up on the bluff where the Indians were supposed to have been seen we could see across the valley, see Reno, and his three companies, about thirty-five Indian scouts, going right to the Indian camps. We could see the Indian camp, plainly. Custer never did go to the ford of Little Big Horn, where Creek [ran] *into it, it being about a half mile from the ford of Little Big Horn to the place where we turned to the right.*

(Walter Camp Collection, box 5, folder 7, BYU Library.)

4. Did Knipe see Custer order Rees dismounted at lone tepee because they would not go ahead and engage Sioux? Knipe says did not see this and does not believe anything like this took place.

(Camp MSS, field notes, box 2, folder 8, Daniel A. Knipe, Lilly Library.)

5. Herendeen's account that Custer delivered orders to Reno direct when he told him to charge the village agrees with what Knipe says. Knipe says Custer motioned Reno to come over and then they rode side by side and Custer talked to him direct. Herendeen says this was ¾ mile from village.

(Ibid.)

6. Knipe sometimes has thought that his seeing Indians on the ridge is what determined Custer to turn to right and cease to follow Reno and may have been responsible for the plan followed by Custer. Knipe says that as soon as . . . he saw 60 to 75 Indians on hill . . . north of where Reno was corraled, he reported to Serg. Bobo, who reported to Harrington and Harring-

orders from General Custer to go back and order McDougall to follow him with pack train and to hurry up.[7] Knipe met Benteen[8] a little west of burning tepee[9] and passed on to McDougall a little further east.[10] He met McDougall and delivered orders.[11] His orders were: "Go back to McDougall and bring him and the pack train straight

---

ton to Tom Custer and Tom Custer to General Custer. General Custer immediately turning to the right in direction of Indians. Suggestion that this event may have been what decided Custer to go down river on that side. Naturally he would not wish to attack the camp without driving these Indians in.

(Ibid.)

7. The order Knipe carried to McDougall was if any packs got loose to cut them *unless ammunition packs*. Besides what he was to tell McDougall, Tom Custer said: "And if you see Benteen tell him to come on quick — a big Indian camp."

(Ibid.)

8. Did Benteen tell Knipe he thought you had made a *mistake* in the officer and then tell you where you would find McDougall and did you meet Benteen east of the watering place? Edgerly says Knipe met Benteen east of watering place. Knipe says no. How far east of Benteen did find packs? *2 miles.*

(Ibid.)

9. We quote here from a letter written by Daniel A. Knipe on October 9, 1910, at Bristol, Pa., to Walter Camp:

In regards to the place that I met Benteen he had left the place where he was watering his horses. When I first saw him that was what he was doing watering, and it was about one mile as you say from where I met McDougall. I was not in sight of McDougall when I met Benteen; it was just after he crossed the Dry Creek and if you remember that there is a little valley up that Dry Creek. Benteen was closer to McDougall when he was at the water hole than he was when he met me I would say one-half mile farther from him.

(Walter Camp Collection, box 5, folder 7, BYU Library.)

10. When Knipe on way to McDougall with message he passed band of Rees and not knowing whether they were friends or Sioux put cartridge in gun and got ready to fire in case they attacked. [Told] Knipe about my difficulty in reconciling time of retreat of Rees with ponies with Knipe's statement as to where he met them. Knipe says he could not be mistaken. There was a small party of them — ½ dozen or more. He was within about 200 yards of them. *They passed to my right and went on ahead. When I turned to right to go to Benteen they gained on me. (They had the herd down to a dead gallop and were certainly losing no time in quitting the valley of the Little Bighorn. They were raising a tremendous cloud of dust and were giving voice to more kinds of yells and "yips" and "ki-yis" than I had heard in many a day.) Soon after this I saw Benteen coming and turned to right and went over that way waving my hat. Benteen and his command then turned to his right and came over to meet me.*

(Camp MSS, field notes, box 2, folder 8, Daniel A. Knipe, Lilly Library.)

11. Knipe met Benteen at the creek not far from the burning tepee . . . about 1 mile west of lone tepee. Knipe met head end of pack train about at lone tepee. Packs strung out about a mile and met McDougall about ½ mile east of lone tepee. When Knipe got to north branch of Benteen Creek . . . he saw Benteen over south at main Benteen Creek and he waved his hat and Benteen turned to right (north) and came over that way and Knipe turned to right and passed Benteen and told him that "they want you up there as quick as you can get there — they have struck a big Indian camp."

(Ibid.)

across the country. Tell McDougall to hurry the pack train to Custer and if any of the packs get loose cut them and let them go; do not stop to tighten them." Knipe rode back at head of pack train and brought it to Reno who had already retreated and Benteen already with him. Ben Hutchins, Lieut.,[12] killed crossing river and Lieut. Wallace tried to get him out. Right away whole command at about half past 2:00 p.m. went forward to highest point about ¾ mile north of place of fortification and stopped there about ½ hour and then Indians rode up and fired and then whole pack of Indians came up and charged Reno about 3:00 p.m. (This differs from Godfrey's account). Indians fired until dark and then stopped and began again next day and kept up all day.[13] Next day, 26th, men went down to river with camp kettles to get water and Indians kept them from getting any, some of the men being wounded. Evening of 26th Indians moved camp about sundown but warriors kept shooting until dark.

Capt. Keogh's old horse Comanche (claybank in color) was the only survivor of Custer's battle. He was found on battlefield with six wounds and was taken (limped his way) on night of 27th . . . along with Reno's wounded up to steamer Far West which Terry had brought up as far as mouth of Little Big Horn. . . . Knipe says that from time Custer parted from Reno his command (Custer's) went at trot and gallop all way up the bluff and that when Custer's men saw Reno charging northward on opposite side of river Custer's men broke into rather wild disorder and began waving their arms, yelling and urging their horses ahead at break neck speed (This may have been mistaken by Godfrey for the cheering he speaks about). In this wild run many of the men got in advance of Custer and the last words Knipe heard Custer utter were: "Hold your horses, boys; there are Indians enough down there for all of us." Knipe says it was a trot and gallop all the way to this point and beyond and that no halt was made by Custer to cheer

----

12. Reference here is to Second Lieutenant Benjamin Hodgson of Co. B, 7th Cavalry.

13. Was Knipe on H Co.'s line all time June 25 and 26? Says was on Co. B line June 25. Next morning when Benteen wanted help he went up with McGuire, Thompson, Whittaker on H Co.'s line. On hill did Benteen have all of men detailed with the packs? *Part of packers details were there.* . . . Knipe on Reno Hill saw Chief Packer Wagner when spent bullet hit him in head and *I thought he had been killed. He kicked around awhile and finally sat up and began feeling of his head.* . . . Knipe says that at one time when Indians were charging in force many of Benteen's men left their line and had retreated half way down to the hospital, when Benteen rallied them.

(Ibid.)

Reno. Shortly after this Knipe was sent back to carry word to Mc-Dougall, and Trumpeter Martini was sent with message to Benteen. Goldin, whom Cook sent to Reno, must have left before Knipe, and Martini must have left last as, according to Benteen's story, Martini reached him after Knipe passed going to McDougall.

Knipe says every man in Custer's command,[14] including Custer, was stripped and that many were mutilated with arrows and hatchet blows across forehead, these men being probably not quite dead and killed by squaws in that way. Knipe says Custer had only one wound and that through chest.[15] Says he had good look at him as he lay with

---

14. July 20, 1908, letter from Knipe to Camp (see fn. 3):

The officers and soldiers seemed to be killed in about the position they were formed in the line of march. The horses were killed and scattered all over the hill, and at the point where Custer lay.... There was not hardly any horses around where he was lying when found. The soldiers lay thick at this point. Custer was lying across two or three soldiers, just a small portion of his back touching the ground....Custer had no clothing on whatever, nor none of the soldiers. There was nothing left but a foot of a boot, the leg of this being gone, on Custer. There were no mutilated soldiers at this point, except Cooke, who was near Custer, and the mutilating of him was just a long gash on one of his thighs. Custer's wound was in the left breast, near his heart, just one shot. I saw Sergeant Bobo, Finley, Finkle, they were lying along the line of march as the company was retreating for the last stand. Sergeants Finley and Finkle were both mutilated very badly. They showed to be wounded. Their horses were lying near them. Bobo was not mutilated at all.

(Walter Camp Collection, box 5, folder 7, BYU Library.)

15. Asked Knipe if ridge where monument now is was so level and wide . . . Says no, says *was narrower and Custer laid on very peak of it.... On . . . 27th perhaps 3 or 4 o'clock, Capt. Benteen and his company were saddling up to go over to the battlefield, and as I had been with him throughout Reno's siege I asked permission to accompany him, to see if I could locate the dead of my own troop C. He answered by saying that I could if I had a horse. Upon my giving an affirmative reply he said, "Yes, come along with us." I fell in behind and went along with him. We went down to Dry Creek, on about the same route which I now believe Custer followed, and then down Dry Creek nearly to the ford of the river. From here went direct to the battlefield, and the first dead soldier we found was Serg. Finley of my own company at point marked. His body was stuck full of arrows. The dead lay plainly in sight, all being stripped of clothing and we passed on toward Calhoun, finding Serg. Finckle on the way between Finley and Calhoun. Turning back to the left at Calhoun I passed along in the direction of where the monument now stands and about two-thirds way to where Keogh lay I recognized the horse of 1st Serg. Bobo of my own co. The horse had evidently been ridden along the ridge close to the gully, for he had slidden down the bank, into the gully, and died there. When I came to the pile of men lying around Capt. Keogh I recognized Serg. Edward Bobo. While Benteen's men were in ranks as they passed around I was free to go by myself. Arriving at end of the ridge I recognized the bodies of Genl. Custer, Boston Custer, Cooke, Lt. Smith and others, but did not see Tom Custer, my own captain. As I had him particularly in mind I cannot understand how I came to overlook him but the bodies were badly bloated after lying two days in the hot sun and in some cases identification was difficult or impossible. I next went along the line of dead bodies toward the river, and riding along the edge of the deep gully about 2000 feet from where the monument now stands, I counted 28 bodies in this gulch. The only one I thought I recognized at the time was Mitch Bouyer. I am not positive about this, as I did not go down in the gulch for closer inspection. I recall that, as the matter ran through my mind at the time, I was then well enough satisfied that the corpse was that of*

---

small of his back across another dead soldier and that there was neither wound in his forehead nor burned powder marks on his forehead or face.

Says that only 3 tepees[16] were left on the site of Indian camp and that these were piled full of dead Indians wrapped in buffalo skins, as for burial. He estimates that there must have been at least 60 dead Indians found thus.[17] Says that most of their tepee poles were still on ground, they having taken away only enough for travois. They also left large quantities of dried buffalo beef, kettles and other utensils, evidently having more of these than could be carried off.

Knipe tells how, when besieged on Reno hill, the chiefs would try to urge on their men. There would be a lull in firing and then some Indian would cry out a command in a loud voice easily heard round about. The interpreter at times would report the chief as saying to his men that they could easily get the soldiers (white men) if they would only try a little harder.

Knipe says Benteen acted very bravely and walked about exposed to fire much of the time.[18] When the soldiers would remark that he was "drawing the fire" he would say: "Well they will fire about so often anyhow" etc. Knipe was duty sergeant being outranked by the first or orderly sergeant.

Sturgis was Col. of 7th Cavalry and Custer Lieut. Col. The young Lieut. Sturgis killed with Custer was his son, who had gone out to see the fight, not being in command. . . .

Bouyer. Having seen these bodies in the gulch I am at a loss to understand the absence of markers there. I have heard and read much about the mutilation and scalping of the men on the Custer battlefield. I cannot recall seeing a single body that was scalped, and I do not think, as a general thing, that the bodies were mutilated any more than was necessary to cause death wherever life still lingered with the wounded. What seemed to be a common method of doing this was to chop open the head across the forehead or across the eyes. . . .

(Camp MSS, field notes, box 2, folder 8, Daniel A. Knipe, Lilly Library.)

16. July 20, 1908, letter from Knipe to Camp (see fns. 3, 14):

As I did not tell you before much about the dead Indians in the camp in the three tepees, I will tell you now: I cut the buffaloe robe from around one of the Indians to see what was buried with the Indian, and I found one piece of rawhide about two feet long lie full of white people's scalps. Some of them were women's scalps, with hair several feet long. These scalps I left there with the dead Indian.

17. *There were three tepees full of dead Indians in the village. I did not count them, but I estimate there was something like sixty-five or seventy dead Indians in these three tepees. They were already tied up in buffalo robes, ready for burial.*

(Ibid.)

18. Knipe said once when Benteen came back from a visit to Reno he (Benteen) said: "I found him lying in the same place where I saw him before."

(Camp MSS, field notes, box 2, folder 8, Daniel A. Knipe, Lilly Library.)

It is important to note Knipe's statement that just before Custer separated from Reno at mouth of Benteen Creek Knipe saw a considerable band of Indians on the bluffs just north of Reno hill. He estimated that there must have been 60 or 75 of them. Says he called the attention of his orderly sergeant to them. When Custer with his 5 companies turned northward from Benteen Creek he was going straight in the direction of these Indians. Knipe says the Indians must have been ¾ mile or a mile away. These really may have been the Indians who signaled or sent word to Gall instead of (Iron —?) whom Godfrey speaks of signaling to Gall from "the high point." It does not seem likely that after Reno had begun firing that Gall could have heard an audible signal from across the river. It appears to me that Gall's information of Custer's approach must have come to him before Reno had advanced to his first fighting position, because Custer was going north parallel with Reno across the river and fully abreast of him, in full view from the Indian camp and also in full view of Reno's men. The probability is therefore that information of Custer's approach came to Gall while Custer was still a considerable distance south of a point opposite from the Indian camp. Knipe is very positive and emphatic in expressing his recollection that Custer and all his men proceeded north along the bluffs so far west that they had full view of Reno's men and the Indian village all the time instead of some distance back and out of sight as stated and mapped by Godfrey. Knipe says that Custer was trotting and galloping along with companies in columns of twos, all 5 companies abreast, the men cheering and eager for a fight and that after the highest point on the bluffs was reached, the men, through their eagerness, broke into something like disorder, as previously noted. If this was the case Gall certainly must have known of the presence of Custer's command before he (Gall) was well engaged with Reno.

Knipe is of the opinion that Custer first tried to ford and charge the Indian camp at the mouth of Dry Creek (Reno Creek). His reason is that a dead trooper, with his dead horse, were found on the west side of the Little Big Horn at this point, or practically in the Indian Camp. This is not, however, conclusive evidence, as the soldier may have been attempting to escape from Custer hill and was forced by pursuers to take a route to point where he was found. Godfrey's theory seems more plausible. By the time Custer got to Reno Creek the Indians must certainly have become thoroughly apprised of his approach and had preparations well under way to meet him. By this time also Custer probably had full understanding (tried to verify this by observation on the ground) of the extent of the Indian village, and his route, as mapped by Godfrey. Would indicate that he was making for some point from which he could charge the north end of the village. His course in turning down on the ridge ending in Custer hill would bear out this idea of his plan. By this time, however, the low country intervening between his position and the village may have been thickly filled with Indians, which would compel him to give up his plan of attack on the village and make a defense instead.

If Godfrey's account obtained from Gall is correct concerning the dismounting of Calhoun's and Keogh's companies back by the spring, and that the lead horses remained there until stampeded by the Indians, how does it come that no dead soldiers were found back there or between there and Custer hill?

Interview with
John Martin,
October 24, 1908[1]

Trumpeter Martin, Orderly for Custer on June 25, 1876, Voss
Chief Trumpeter. . . . Three trumpeters: John Martin, H Troop;
Dose of G Troop; Bishop (?) of C Troop.[2] Martin says these were the
only orderlies Custer had that day and that he is certain about it. Martin says that 1st Lieut. James A. Nowlan (Henry J. Nowlan) was regimental quartermaster but was left back with the wagon train at Powder
River.

Martin says at mouth of Rosebud Mitch Bouyer told Terry where
Sitting Bull's camp was located. Then officers desired Bouyer to con-
duct them to the village, and Bouyer said he had previously been with

---

1. Camp MSS, field notes, John Martin, folder 3, Lilly Library, Indiana
University.

John Martin (Giovanni Martini) was born in Italy in January 1853 and
came to the United States in 1873. He enlisted as a trumpeter and was assigned
to Company H. He carried the last message from Lieutenant Colonel George
Custer to Captain Frederick Benteen and was in the hilltop fight. He reenlisted
and served in the 3rd Artillery for thirteen years and transferred to the 4th Artillery. He was promoted from trumpeter to sergeant in 1900. He participated
in the Black Hills expedition in 1874, the Sioux campaign in 1876, the Nez
Perce campaign in 1877, and the Spanish-American War. He retired as a sergeant
on January 4, 1904, and resided in New York City until he died on December
24, 1922. He was buried in Cypress Hills Cemetery, New York City.

2. Henry Voss was chief trumpeter and William H. Sharrow was sergeant
major of the regiment. Both were killed with the Custer column. Henry C. Dose
was a trumpeter in Company G and was killed with the Custer column. There
were two brothers, Alex and Charles H. Bishop in the 7th Cavalry, but neither
was in Company C. Martin may have been referring to Charles H. Bischoff, but
Bischoff was on detached service at Yellowstone Depot. The trumpeter in Company C was William Kramer, who was killed on June 25, probably with the
Custer column.

Sitting Bull and that Bull had offered 100 ponies for his head and that he would go along, and the Indians would kill him if they could get him; and Custer said in that case the whole command would meet the same fate.

Did not see Indians on ridge . . . when Custer separated from Reno. Says that before Custer reached high ridge he marched in columns of twos with gray horses in center of column.[3] His description of route agrees with Curley and Knipe exactly. Martin says Custer's trail passed along where Reno retreated to. Then Custer halted command on the high ridge about 10 minutes, and officers looked at village through glasses. Saw children and dogs playing among the tepees but no warriors or horses except few loose ponies grazing around. There was then a discussion among the officers as to where the warriors might be and someone suggested that they might be buffalo hunting, recalling that they had seen skinned buffalo along the trail on June 24.

Custer now made a speech to his men saying, "We will go down and make a crossing and capture the village." The whole command then pulled off their hats and cheered. And the consensus of opinion seemed to be among the officers that if this could be done the Indians would have to surrender when they would return, in order not to fire upon their women and children.

Then command "Attention" "Fours right" "Column right" "March" was given and command went forward down off the hill and then "Column left" and whole command passed down ravine toward dry creek.[4] Martin thinks he continued about ½ mile farther when Cooke halted and wrote message to Benteen and gave to Martin and then Custer spoke to Martin and said: "Trumpeter, go back on our trail and see if you can discover Benteen and give him this message. If you see no danger come back to us, but if you find Indians in your way stay with Benteen and return with him and when you get back to

---

3. Custer never left his command to ride to the high point to wave his hat, as is sometimes reported. When Custer was on the high point his whole command was there with him, sitting on their horses. As soon as the command left this high point everybody passed out of sight from Reno's position and went down the hollow toward Dry Creek. *I do not remember seeing Mitch Bouyer or the Crow scouts at this time. They might have been somewhere in the vicinity and I did not see them.*

(Camp MSS, field notes, John Martin, folder 3, Lilly Library.)

4. Did Custer *follow the bottom South Coulee all the way* and make turn into Medicine Tail or cut across the hill and save some of the distance? He doesn't seem to think Custer cut across the hill. *No, Custer followed coulee all the way.*

(Ibid.)

us report." Martin started back on trail before got up the hill (that is up to high point where whole command had halted) he heard heavy firing in the direction of his right. It might also have been Reno's fire which he heard as that would have been to his right. He afterward supposed was at Ford B. After this he met Boston Custer going to join the command. When Martin got to top of ridge he looked down in village and saw Indians charging like swarm of bees toward the ford, waving buffalo hides. At the same time he saw Custer retreating up the open country in the direction of the battlefield. (He did not tell this at the Reno court of inquiry because he was not asked the question. He thinks that in Reno court of inquiry it was not desired that he should tell all he knew and said that afterward he never was invited by officers to discuss what he knew of the battle and never volunteered to do so.) The Indians were firing straggling shots. About this time Martin was fired on by Indians in the bluffs between him and river and they hit his horse on hip, and blood spattered on Martin's back.[5]

Martin now rode fast and met Benteen on Benteen Creek and came back with him. Martin says when he gave message to Benteen, Benteen asked: "Where is General Custer?" Martin said: "About 3 miles from here." Benteen said, "Is [Custer] being attacked or not?" and Martin said: "Yes, [he] is being attacked" and said no more. Martin is positive that he did not tell Benteen . . . that Indians were "skid-daddling." . . . Ask Martin if when he returned and did not see Reno if he saw any Indians where he afterwards learned Reno to be. *No — saw neither Indians nor Reno nor any fighting.*

Martin says when Benteen got up Reno came up without any hat and said: "For God's sake, Benteen, halt your command and wait until I can organize my men." After Martin got to Reno Heights did Benteen or Reno consult him as to direction of Custer? *No,* Martin says. *No. Benteen had the heel of his boot shot off on the hill. He turned around and looked at it and said: "Pretty close call — try again."* Martin says he certainly saw 4 Crows with Reno on the hill during the two days.

Martin says careful search was made of whole country for dead men down to river — that detachments were sent out and that Serg. Butler was found in this way.

---

5. Martin says he met Boston Custer after his horse was hit and that Boston Custer called attention to the fact that his horse was limping.

(Ibid.)

Martin saw Serg. Butler of L Troop and says his horse was dead with him. Does not think he could have been carrying message because Butler was not an orderly that day. Martin saw the heap of dead men in deep gully between Custer and the river. Says that one of the first sergeants with whom some of the men had left their pay for safe keeping had about $500 in paper money torn up and scattered all over his body. Martin says on Custer battlefield there were not half as many dead horses as dead men. Martin says that one of Cooke's sideburns was scalped off, skin and all, and this corroborates what others have said. Martin describes Custer's wounds as do Tom O'Neill and Hammon. He also describes Tom Custer's wounds as did Hammon. Keogh had a gold chain and Agnus Dei Catholic emblem on his neck which the Indians had not taken and Benteen secured this.

Martin saw the dead Indians in the brush on river bank in village. Says there was a big pile but did not count them. Martin says horse Comanche followed the troops down to boat of his own accord when wounded were taken down and was not led. When found, they thought he would die and not worth while to take away.

Martin says that when Genl. Terry came up on the 27th, Terry took him to the spot where Martin started back from Custer with the message and Martin described the ground and incidents to him precisely.

Interview with John Martin, May 4, 1910[1]

Custer first halted on Weir's hill and took a look at village (from this point he could see only about ⅓ of it — Hunk and Blackfoot villages — WMC).[2] *Here he turned column to the right and went down coulee to Dry Creek[3] and turned to left and followed Dry Creek straight for village. About half way down to Little Bighorn we came into full view of the village* (The first time he had seen south end of it — WMC)[4] *and here he halted the command and Cooke[5] wrote out the message to Benteen, and I started back with it on the trail.[6] I did not follow Dry Creek all way back to coulee running north and*

---

1. Camp MSS, field notes, John Martin, folder 3, Lilly Library.

2. Martin says whole column passed over the high ridge from which they could plainly see village and children and dogs in it. Martin says he was with Custer after he passed the high ground and left him just as the command started down a ravine to get off the bluff, somewhat to the right of highest ground and about 1000 feet from it.

(Camp MSS, field notes, Custer's Trail at Little Bighorn, box 2, folder 6, Lilly Library.)

3. In his notes Walter Camp often used the term Dry Creek to describe Medicine Tail Coulee.

4. Martin was seemingly confused at this point. In another note Camp says of Martin, "When started out with message had not seen village from this coulee."

(Camp MSS, field notes, John Martin, folder 3, Lilly Library.)

5. Martin said Cooke told him to follow back on same trail and after he had gone 500 or 600 yards or perhaps ¾ mile, *I got on same ridge from which Genl. Custer saw the village the first time and on looking down on the bottom I saw Major Reno and his command engaged already, but I did not pay any attention to that.* Thinks that from time he saw Reno he was 15 or 20 minutes getting up to Benteen.

(Camp MSS field notes, Custer's Trail at Little Bighorn, folder 6, Lilly Library.)

6. Thinks he left Custer 2 miles north of Reno Hill. After he left Custer he traveled up hill for some distance.

(Ibid.)

103

south but cut across the high ground. When I got up on the elevation I looked behind[7] and saw Custer's command over on the flat and Indians over in the village riding toward the river and waving buffalo hides. The battalion appeared at this time to be falling back from the river. This is the last I saw of the 5 companies alive and it was only a hasty glance.

I kept on up the north and south coulee and soon met a mounted man whom I recognized as one of C troop, but whose name I did not know. He inquired where the command was, and I told him down the coulee quite a distance and that he had better fall back to the pack train, as he would likely be cut off by the Indians before reaching the command, but he kept on. After this I met Boston Custer[8] and went on to Benteen.

As Benteen approached the river[9] we turned to the north along the bluffs just above the river and there met three Crow scouts who pointed out Reno's men who were now retreating across the bottom. It has been asserted by some writers of late years that Custer's command

---

7. *Met Boston Custer half way between medium coulee and Weir Hill. Boston asked me where Custer was and if he had been attacked and I said no. Soon after . . . met the two men. After this I heard a volley and looked back and saw Custer retreating back from the river.*

(Camp MSS, field notes, John Martin, folder 3, Lilly Library.)

8. On his way to Benteen with the message he met first Boston Custer on the bluffs and farther along on the bluffs two enlisted men who were together and inquired for Custer's command. This is another good proof that Custer hesitated and stopped some considerable time after he came in sight of village.

(Camp MSS, field notes, unclassified envelope 130, Lilly Library.)

About meeting Boston Custer, when going back with message and after, he heard firing. Told him he had better look out as there were Indians around and Boston Custer said: "Well I am going to join the command anyhow . . ." It would seem that if the meeting of Boston Custer was a fact Custer must have remained some time in vicinity of ford or else Boston Custer must have cut a big circuit and joined command on the high ground. However, it might have been Reno's firing that Martin heard, in which case Boston Custer may have had time to over-take the General before reaching Ford B. The meeting of Boston Custer and the fact that he died with the General can hardly be reconciled by any other explanation.

(Camp MSS, field notes, John Martin, folder 3, Lilly Library.)

9. Martin says that Benteen followed Custer's trail (Important): *We marched on Gen. Custer's trail and when we got up this ridge from where I saw Maj. Reno fighting on the bottom we saw Maj. Reno's command and the Major himself, the men still retreating on the bluff.* (Ask Knipe how far he found McDougall back of Benteen and whether he remembers Martin's coming back to McDougall). Martin says his own company was with Benteen. He says packs got up to Reno in 10 or 15 minutes behind Benteen, and in another place he says 3 hours. Says it was 1½ hours after McDougall reached Reno Hill before the whole command went in direction of Custer. Says he found Benteen 3 or 4 miles from where he left Custer.

(Camp MSS, field notes, Custer's Trail at Little Bighorn, folder 6, Lilly Library.)

never got nearer the river than where he was found dead, but I know this to be incorrect for I myself was with General Custer when he was much nearer the river than is the point where he was found dead and I saw him and his command right down on the flat within a few hundred yards of the river, retreating from it. Until late years no one ever seemed to doubt the fact that Custer went to the river at the place which I state.

When Benteen met Reno on hill, Reno requested him to halt his command, etc. Benteen pulled out Cooke's note and showed it to Reno. Reno was bareheaded and much excited and exclaimed: "Well I have lost about half of my men, and I could do no better than I have done."

In Benteen's charge the Indians had formed in the gully and were coming up the hill. We charged out, old Benteen right in front of us. Before this charge the Indians had been close enough to throw stones into our lines. When we charged out we killed three of them. The Indian who was killed and whom the other Indians could not get away was killed on evening of June 25.

I showed (on June 27) Benteen where I left with note from Custer, and Benteen estimated the distance to be 600 yards to Ford B. Did not go down there with Terry on June 27.[10] Reno introduced me to Terry when Terry came up and [Reno] said: "Gen. Terry, here is the man who carried the last message from Custer." Terry then asked me several questions as to how far I had been with Custer, etc. and then said: "Well, you are a lucky man and I wish you good fortune."

In the village I saw the two tepees with dead Indians in them and only about 100 yards away on the river bank there was a pile of dead Indians under a tree with blankets thrown over them. . . . Saw body of white man in village where Knipe showed me but says body was in a tepee.

---

10. Again some confusion in Martin's statements, since in another note Camp quotes Martin:

On June 27 I accompanied General Terry over all this ground and explained these matters to him in detail.

(Camp MSS, field notes, John Martin, folder 3, Lilly Library.)

★

105

Interview with
Thomas F. O'Neill[1]

Tom O'Neill's story given to me personally on October 12 [probably 1919] in Washington D.C. O'Neill says Custer came within 300 or 400 yards of river before he turned up to the right. He remembers the ford where Reno crossed as at a high bank. The trail split and went around a little rise of ground on which some of the Rees were sitting holding a council and discussing the numbers of the Sioux. One of these was picking up handfuls of grass and dropping it and pointing to the Sioux, who could be seen down and across the river, indicating that the Sioux were as thick as the grass. He [O'Neill] went to left of this knoll and down to the river through a dry ravine. On other side of river there were timber and fallen logs and took some time to get through. When about half way down to where skirmish line was formed he saw Custer and his whole command on the bluffs across the river, over to the east, at a point which he would think was about where Reno afterward fortified, or perhaps a little south of this. Custer's command were then going at a trot.

He says that on the skirmish line there was no very hard fighting and thinks that but few effective shots could have been fired. The skirmish line could not have stood to exceed 20 min. The men were in good spirits, talking and laughing and not apprehensive of being defeated, and the Sioux, toward the village, were riding around kicking

1. Walter Camp field notes, folder 83, BYU Library. Thomas F. O'Neill, born in Dublin, Ireland, was a private in Company G. He enlisted for the second time on January 17, 1872. He was cook for Lieutenant Donald McIntosh on the Sioux campaign until June 25. He retired as a first sergeant and died on March 23, 1914. His account is also in *The Pacific Monthly*, July 1908, p. 109. A copy of a three-page letter from Sergeant Thomas O'Neill to Brigadier General E. S. Godfrey with his account of the fight is in the Manuscript Room, New York Public Library.

up a big dust but keeping pretty well out of range.

Presently they saw the Sioux going around the left flank, which extended to a point about half way to the hills to the west. The men then ran to their horses and from behind the little rise of ground between timber and open plain they lay and fired at Indians for some time, Lieut. Hare occasionally borrowing a gun from Lieut. Wallace to try his marksmanship on the Indians as they would circle around.

About this time there was a cry that the Indians were getting at the horses over toward the left flank and he [O'Neill] went with McIntosh and whole troop to investigate. They found the river at their back and no Indians in that direction. Reno was in the timber and apparently not excited. They then returned and found hot fire in front and men calling to hurry up as the Indians were pressing. In about 10 minutes Capt. Moylan ordered Troop A to mount. Hodgson inquired "Where you going Moylan?" and Moylan said he was going to charge. Lieut. Varnum remonstrated and said: "For God's sake men let's don't leave the line. There are enough of us here to whip the whole Sioux nation." Nevertheless the stampede was started and could not be stopped.

As he (O'Neill) was mounting, his horse was shot, and seeing a horse without a rider, he mounted it; but immediately Trooper Martin came up and claimed the horse and so he gave him up to Martin, who was killed on the retreat. He then, with some others, followed on after the retreating column on foot. The Indians were riding on the right flank of the mounted men firing into them, and the first he knew he saw them behind coming for him. He then decided to get back to the timber and met Indians pursuing the column. When they would get too close he would take aim, and the Indian aimed at would hang over on opposite side of pony and pass on and in this way he stood off those inclined to get too close until he got to timber without being ridden down. One large Indian, however, rode right up onto him from behind, but he turned and shot him through with his carbine and Indian fell off. One dismounted soldier with him was killed getting to timber.

He quickly reached the south side of the timber and as he ran in he saw De Rudio[2] and soon joined. O'Neill going back to timber passed McIntosh coming out on McCormick's horse. McIntosh asked O'Neill where the command was. He next passed Rapp, the last man out who was leading McIntosh horse. Rapp inquired for "Tosh." The Indians soon came up and killed Rapp. Scouts Billy (probably Bob) Jackson, half-breed, and Gerard with their horses tied some distance

2. For information about Charles De Rudio, see footnote 1 on p. 82.

away. De Rudio's horse had gotten away from him. Jackson and De Rudio were in buffalo wallow. Here they lay and watched the Indians passing back and forth out in the open. They immediately prepared to resist, but waited some time and no Indians came in.

Gerard's horse began to whinny, and Jackson pulled a large bunch of grass, stuffed it into the horse's mouth, and tied it fast to keep the horse still. They could hear Indians all around and moved very cautiously, not going any considerable distance until after dark. During the afternoon they heard firing in direction of Custer, at one time three volleys, and O'Neill thinks all firing in direction over about 5:00 p.m. as nearly as he can estimate.

About 10:00 p.m. the four men and two horses cautiously crept through and out of timber and started up the river, De Rudio and O'Neill hanging to horses' tails. They soon began to find dead men and recognized Lieut. McIntosh in the hazy moonlight. They soon met a small party of mounted Sioux who turned to the right and evaded them. They had heard the firing on Reno during the afternoon and evening, but as all was quiet after dark did not know whether the command had perished on the bluff or retreated. They looked at bluffs on east side and thought them too high and thought best thing would be to go back to Ford A. On the way up the river O'Neill requested Gerard to ride his horse into the water at one point to discover how deep it might be, but Gerard refused to do this and so O'Neill waded in and suddenly stepped into a hole up to his neck.

He floundered out and they went farther up the river. All took drink of water and crossed to the island and at the north end of the island ran into a picket party of Indians with their ponies, about 10 Indians, who called out in Sioux. Here Gerard and Jackson wheeled horses and went back north the way they came and this was last seen of them. The Indians 15 yards away were frightened and jumped horses into river.

De Rudio was behind, and O'Neill squatted, drew his pistol, and prepared for the worst. He heard footsteps and when he saw the cap he recognized De Rudio who said, "O'Neill, they're all gone." They wandered about island looking for place to cross main stream when they became tired and worn out and sat down and rested. Boots full water and clothing wet, he [O'Neill] stripped and wrung out clothing. Now startled by clatter of hoofs and sound of voices. They now waded over to the island but found deep water on east side of it.

Just as it was coming day they heard voices coming up the river on the east bank, and De Rudio ran out exclaiming "Tom Custer!" "Tom

Custer!" O'Neill ran out but immediately warned De Rudio that the men were Indians and not soldiers, and straightway the Sioux began firing at them. At this De Rudio and O'Neill retreated back through the timber on the island in great haste, making for a big clump of bushes only to find seven or eight mounted Indians looking for them. O'Neill, seeing that they were discovered, discharged his carbine into the bunch of redskins, and De Rudio fired two revolver shots, whereupon the Indians were surprised, thinking they were being charged upon by some body of troops. The Indians' ponies were also thrown into fright and were jumping against one another. Turning behind clump of brush and keeping out of sight now to the eastward 150 yards nearly to main river bank, they found trees washed up in a flood against stumps enclosing a triangular space and into this they jumped and decided to try to stand. The Indians saw the direction they went and fired about fifty shots into the brush in that direction, bullets striking the logs all about them. O'Neill now thought they were as good as gone and took off his cartridge belt in which he had, as he remembers, about 25 carbine and 12 revolver shots left. He was resigned to stand here to the last and shook hands with De Rudio thinking that the last would soon be "wound up."

Fortunately the Sioux did not follow them up, probably thinking they had escaped, and at this point they lay all day. Soon the fight against Reno on the bluff started up, and some of Benteen's firing came right down over their heads. Some of the Indians being between them and Benteen, they could hear the Sioux talking quite plainly.

O'Neill says this was the longest day he ever experienced, as they were eagerly waiting for night to come so they could get out. At last darkness came and they made their way up the river, thinking to cross at Ford A and go back on the trail toward the Rosebud. They were very hungry, having had only 3 pieces of hardtack since the morning of the day before — the 25th. O'Neill said he was so thirsty his mouth could make no saliva, and the hardtack was so dry that he could not swallow it and had to blow it out of his mouth as dry as so much flour.

As soon as they got into the water they drank to their fill and were greatly relieved. He thinks they must have missed the ford and gone on past it, but they waded across with the intention of going to the deserted village at the burning tepee, where they hoped they might perchance find some piece of dried meat or unpicked bone left by the Sioux two days before. On their way up Benteen creek, when about a mile from the river, O'Neill heard the braying of a mule away off to his left, whereupon he nudged De Rudio in the ribs and asked him if

109

he also had heard it. De Rudio had heard nothing (being hard of hearing) and was skeptical of O'Neill's opinion that the command might be up there. O'Neill, however, was determined to try and so they started off in that direction. Eventually they heard voices but were too far off to be sure whether it was English or Sioux. They were determined to find out, so they crept stealthily on, listening awhile and then creeping nearer. Finally a voice he could recognize (Serg. McVey, Troop A) loudly cried out:[3] "Hello, Mac," and a number of voices answered back: "Who's there?" and received the reply: "Lieutenant De Rudio and Tom O'Neill." De Rudio was now no longer in doubt, confidence so genuine that he outran O'Neill and got to the command some distance ahead of him. O'Neill helped bury the dead on June 28. He and Hammon[4] personally dug the hole in which Genl. Custer was buried and lay the body in it.

Lieut. Wallace wrote the General's name on a piece of paper, rolled it up and inserted it in an empty cartridge shell and put it by a little stake driven by Custer's head. Before he was covered, Dr. Porter took locks of hair of all the officers.[5] His description of Custer's wounds tallies well with Hammon's. Says was shot clear through head back of both temples and through the chest. Tom Custer was disemboweled but breast not cut open. He recognized him by looking at his face.

---

3. David McVeigh of Company A was a trumpeter, not a sergeant, as mentioned by O'Neill.

4. John E. Hammon was a corporal in Company G. A typescript copy of his statement to Charles E. Deland, February 28, 1898, is in the Dustin Collection, Custer Battlefield National Monument.

5. Editor's note: In those days people made hair pictures (many of these are on exhibit in local museums), watch chains, and other things from hair. Human hair had a cultural significance then that no longer exists today. Perhaps Dr. Porter intended to give the locks of hair to the families of the deceased.

Interview with
Stanislas Roy[1]

On 5th of June got caught in snow storm between Hart [Heart] river and O'Fallon creek and very cold weather. . . . Roy says wagon train went no further than Powder river. Did not go to Rosebud and then return to Powder. . . . Indian graves were in hollow between Miles City and Rosebud.

About Ft. Keogh is where Reno came in off his scout. Between here and the Rosebud we came across low ground with Indian graves in trees. G troop men tore them down and robbed them and threw bones into Yellowstone. Some of the men told McIntosh that G troop might be sorry for this. . . . On trail along Rosebud Indian ponies had eaten grass off each side for long distances. . . .

Roy says when started at noon 6/22 left camp in timber about mile east of mouth of Rosebud and cut across hill and struck Rosebud some distance from river, crossing it and continuing up west side of it. His account seems to indicate that Custer followed a route now marked by the road.

Roy says always heard that Bob Jackson and Billy Cross never forded at Ford A. No one remembers seeing them in the valley fight or on west side of river at all. About 50 yds. timber on west bank Ford A. . . . Reno's advance was cos. G, A, M in this order. . . .

1. Walter Camp field notes, folders 50 and 99, BYU Library. Stanislas Roy, born in France, was a sergeant in Company A, 7th Cavalry. He enlisted in the 7th Cavalry in 1869 and again on January 19, 1875, at age 28 (in Cincinnati, Ohio). He was awarded the Medal of Honor on October 5, 1878, with the citation, "Brought water to the wounded under most galling fire of the enemy and at great danger to life." He participated in the Nez Perce campaign and the engagement at Bear Paw Mountain during October 2–4, 1877. He died at Columbus Barracks, Ohio, on February 10, 1913. His correspondence (1909–1912) with Walter Camp is in the Walter Camp Collection, BYU Library.

After passing ford we formed in line and while forming I heard some of the men say "There goes Custer." He could be seen over on hills to our right and across river. *Dismounted about 200 yds. in advance of timber and skirmish line advanced to point of timber. G on right, A next, and M on left.* He is sure there was no timber to right of line. Some Indians were in timber in advance of right of skirmish line and were firing on skirmish line in an oblique direction — toward the southwest.

Skirmish line extended west from point of timber and not where I have it on the map. Roy saw Charlie Reynolds dismounted and wounded with pistol in hand trying to follow troops in retreat. Roy says, *After my horse was wounded he seemed to be crazy and I could not guide him but he went right, and I stuck to him and he carried me through all right.*

Ordered in from skirmish line and went into timber about 50 yds. to get horse. Met Wallace[2] mounted and leading G Troop out. I asked (no one in particular) where my horse was and Wallace said "Grab any horse you can get and get out of here." Says all went out of south side of timber. Thinks was on skirmish line full 20 minutes. Shot away about 20 rounds of ammunition. Saw ravines over toward hill full of Indians shooting oblique to line. Also saw Indians across river opposite the timber circling around toward east. Saw them through timber.

When went in saw Gilbert[3] coming out of timber with 4 horses, one of which was mine. I mounted up and followed the column and yelled to Gilbert to follow the column and "git." I was behind Gilbert and very late in getting out of timber. About 75 or 100 yds. from timber I saw Charlie Reynolds dismounted and wounded with pistol standing still and showing fight. Soon after this my horse was shot through jaws just back of mouth. Horse went down and then jumped up again and I mounted. My sling belt flew over my head when horse fell and lost my carbine, so that when I mounted had only pistol. Got safely to river. Water about belly deep to horse. Started immediately up the bluff. Horse bleeding badly and abandoned him

---

2. *When I entered the woods I said to Wallace: "Lieutenant, I cannot find my horse." M and A Troops had already gone out and Wallace said, "Take any horse you can find and get out of here quick, or get on a horse behind some one. Get out any way that you can on a horse."*

(Walter Camp field notes, folder 99, BYU Library.)

3. Private John M. Gilbert was in Company A.

going up bluff. The talk was that Reno would go to Custer and I said to Moylan "Captain, I am dismounted." He said, "Well, get one," which I was, of course, very anxious to do because it would have been very dangerous to have been dismounted had the command left the place. (About 10 minutes after getting to top of bluff, Benteen came up and there was talk about going to Custer and then happened to talk with Moylan about getting horse.) *I then went about halfway down to river and got my horse.*

Soon after Benteen came up, Weir went out and later came back and Sioux after him. Heavy firing till dark. King wounded evening of 25th.[4]

On evening of 25th we made breastworks. After firing ceased, Reno came up and said to Moylan, "Have one noncommissioned officer volunteer to go in charge of six volunteers to go out and stand picket in front of Co. A line." Moylan called one noncom officer after another to volunteer for this duty. Heyn was wounded. Called Serg. Fehler and he refused to volunteer. Serg. McDermott would have gone but Moylan did not want him to go — said he wanted McDermott to be first sergt. in place of Heyn. Sergt. Easley gave as his excuse that he had been on guard night before. Next Moylan called me and I said I would go if men would volunteer to go with me. Next privates called on, and the following volunteered — Conner, Gilbert, Bancroft, McClurg, Harris. Another man whose name I will not mention volunteered but backed out at the last minute before starting. I then said I would stand with one of the men on one relief. After men volunteered I went to Reno for orders. Reno told me to have the men sneak out one at a time. The Sioux were still out there galloping around. We could hear them plainly. Reno told me to have two stay awake at a time and to talk to each other so as to be sure to keep awake. We were all very much in need of sleep. He also said that if Indians opened fire very early next morning, to scatter and run for the breastworks but not to go in a bunch. The picket was carried out exactly as ordered by my detail, and at dawn when Sioux opened fire we were lying in grass and sage brush and we retreated to line safely and in good order. I was then complimented by my capt. for duty that night.

Fighting started at daylight on June 26 and very heavy until about

---

4. George H. King, corporal, Company A, died on July 2 of the wound received here. He was buried on the north bank of the Yellowstone River at the mouth of the Bighorn River.

10:00 a.m. We could see them riding around us by the hundreds like race horses. They fired at us so heavy that cut down all of sage brush in front of us. A little rain fell about noon of 26th, and men held ponchos to catch some of it but did not get much.

On a.m. of June 26 F. C. Mann, citizen packer, was killed. He was behind breastwork with carbine on A Co.'s line. He was aiming a carbine over a breastwork about 3 ft. high, and after he had been observed in this position about 20 min., some one made remark that "something must be wrong with the packer." Upon going up he was found stone dead, having been hit in the temple and killed so quick that he did not move from position sighting his gun.

About 11:00 a.m. June 26 we dragged up more dead horses and extended our line up toward Benteen's position and gave better protection to the men. Benteen saved the command, according to my opinion. He was a very brave and nervy man. We became thirsty and chewed grass to get saliva in our mouths, and Cowley[5] went insane from thirst and did not recover for some time. We had to tie him fast on June 26.

After Benteen's charge the cry for water was very loud, especially the wounded. Some of the enlisted men would propose that some of the men should volunteer to get to the river for this purpose. This talk went around, and finally the officers said if any of the men wanted to volunteer they might do so. Not long after this 19 men volunteered to go, and officers thought this would be too many, but said 12 might go. It was decided that we would take 2 canteens to a man and about 6 2-gal. camp kettles in the party. Sergt. Fehler was one of the sharpshooters and four others. They could command the timber on west bank and kept the Indians from getting thick in there. Nevertheless there were many skulked along the river bank in position to fire on anyone attempting to get water.

In going down from top of bluff we had to run across an open space about 100 yards wide to get to head of ravine. From here to river we were concealed from Sioux. We got down to mouth of ravine and could see Indians in brush on opposite bank of river, but we did not want to shoot, to bring an engagement. Ravine 20 yds. from water. Madden was third man to rush for water and was hit and leg broke, but he crawled back to cover unassisted. He was a big, heavy man and his wound was very painful and requested to be left down there as

---

5. Private Cornelius Cowley was in Company A.

114

it hurt him to be disturbed. He thought he would be safe down there. He was carried up some time before dark.

Water party Roy, Gilbert, Madden (K Troop), Wilber (M Troop), Bancroft, Harris, Voit, Peter Thompson, Goldin, Tanner, Coleman (B), Boreen;[6] Roy says he is not sure about the last 3 names.

I was fifth man to dash for water. In ravine we numbered ourselves off and said that as each man's name was called off he could go or not as he would choose. The first man, whose name I do not remember, came back with a kettle full and we all took a drink, the first in 36 hours. I think Wilber was fourth, and he was wounded. After Madden was hit, he crawled back and we gave him water and nursed him and there was then an intermission of about one-half hour before anyone went again. Altogether we were there in the ravine about an hour getting water. We would rush and fill the kettle from the river and then fill canteens from the kettles.

In about one and one-half hours after starting we got back to the top of hill with water, and Varnum was put guard over it. Dr. Porter[7] issued water to the wounded, but there was not enough to give them all they craved for. The fight was still on, and toward evening the Indians slackened their fire and withdrew. That night we dug pits toward

---

6. Stanislas Roy, Co. A; John M. Gilbert, Co. A; Michael Madden, Co. K; James Wilber, Co. M; Neil Bancroft, Co. A; David W. Harris, Co. A; Otto Voit, Co. H; Peter Thompson, Co. C; Theodore Goldin, Co. G; James J. Tanner, Co. M; Thomas W. Coleman, Co. B; Ansgarius Boren, Co. B. Of this group, Bancroft, Harris, Voit, Thompson, and Goldin later received the Medal of Honor for bringing water to the wounded.

7. The account of Dr. Henry Rinaldo Porter, who was acting assistant surgeon with Major Reno, was published in the *New York Herald*, 11 July 1876, as "The Terrible Sioux Doctor Porter's Account Of The Battle," and in the *St. Paul Pioneer Press* 12 July 1876, as "The Indian Battlefield." An abstract of his testimony before the Reno court of inquiry is found in Frances Chamberlain Holley's *Once Their Home or Our Legacy from the Dakotahs* (Chicago: Donohue and Henneberry, 1890), pp. 247–49. An extract concerning Dr. Porter is found in Joseph Mills Hanson's *The Conquest of the Missouri* (Chicago: A. C. McClurg & Co., 1909), pp. 293–95. Dr. Porter's own story is found in *Compendium of History and Biography of North Dakota* (Chicago: George A. Ogle & Co., 1900), pp. 160–62. Henry Porter was born in New York Mills, New York, on February 3, 1848, and graduated from The Georgetown University School of Medicine in 1872. He served in Arizona with the 5th Cavalry as an acting assistant surgeon and later moved to Bismarck, Dakota, where he served as an acting assistant surgeon for the army at various times. He died on March 3, 1903, in Agra, India.

river to guard water route and carried up plenty of water for the use of the men. That night Gerard and Bill Jackson, De Rudio, and Tom O'Neill came in. I heard De Rudio yell "Hello" and guard George Bott of A Troop was on post and challenged him and he answered "Lieutenant De Rudio," and the officer of the guard gave orders to "advance" him and he came in. There was great rejoicing as we had supposed they had been killed. We had seen Indians leave the valley on evening of June 26 but thought it might be a ruse. On morning June 27 took horses down to water. It was a pitiful sight to see the poor animals plunge their heads in the water up to their eyes and drink.

Seventh Infantry came up and camped in bottom about where McIntosh was killed. The officers of Gibbon's command gave up all their sugar, lemon, and other luxuries for our wounded.

On 28th . . . I was detailed to help shoot about 20 wounded horses scattered down on side of bluffs which had been left on retreat up bluffs on June 25 and wounded horses that had strayed out from Reno hill during 2 days fight, some of which had been turned loose after being wounded.

On June 28 a.m. we went over to Custer battlefield to bury the dead. We carried our wounded over to camp in village opposite Custer battlefield. Some of these were on horses, but about 30 had to be carried by hand on blankets. They were carried in reliefs, and the Infantry helped us out. We then formed skirmish line and buried the dead. On the way over we followed what we supposed was Custer's trail and at one point it led down pretty close to the river.

The first dead body we came to was that of Corpl. John Foley. I heard several say: "There lies Foley of C Company." I saw him and recognized him easily, as he had bald head and black hair. He was of middle age and I knew him well. Foley was at least three-fourths mile in advance of the first group of dead at C.[8]

The next body we came to was that of Sergt. Butler, and from him to first group of dead at C the distance was considerable. He lay probably one-half way from Foley to C. There was no dead horse near either Foley or Butler. I helped to bury the bodies on west slope of ridge, and we wound up with E Troop men over near the gully. I

---

8. When we went to bury the dead on June 28 we did not follow Dry Creek to the river but cut straight across to the battlefield, going over the little rise between the two coulees. The first body we saw was that of Corpl. Foley of Co. C on this rise, just over toward the coulee running up to the battlefield. Butler lay 200 or 300 yds. beyond and across the ravine.

(Walter Camp field notes, folder 99, BYU Library.)

then took sick to my stomach from the stench and went to river to get a drink.

On way down to boat with wounded we made a night march and Capt. Marsh of Far West had pine torch lights to light us for the last 5 or 6 miles on way to boat. We took reliefs in carrying wounded. Some on blankets, some on travois on horses and mules. It was a slow and exceedingly laborious job.

We lay in camp some days at mouth of Big Horn and then marched over to Rosebud. Having heard that Sioux were on Rosebud, Gen. Terry started up that stream. This was about three weeks after Battle of Little Bighorn. We had scouts out, and all of a sudden one day these came in and reported big force of Sioux coming down river to meet us. There was much of a stir with us and the old 7th again formed a skirmish line and got ready for battle. In a few hours it developed that our supposed enemy was Gen. Crook with large force — over 2,000 men. We first saw a lone rider coming in the distance, and when he got up to us he proved to be scout W. F. Cody, later better known as Buffalo Bill of circus fame.

In Crook's command there had been a similar activity upon sighting our advance scouts, who like those of Crook's, were Indians, and each had mistaken the other for Sioux. The two commands joined forces, but there was no fighting soon. The Sioux were not to be caught by a force superior to their own.

Interview with
Roman Rutten[1]

Approaching Ford A, Rutten's horse, as soon as he smelled Indians, began to act up badly and he could not control him. The only thing he could do was to continually circle him around the 3 troops. The horse kept this up after passing Ford A and when got down near the skirmish line, the horse lunged ahead of the command and took him considerably nearer the Indians. He therefore circled him around to the right, and came back through the timber and joined command.

Rutten was not wounded in this movement (as Wm. E. Morris states) but was wounded in the shoulder on the hill the next day. Says Sergt. O'Hara was first man killed, and he fell on skirmish line.[2] Soon all went into the timber and began to mount up. He heard 1st Sergt. Ryan ask Capt. French where they were going or where he (French) thought they had better go, and while French's mind seemed to be diverted for the moment, as though he was considering what answer to make, Reno rode past to the border of the timber and cried: "Everybody follow me."

Lorentz was hit in the timber, and Streing outside but near the edge of the timber.[3] As Rutten left the timber, a solid line of Indians, as many as 200, he would think, rode up on his right and had stopped or nearly stopped, and were doing some very loud yelling as the soldiers

---

1. Box 2, Camp MSS, field notes, Little Bighorn, Battle of 1876, III, Lilly Library. Roman Rutten, born in Baden, Germany, was a private in Company M, 7th Cavalry, and was wounded in the right shoulder in the hilltop fight on June 26. He recuperated from his wound in the hospital at Fort Rice, Dakota. He enlisted on July 17, 1872, in Philadelphia at the age of 26.

2. Sergeant Miles F. O'Hara, Company M, was killed by a shot through the breast in the valley fight.

3. George Lorentz, private, Company M, and Frederick Streing, corporal, Company M, were both killed in the valley fight.

were getting out of the timber. A few of these Indians were firing into the retreating soldiers but most of them were giving vent to a variety of Ha Ha's and Haw Haws, apparently being about as badly excited as the soldiers and apparently undecided as to what movement the soldiers were about to execute. Rutten was not long in leaving these unwelcome spectators behind, but there were already Indians ahead and plenty of them riding along on the right. A little way from the timber Isaiah's horse had been shot down, and the colored man was making a stand, down on one knee, cooly firing his sporting rifle.

Isaiah and I were intimate acquaintances, and as I passed him he looked up at me and cried out, "Goodbye Rutten." Corpl. Scollin fell in some low or soggy ground not far from the timber, and beyond this some distance was Lieut. McIntosh trying to make his way.[4] He was singled out by himself, and he was trying to urge his horse along but was not succeeding well. His lariat was dragging, which seemed to bother the horse. McIntosh was surrounded by twenty or thirty Indians, who were circling about him, apparently determined to get him.

Rutten's horse now smelled Indians stronger than before and he knew exactly what to do, without any communication by bit or spur, so that all Rutten had to do was to stay in the saddle. The horse tore right across the circle of Indians of which McIntosh was the center, and on he went. The horse did not like the sight of Indians at the right, and so he veered to the left among some stumps and logs, but these were no obstacle to him. He did not take time to run around any of these but jumped right over them, keeping a straight course.

When I reached the river, the water ahead of me was full of horses and men struggling to get across. I thought I had better keep out of the muddle and so turned my horse downstream. The opposite bank was high and steep, and men were riding both upstream and downstream trying to find some place to get up. Finally the mob of horsemen made for a narrow trail cut by buffalo in going for water, which cut through the steep bank at a moderate incline. Before I reached it, a horse had fallen exhausted or shot right in this cut and was choking the passage, but he was pulled out. How it was done and so quickly, I did not see nor did I stop to inquire. The run up through this cut was a hard test of horse flesh.

---

4. Donald McIntosh was first lieutenant, Company G.

119

Rutten tells how in the fight on the hill during a.m. of June 26 Benteen came over and told how rapidly he was losing his men and that if he did not get assistance soon, he could not hold his hill, and he quietly remarked that if his hill was carried by Indians the remaining six companies would not last long. Benteen discussed the matter with Reno, who finally said he might take one of the companies on that side, and Benteen, without discussing which one he was to have, said: "All right, I will take French." French was informed about this and immediately went along the line and told his men to be still but be ready, when he would give the word, to jump up and run for Benteen's line. Benteen's line, being on the highest ground in the vicinity,[5] the men going to his assistance would be clearly exposed for some 100 yards while going up the slope. At French's word all the men present, but not all of the available men of the company, leaped to their feet, scattered, and started up the hill. In this run Wilber was wounded. Rutten heard the Peter Thompson story and also about the man (Nathan Short) who got to the Rosebud. Rutten says Botzer was acting 1st sergeant of Co. G. Rafter says this is so. Says Alex Brown was with packs. Vickory (color sgt.) was carrying one flag (regimental) for Custer. Sergt. Robert Hughes, Co. K, was carrying another flag for Custer. There were two flags — battle flag and regimental flag. Hughes probably carried battle flag. Rutten says Francis T. Hughes of Co. L was the last man of 5 cos. coming down Sundance Creek. He had a big black horse which he could not control and could not ride him in the company and so followed behind.

---

5. We quote here from a letter written by W. O. Taylor on December 12, 1909, at Orange, Mass., to Walter Camp:

I do not know if M, K, B, G, and D Troops made any attempt to fortify their positions at that time, or not, and as for H Troop I know that during the forenoon of the 26th, I with others was ordered to take from our barricade anything we could carry, up to the position held by H Troop, I think this was done by the request of Capt. Benteen, as they had no protection and were suffering some loss, and our barricade was perhaps longer than was actually needed 'for the number of men behind it, in carrying our loads up to Benteen's position we were exposed for a part of the way to severe fire from the Indians, when we arrived there Benteen's men were all lieing flat on the ground with no protection at all that I saw, and no evidence of any fortifying the night before by that troop; leaving our loads on the ground we returned at once to our barricade, where a few moments later, F. C. Mann, a civilian packer, lieing not over two feet from me was shot in the head and instantly killed, he had been doing some long-range shooting, and raising his head just a little above the works for another shot, was struck, and expired without a sound.

(In Walter Camp Collection, box 6, folder 2, BYU Library.)

120

Interview with Jacob Adams, October 14, 1910, Vincennes, Indiana[1]

I was with the packs, and before we came to the bluffs where Benteen and Reno were, we halted the packs back on the low ground. While lying there we saw a single horseman coming toward us pretty fast, and although we could not tell whether he was a white man or Indian, I said I would go out and meet him and did so. His horse had been running and was about winded. He was a white man about forty-five years old, sandy hair, thick set man, with a goatee and moustache. He said he thought they were fighting up ahead. Said his horse had run away with him and he could not control him. He joined the packs there with us.

I went with Benteen over to Custer battlefield on p.m. of June 27. Down near the river and before we came to any dead men we found three or four dead horses. Custer lay within a circle of dead horses on a flat place at the end of the ridge. Tom Custer lay back of him and not near the horses. Quite a distance east of Custer (down near Keogh and between Keogh and Custer) the dead bodies lay thick, and among these were identified dead men from all of the five companies. We came to the conclusion then and there that the fight had been a rout, a running fight.

When we found Old Comanche he was sitting on his haunches,

1. Walter Camp field notes, folder 43, BYU Library. Jacob Adams was a private in Company H, 7th Cavalry. He was with the pack train on June 25 in the hilltop fight and in a water party on June 26. He was born in Stark County, Ohio, June 25, 1852. He enlisted in 1873 and was with the 7th Cavalry detachment that arrested Rain-In-The-Face at Standing Rock Agency in 1875. After he was discharged in 1878, he resided near Vincennes, Indiana, and later near Kalamazoo, Michigan. His account, "A Survivor's Story of the Custer Massacre on the American Frontier," is found in *The Journal of American History*, 1909, 3:2.

braced back on his forefeet. We lifted him up in his feeble condition and he followed us around.

Bodies were mutilated in every conceivable way. One dead body had one leg nicely cut off, as with a sharp knife, at the hip joint. It was done so carefully that the bowels had not come out. Bodies were mutilated in every conceivable way, some being set up on elbows and knees and the hind parts shot full of arrows. On our way back to Reno hill we crossed the river and rode through the village, and on the way we saw a body of horsemen coming. Benteen looked through his glasses and said he thought they were Indians, and Reno told him to command the co. Benteen had us draw pistols, ready for a charge, when we discovered them to be a troop of the 2nd Cavalry.

Lieut. Gibson and I went to McIntosh's body. The fire had run through the grass and scorched it. Gibson wanted me to get a pack mule and take it up on Reno hill, but I disliked the job and told him I knew of no way to pack it, so he decided to have it buried where it lay, and I buried it there.

On the trip over to Custer ridge on June 27 Sergeant Geiger and I were in the rear with a pack mule loaded with ammunition. When Benteen got ready to charge, I rode up and joined the line. Geiger ordered me back and made all kinds of threats, but I told him if they were going to charge through Indians I proposed to be with the charging party and not in the rear with him and the mule where we would surely be gobbled up."

Says that on the hill Benteen had the heel of his boot shot off. In bottom Isaiah's body lay not farther from timber than 40 or 50 yards. Charlie Reynolds's body lay farther from the timber.

After we left Pease Bottom, we camped north side of Yellowstone, opposite Rosebud. After we broke camp there I saw a dead soldier and dead horse south of Yellowstone and within sight of Yellowstone — only a few miles from it. The body was then thought to be one of L troop men who had been with Custer and scalped. The carbine was with the body and all equipment, and the leather sling was still over the shoulder. We concluded that both the man and the horse had been wounded and had gotten that far and given out. This find was considered no unusual thing, and I do not suppose one of our officers would have gone to see it if he had heard about it.

122

Interview with
John McGuire[1]

McGuire says Custer was arrested by Terry's order twice before got to Powder river for trying to advance too far ahead of column with escort and without permission. Three cos. made a scout up Little Missouri River under Custer himself.

Reno's scout out 12 days. C Troop was along, thinks B Troop along, also D crossed divide, hit Powder and Tongue and then crossed divide, hit Tongue and Rosebud.

Two Gatling guns along. There were a few infantrymen with the Gatlings. Each Gatling hauled by four horses. At some of the ravines had to unlimber guns and unhitch horses and haul over by hand. Passed over very rough ground, rougher than they found beyond Rosebud. At one time men lifting and pulling guns got tired and gave up, and other men had to be sent back to get them up. They were abandoned only temporarily at any time. Never were abandoned with thought of leaving them. Thinks it a great misfortune were not taken to Little Bighorn, as ground was not nearly so rough as had been back on Reno's scout. On Reno's scout one of B troop's pack mules fell down in the water and spoiled the provisions and this is one reason why ran short of rations . . . ran out of provisions and thought would starve before found Custer and rest of regiment.

Left band at Powder River and took horses to go on expedition to Little Bighorn. Hardtack which fell off mule on night of June 24. Says reason Sioux scouts broke into boxes was to carry back hardtack as trophies to show their chiefs how close they got to soldiers.

---

1. Walter Camp field notes, folder 73, BYU Library. John McGuire was a private in Company C under Captain Tom Custer. He was with the pack train on June 25 and was wounded in the right arm in the hilltop fight on June 26. He was sent back to Fort A. Lincoln on the steamer *Far West*.

Saw where Indians had killed buffalo on Rosebud, and Mitch Bouyer[2] told him that Indians had herded buffalo ahead of them and that such was reason for such a big trail, which in some places was spread out all over the country. Says Custer had kept Bouyer ahead of column all along. Bouyer said he had told Custer there must be a very large village ahead and Custer said: "Show them to me," meaning he would believe it only after he would see them.

Mitch Bouyer a good trailer. Had lived among Sioux in boyhood. Was about 30 years old. Bouyer told McGuire that from what he saw of signs Indians must be very thick ahead of them. Said "There are too many for this outfit, and if we get up to them they will recognize me and that will be the last of Bouyer. Nevertheless I have been drawing $10 per day from the government and intend to stick it out."

Thinks there were 30 Rees. Saw them go back with herd of Sioux ponies and no officer with pack train tried to stop them. Says that when pack train[3] got up all was in confusion with all six troops there with Reno and Benteen. Did pack train start toward Custer when Godfrey, Benteen, and others moved down that way? *Yes, went to top of ridge where could see Weir out ahead.* Did he see any ammunition boxes opened while waiting to start? *No.*

Says several times Indians got close enough to fortifications to shoot arrows and throw stones into the lines. After being wounded went down to hospital, where the wounded were placed under a fly tent. *Every little while a bullet would go whizzing through the tent, and it seemed to me that the wounded were in as much danger of being struck again as they would be on the line.*

Point out on map where ammunition mule got loose. *Yes, back*

---

2. Antoine Bouyer says Mitch Bouyer's name is Michel Bouyer. Mitch's father was a full blood Frenchman who was killed by Indians while trapping. Mother of Mitch was full blood Santee Sioux. He was married to three Sioux. John Bouyer, brother of Antoine and Mitch, was hung for murder. F. G. Burnett says Mitch Bouyer was about 5 years older than he. Burnett is (Sept. 18, 1913) now 70.... Mitch Bouyer's widow married Wind (commonly called Big Wind) and lived on Big Horn. She died in 1916.

(Camp MSS, field notes, Walter Mason Camp, box 2, folder 9, Lilly Library, Indiana University.)

3. John McGuire says there was a detail of a non-commissioned officer and 7 men with each company's pack mules. Officers say the detail was 1 non-com officer and 6 men. This makes at least 96 or 84 men. Besides these there were strikers, cooks, headquarters details, and men leading officers' extra horses to the number of two or three to each company, or 30 men. Besides the above there were 11 men citizen packers, making at least 125 men all armed. With McDougall's men of B Co. he thus had a larger battalion of fighting men than either Reno or Benteen.

(Walter Camp field notes, folder 79, BYU Library.)

on trail, which was south of Custer's trail as explained by McDougall. Catching the pack mule — the mule started back on the trail. McGuire was just then tying Hanley's horse and Hanley said: "Where is my horse?" *I said, "I have him here." I then threw the reins over the horse's head, and Hanley rode off after the mule, and I went on foot. Hanley got around on the flank, and the mule turned him my way. When the mule saw he was being headed off, he turned and ran back into the herd. Neither Hanley nor I got our hands on him.*[4]

Says when Peter Thompson came back, Sioux were already firing and [McGuire] said to those around him, "Don't fire — there comes Thompson with his horse."[5] Thompson came along with his horse and as he approached, McGuire said, "Thompson, hand me your horse. I have room on my line." *Just as he handed him to me, the horse was struck on the left flank near the heart and almost instantly killed.* McGuire says he heard the story Thompson told about Bill Jackson and stirrup gone but thinks it might have been Bob Jackson instead of Bill.

McGuire says he saw Peter Thompson go for water after being wounded and before wound was dressed. He went early in forenoon on June 26.

Was there any particular reason for Thompson and Watson keeping still about their manner of escape? *Yes, the company filled up with new men in the fall who would not understand such discussions, and the old men never said much about questions of this kind.*[6]

---

4. See the account of Richard P. Hanley.

5. *Although Trumpeter Martin and myself* [Daniel Knipe] *were the last messengers sent by Gen. Custer, we were not the last men to leave his battalion and survive. That distinction belongs to Peter Thompson and James Watson of my company. I have personal knowledge of Thompson's movements that day as I saw his horse standing on the bluffs when I went out with Co. H, and I later saw Thompson himself coming up the bluffs from the river and heard him then say that he had left his horse standing and followed on after Custer about until cut off and turned back by Indians.* Knipe says when column went down in direction of Custer, he went with Co. H and saw Thompson's horse standing near head of hollow down which Custer marched. *When I saw Peter Thompson coming up the bluffs on foot with his carbine and knowing that he had been with his company all day, I said: "Thompson, where in the devil have you been?" He said: "Well, my horse gave out and left me afoot; and I tried to catch up but could not make it." I then told him that I had seen his horse some distance back of us on the bluffs.*

(Camp MSS, field notes, Daniel A. Knipe, box 2, folder 8, Lilly Library.)

6. The following is an extract from a letter dated December 20, 1922, written by Walter Camp in Chicago to an unidentified correspondent, a copy of which is in the editor's possession:

I will reply hastily to your letter of 16th inst. covering the Peter Thompson story. Candidly I do not know what to think about his story in its entirety. I have discussed it with

McGuire says that among C troop men it was always the opinion that John Brennan and John Fitzgerald fell back from Custer's 5 troops out of cowardice and in that way did not get into the fight. Says that they . . . often joked about it afterward.

On boat going down there were 51 wounded white men and one Indian (White Swan).

Heard of Nathan Short. He got good distance toward Rosebud. Had bobtailed horse. Only bobtailed horse in co. Had initials on cartridge belt.

---

six or eight officers who were at Little Bighorn on June 25 and 26, 1876, with Reno, and not one of them believes it. I heard the story first in 1906 and made some investigations. Here is a strange thing — a good many enlisted men heard his story in 1876, but not one of the officers I talked with had ever heard of the story until I told it to them, some of them in 1908. . . . Now about the Crow dragging a squaw, about Custer being down at the river, and the Sioux Indian on the boat with the wounded on the way to Ft. Lincoln all that is unbelievable — it is impossible.

Thompson did not meet Weir's troop when he came out of the bottom. If he says he did he is mistaken. I have talked with a half dozen or more of that troop about their advance toward Custer and no one of them ever heard anything about Thompson. Old Sergeant [Thomas W.] Harrison and Sergt. [Cornelius] Bresnahan, whom Gen. Godfrey and I met in 1916, and talked over that whole matter of Weir's advance were very clear about all details, and neither of them saw or heard anything about Thompson. Neither did Weir's troop pick up any played-out horses that p.m. There were, however, some played-out cavalry horses rounded up on June 27 and shot — ten or a dozen of them; and it is a fact, supported by the best testimony, that some of Custer's horses did play out and were left behind just before the Custer battalion got into the fight. I have evidence of that independently of Thompson. . . .

Thompson did not claim, to me, that he struck Weir's company at all. He did tell me about seeing Custer down at the river, about the squaw being pulled by a lariat by a Crow and the hostile Indian on the boat, etc. I tried to discuss with him the impossibility of these things but there was "nothing doing" and I saw that he would take offense if I persisted. This was in 1910. My conclusion is that the story cannot be accepted in its entirety, although a good deal of it is plausible. The Crows who were there June 25, 1876, never heard anything about one of their number lariating a Sioux squaw. I went through all that with the four surviving Crow scouts, so Thompson is mistaken about that. If some things in Thompson's story could be eliminated it could be given historical standing, but as it stands published it cannot be reconciled with known facts. It could be edited into good shape but I hardly think the historian would have the moral right to do that.

Interview with Richard P. Hanley, October 4, 1910, Boston[1]

Said the ammunition was packed in appareros [aparejos: pack saddles] and not on sawbucks, like the hardtack and other supplies. Each mule carried two boxes of cartridges containing 1000 cartridges to the box.

The mule that tried to stampede into the Indians on Reno hill was old Barnum. He went down past Moylan's line and on east toward the hill. The shots from the Indians cut the ground all around, and Hanley thought he would be killed. However, he felt responsible for the mule and thought he would be blamed if the mule got away, so he drew his revolver, intending to shoot the mule down if he could not catch him and lead him back. The mule got out about half way to where the Indians were circling around. Hanley finally headed him off and he ran back into the herd.

Hanley says that Peter Thompson,[2] John Fitzgerald and John Brennan were not with the packs on 6/25/76 but were with their com-

---

1. Walter Camp field notes, folder 43, BYU Library. Richard P. Hanley, born in Boston, was a sergeant in Company C. He was with the pack train and in the hilltop fight. His fifth enlistment was on September 30, 1873. He was awarded the Medal of Honor for recapturing Barnum, the stampeded mule. Hanley retired as a sergeant and resided in Boston.

2. We quote here from a letter written by Daniel A. Knipe on July 20, 1908, at Marion, N.C., to Walter Camp.

There was a man by the name of Thompson in Troop C . . . that was wounded on the hill with us at Reno's stand. He was wounded in the arm. . . . this man was with Custer close to the ford where he first attempted to cross. He lost his horse by some means down there and came walking to the top of the hill, where Reno's stand was made. He was with Custer and his men when I left them. His horse's giving out left him to turn off to the left of the march and he got lost from the five companies and came back, but told us the direction they had gone when he came back to us.

(In Walter Camp Collection, box 5, folder 7, BYU Library.)

pany and straggled back from Custer after the packs reached the bluff at river.[3] He does not know just when they got back.

In 1877 Co. C was on road between Bismarck and Black Hills guarding it against road agents. Frank Berwald says Co. E was on same duty. Says Sgt. Riley of Co. E was Chief of Police of Cincinnati in 1893 or 1894 but did not make a success of it. Says Corpl. Edward Clyde of Co. F was in 4th Cavalry after being in 7th Cavalry.

Hanley says when went to capture Rain-in-Face he was along and went down on ice. Says he was in store when Tom Custer grabbed Rain, and Tom had two enlisted men to help him. Had Rain in corral all night and early next morning started with him for Ft. Lincoln.

On Reno's scout Harrington commanded Co. C. Had pack mules along, and Hanley had charge of his co. packs.

---

3. See Daniel Magnussen's *Peter Thompson's Narrative of the Little Big Horn Campaign 1876,* published in 1974 by the Arthur H. Clark Co., Glendale, California. This is Thompson's story which first appeared serially in the *Belle Fourche Bee* (S.D.) in 1914 as "The Experience of a Private Soldier in the Custer Massacre."

According to Knipe's account, Thompson must have got back to Reno from Custer's command after the arrival of McDougall because Knipe saw him walking back, and Knipe arrived with McDougall. Peter Thompson came walking back after McDougall arrived and said that his horse gave out somewhere down in low country and he had to fall out. He left the horse standing, then wandered around and got lost before finally back tracking and finding his way back to Reno on the heights.

(Walter Camp field notes, folder 15, BYU Library.)

Interview with George W. Wylie, October 16, 1910, Junction City, Kansas[1]

When Benteen's battalion was approaching the point where Reno retreated up, Wylie saw the last part of Reno's retreat out of the valley. Just as Weir started toward Custer on June 25, the troop met Billy Cross coming in opposite direction from that in which the troop was moving (that is, Cross was coming south along the bluff) with a handkerchief tied around his head.[2]

Soon after Benteen joined Reno on hill, Capt. Weir started to open up communication with Custer, and the troop marched out along bluff until came to a jumping-off place from which could look down upon the hollow of Medicine Tail coulee. Men dismounted and put horses behind Edgerly peaks and behind hill to east, and men formed line over this hill from east to west. Seeing many horsemen over on distant ridge with guidons flying, Weir said, "That is Custer over there," and mounted up ready to go over, when Sergt. Flanagan[3] said: "Here, Captain, you had better take a look through the glasses; I think those are Indians." Weir did so and changed his mind about leaving

---

1. Camp MSS, field notes, Walter Mason Camp, box 2, folder 9, Little Bighorn, Battle of 1876, Lilly Library. George W. Wylie, born in New Orleans, enlisted on March 17, 1873. He was in the Little Bighorn River fight in 1876 and the Nez Perce campaign in 1877 and was wounded on September 30, 1877, in the Snake Creek fight. He was in the Wounded Knee Creek fight on December 30, 1890. He retired as a first sergeant and resided in Junction City, Kansas.

2. William Cross was a half-blood Dakota Sioux scout in the Sioux campaign of 1876. His story, as told to a news correspondent, is in the *Chicago Tribune,* July 15, 1876. Cross died in 1894 on the Fort Peck Reservation, near Culbertson, Montana.

3. James Flanagan was a sergeant in Company D. He was born in County Clare, Ireland. He served in the Civil War. He died in 1921 in Mandan, North Dakota.

the place. Accordingly the men were dismounted and the horses led behind the hill.

The Indians soon came up in great force, and the men were mounted up and started back along the ridge in column of twos on a walk. After going some distance the Indians had arrived on Edgerly peaks and opened up a hot fire. Corpl. Wylie had a ball shot through his canteen, the staff of the guidon he was carrying was shot off, the flag dropped, and Vincent Charley was shot and fell off his horse. Wylie got down to pick up the guidon. At the same time Edgerly was stooping over Charlie and told him to lie quiet and he (Edgerly) would return and rescue him. Here Edgerly had difficulty in mounting his horse. This was some distance south of Edgerly peaks (and probably about opposite the ravine on east side of bluffs in which the cedar trees are growing). Says no other troop got as far in the advance as D troop. Does not recall seeing Corpl. Foley ride down pursued by Indians and never heard of it. This refers to what Flanagan told me.

On his line on the hill Benteen had, besides his own company, men from all the other companies drawn from details with the packs. On Reno hill Liddiard, Co. E, was killed while taking aim at some Indians that Benteen was pointing out to the men. There were several men there talking, and Liddiard,[4] who was a good shot, lay down to take aim talking at the same time. It was noticed that he had stopped talking, and seeing his face turned down and the blood running around the rim of his hat was the first intimation that he was dead.

On Custer ridge the body of Trumpeter John W. Patton[5] lay across Keogh's breast when first found. Wylie had opportunity to see only a few bodies around Keogh and was then sent out as vidette to watch for Indians.

---

4. Herod T. Liddiard was a private in Company E. He was born in London, England. He enlisted on December 4, 1872.

5. John W. Patton was a trumpeter in Company I. He was born in Philadelphia. He enlisted on October 21, 1872.

⭐

Interview with William E. Morris[1]

Lorentz was the man shot through the stomach in the timber and who was left there when Reno retreated out. When he fell off his horse, Neely caught him, and he and Morris tried to lift him upon a horse. But Lorentz was in great distress and refused to be assisted. David Summers was killed just as he emerged from the timber. About half way to the river, Scollin's horse was shot and went down, and Scollin took his carbine and said: "For God's sake boys, don't leave me here." Thorpe stopped and took him on behind his horse and just as he did so this horse was shot down. Thorpe then caught an Indian pony and escaped, and Scollin was left there and killed. Says Sgt. Cary was not left in timber. Geo. E. Smith killed at edge of timber. Turley killed right by Hodgson — only 20 feet away. Meyer and Gordon killed where bluffs begin to be steep (where I took photo of Knipe). Morris with all these men and all the horses hit at same time. The Indians who fired these shots were among bluffs on east side of river, to right and front of Morris as he was ascending the hill. That is, they were in the bluffs and to south of line of retreat up the bluffs. All three men

---

1. Camp MSS field notes, Walter Mason Camp, unclassified envelope 81, Lilly Library. William Morris was born in Boston, Massachusetts. He enlisted on September 22, 1875. He was a half brother of Private Byron Tarbox of Company L, 7th Cavalry. Wounded in the left breast while climbing the bluffs after the valley fight on June 25, he was taken to Fort A. Lincoln on the *Far West*. He was discharged on December 11, 1877, at Fort Lincoln for disability as a private of worthless character. He later became a judge in New York City. His letter to Dr. Cyrus Brady, dated September 21, 1904, is in Brady's *Indian Fights and Fighters*, pp. 401–5. A copy of his seven-page letter to Robert Bruce dated May 23, 1928, at New York City, with an account of the Little Bighorn River fight, is in the Dustin Collection, Custer Battlefield National Monument.

and three horses were hit simultaneously by a volley from these Indians.

Scollin's horse was shot down in the first depression or soft place after leaving timber. He got on Thorpe's horse behind Thorpe and as they struck the second hollow this horse fell and Thorpe caught up an Indian pony running with a dragging lariat. Says McIntosh killed within 20 yds. of river. Morris says he himself was the last to leave the timber except Hare.[2] Hare passed Morris on the way to the river. When Morris got to the river the Indians were between him and the river and they had McIntosh surrounded right on the bank and McIntosh had his pistol drawn and was using it. Getting up out of the water there was a ravine or washout going up to the top of the river bank, like a washout after a hard rain. The whole command passed through this.

---

2. George Lorentz, Frank Neely, David Summers, Rollins L. Thorpe, George E. Smith, Henry Turley, William D. Meyer, and Henry Gordon were all privates in Company M, 7th Cavalry. Henry Scollin (Henry Cody) was a corporal, and Patrick Carey was a sergeant in Company M. Donald McIntosh was a lieutenant in Company G, and Luther Hare was a lieutenant in Company K.

Interview with
Henry Petring[1]

While in the bottom going toward the skirmish line, I saw Custer over across the river on the bluffs, waving his hat. Some of the men said: "There goes Custer. He is up to something, for he is waving his hat." Says Co. G on right of skirmish line next the timber, and a detachment of Co. G was sent into the timber to look after the horses.

In timber Petring, when rest were mounting to retreat, found his own horse killed, so he took Robb's horse. [As I] *emerged from the timber onto open ground, this horse* (Robb's) *was shot from under me. I ran back into the timber and saw a few horses running around loose and caught one of them up.*

My company had now been gone some time and in the confusion I could not satisfy myself which direction they went. My memory does not serve me to say toward what point of the compass I went, but I rode a little and entered the river to ford across and when part way across saw four or five Indians on the bank ahead of me and very near. One Indian, on a cream colored pony, drew up his gun as if to fire, and I, knowing that I was in great danger and would have to act quickly, drew up my carbine without taking aim and fired, and both the pony and the Indian dropped. Then I, in order to get away quickly, jumped down off my horse and started downstream as fast as I could in water waist deep and deeper.

I did not look back until I had gone some little distance, and when I did I saw two of the Indians carrying off the one I had shot,

---

1. Walter Camp field notes, folder 38, BYU Library. Henry Petring, born in Germany, enlisted on December 9, 1874, in New York City. He was in the valley fight and was wounded in the hip in the hilltop fight. He was discharged on December 8, 1879, at Fort Meade, Dakota, on the expiration of his service as a private of good character. He later resided in Brooklyn, New York.

133

and the pony still lay there as if dead. I was then several hundred yards away and back on the same side of the river from which I had started to cross. I immediately went under a stump and later into the thick willows and thought my situation most desperate and wondered if, after all, the best thing I could do would not be to shoot myself.

As I stood in the thick willows, I heard someone coming and looked out in the open, and a gleam of sunshine reflected from a button on his clothing. I thought it might be an Indian, but challenged him, and he replied: "It is Johnson of G Company," and of course I was greatly delighted to see him. We got together, and soon one after another began to come along, and we soon had quite a party — a dozen or more dismounted men. Some had taken ammunition from saddle bags, and we had plenty of it. No Indians came in to molest us, but they set the woods afire. Sergeant Chas. White was wounded and making loud cries, and we were afraid the sound would attract Indians, but they did not come in. Soon after firing the timber, the wind changed and blew the smoke in another direction, and we had no danger from that source.

After being in the timber some time, and as it was getting near sundown, the scout proposed that we try to join the command. Up on the bluff we could see two guidons and a crowd of men but could not make out whether they were soldiers or Indians, but we took the chance and started out of the timber. We saw three or four Indians at a distance, and they fired. Our scout fired one shot but told us not to fire, and we were not molested. We went on to the river, and half forded while we guarded them, and they stood watch while the other half forded, and we all went up the bluffs together and joined Reno's command on the hill.

Says Theo W. Goldin was not left in the timber when Reno retreated. Andrew J. Moore killed on Reno hill on June 26, hit through kidneys just as were getting up to charge out on the Indians. He (Moore) thought he was hit by one of his own men firing from the hospital. Begged the doctor to give him something, as he was suffering terribly. Petring says is dead sure that Botzer was acting first sergt. Henry Dose,[2] trumpeter, orderly for Custer June 25, 1876, was found half way between Custer and Reno with arrows in his back and sides.

---

2. Theodore W. Goldin and Andrew J. Moore were privates in Company G. Edward Botzer was acting first sergeant of Company G and was killed at the river in the retreat from the valley fight. Henry Dose was one of two trumpeters in Company G and was killed with the Custer column.

134

Interview with George W. Glenn, January 22, 1914[1]

Says Isaiah did not start with the command at Ft. Lincoln, but overtook it on the Rosebud with a message. Said he (Isaiah) had orders to go back, but Custer said, "No, you remain with me." Glenn says Isaiah's body was badly mutilated by the Indians.

John Smith, post trader at Ft. Lincoln, went as far as Heart River when the expedition started. He set up his sutler's tent when the men were paid and returned at the same time that Mrs. Custer went back.

At the mouth of the Rosebud we were camped below the boat and above the timber, on clear ground. Bob Jackson was sent back from the mouth of the Rosebud. I am sure I saw him there in that camp, but do not recall seeing him after that. When we left the Yellowstone each soldier carried on his horse twelve pounds of oats, eighty rounds of ammunition, and two horseshoes, one front and one hind shoe. We overloaded ourselves with ammunition to relieve the pack mules.

Many of the men left at the Powder River camp were fellows who played up sick. The officers inquired of the sergeants who were not able to go and such as were thought not to be well and rugged enough were left behind. In each company there was a detail, but there were others who did not want to go, and they pretended to be unwell. In Company H there were none of these, and that is why so few of our company were left there.

Jones was killed on the hill by a bullet that passed through several

---

1. Walter Camp field notes, folder 109, BYU Library. George W. Glenn was born in Boston. His third enlistment was on September 3, 1875, under the name of George W. Glease. He deserted on October 15, 1877, and was apprehended on April 26, 1880. He was dishonorably discharged on July 31, 1880, at Fort Meade, Dakota. He later resided in a soldiers' home in Virginia.

boxes of hardtack. On Reno hill Voigt[2] of Company M was killed while trying to untangle horses, being shot through the head. The horses had become frightened and were badly mixed up, and Voigt was exposing his head above the hill. The men called to him to get down, but he did not heed them. I was carrying on my shoulder a box of pistol ammunition up the hill at this time, and before I got to Benteen's line it was struck by two bullets. Just as I got on top of the hill the Indians changed up at us. Benteen called to Reno to send up reinforcements, and so a company came up and reinforced H, and the two companies drove the Indians back.

Benteen was on his feet all day June 26, and, it being hot, his shirt tail worked out of his pants and hung down, and he went around that way encouraging the men. He would say "Men, this is a groundhog case; it is live or die with us. We must fight it out with them."

Lieutenant Gibson was trying to get out of sight in a pit too shallow and was acting so cowardly that he was in the way of men passing back and forth. Benteen got ashamed of him and told the men to run over him if he persisted in lying there.

Martin met us with Cooke's message before we got to the Little Bighorn. When we tried to get to Custer, we looked down (into Medicine Tail coulee) and saw the country thick with Indians, and some of the men said: "Captain, the Indians are getting around us." Benteen said, "Major Reno, we cannot fight them here. We had better fall back and make a stand somewhere." On our way back the Indians did not press us closely.

In the valley the bodies of McIntosh and Isaiah lay near together.

When Benteen took Company H over to Custer ridge on 27, he went up to the ridge via Crazy Horse gully. The body nearest the river was that of the chief trumpeter Voss, and near to it was that of Kellogg, the newspaper reporter. Both of these bodies were within a stone's throw of the river. In Crazy Horse gully or washout there were bodies lying thick, and some of the men exclaimed, "Here lies the whole command."

Custer's body lay just below the end of the ridge, and within fifity yards of it lay the body of Tom (Boss) Tweed of Company L, who had once been my "bunky" and whom I recognized. His crotch had been split up with an ax and one of his legs thrown up over his shoulder. He was shot with arrows in both eyes. A wounded horse lay near him groaning, and we knocked him in the head with a bloody ax

2. Henry C. Voight.

136

that lay near by, evidently one that had been used by the Indians to cut up or mutilate the wounded.

On our way up the Rosebud to meet Crook, a cavalryman's hat was found near the Rosebud.[3] I saw the hat. It was a white wool hat, with brass crossed sabers and a brass letter "C."[4] It was passed around among the men to see if any one could identify the owner of it. I do not recall that there was any report about a dead man or a dead horse being found with it.

When the Indians passed Poplar River agency going north, they tried to trade a good many watches that they had taken from the bodies of Custer's soldiers.

---

3. We quote here from the letter written on July 29, 1908, by Daniel A. Knipe to Walter Camp:

The dead trooper with his gun and dead horse still lariated to the picket pin was found a few days' journey from Custer's hill. It was not six months before his body was found, but was somewheres about three or four weeks. General Cook's command found him. He was over in the Rose Bud country. He was in the direction of about east, or southeast from the battlefield where Custer was found. I knew the man well. His name was Short, but I do not remember his given name. He belonged to "C" Troop, my company. How I came to know it was Short of my company was that he had his stuff numbered 50, and General Crook reported that the man's number was 50. He was with the company when I left it, on Reno's hill.

(In Walter Camp Collection, box 5, folder 7, BYU Library.)

4. The following is from the November, 1909, letter from Knipe to Camp:

Short wore a light hat with the cross sabres drawn on the front of it with the number "7" between the sabres.... It was a common thing for the men to mark their equipment with their initials for identification. There were very few men in the company who marked their hats as Short did, but I recall very well that he had marked his in this manner. The soldiers all had their hats marked but usually on the inside. I heard Nathan Short's body had been found after we marched from the mouth of the Big Horn to the Rosebud, but I did not see the remains. I only heard that the scouts had found them. I did not see anyone who had seen the body, either, but it has always been my understanding that Crook's scouts had found the body, but I have never heard if they were Sioux or Crows who found him.

(In Walter Camp Collection, box 5, folder 7, BYU Library.)

Interviews with Dennis Lynch, October, 1908, and February 8, 1909[1]

Dennis Lynch born in Cumberland, Maryland, February 22, 1848. Rebellion in 8th Ill. Cavalry 1 year. Enlisted Regulars August 3, 1866. Reenlisted 1871. Reenlisted 1876 . . . in battle Cedar Creek . . . Winchester, Shepherdstown Va., Yellow Tavern, Washita, Black Hills, Yellowstone 73, Little Bighorn, Nez Perce. Served in 8th Ill. Cavalry in Civil War. Enlisted April 1864, under the name of Burns and served under Custer and Sheridan. Was at Cedar Creek and Yellow Tavern and several skirmishes.

Dennis Lynch enlisted in 7th Cavalry August 3, 1866, in Washington, D.C. He was the first 5-year man to enlist in 7th Cavalry. Previous to this all enlistments had been for 3 years. Went to Carlisle and left there 2 months afterwards with 365 recruits for first issue of 7th Cavalry and went to Ft. Riley, where regt. was organized. Went out from Carlisle with Capt. M. A. Reno and Corpl. Pike. He will send me account of doings 1867 and 68 and Nez Perce campaign. Capture of Rain in Face.

At Powder river left recruits with wagon train. Took "swings" and "leaders" (and left the wheel mules) for packs.[2] F troop men with pack train Sergeant Curtiss, Dennis Lynch, Donnelly, 10 men altogether. Had 14 mules for his troop.

---

1. Walter Camp field notes, folder 75, BYU Library. Dennis Lynch was a private in Company F and was on board the *Far West* in charge of the baggage of Lieutenant Colonel George Custer. He was born in Cumberland, Maryland, and enlisted on March 3, 1871. In addition to the Sioux campaign of 1876 he served in the Milk River campaign in 1881.

2. H. L. Scott [says] Custer's pack train was a poor outfit of the kind. It consisted of mules taken from the wagon train left at Powder River and there were but few experienced packers. The equipment was of the "buck" style and there was trouble continually.

(Camp MSS, field notes, unclassified miscellaneous, VIII, Lilly Library.)

138

Lynch says Crows swam horses over Yellowstone at mouth of Rosebud before expedition left there. . . . Lynch said Crows had large broncos — larger than Sioux ponies and smaller than cavalry horses. Crows stripped like Sioux in the fight.

Lynch saw 7th Inf. men carrying dead men out of deep gully. They had "got 7 men on bank" and he remarked: "There are a whole bunch of them in there yet." Lynch says these men in gully were carried up and buried on the ridge. Says Serg. Dave Heaton was one of these 7th Inf. men. (Heaton is now dead.) One of men in deep gully was Timothy Donnelly of F Troop. Lynch identified Briody by sailor's mark on his arm. Vickory and Voss and Donovan lay near Custer. 14 F troop enlisted men lay around Custer. Saw only one man scalped and looked at a good many. 2nd Cavalry and 7th Inf. and 7th Cavalry all helped to bury. Men with pack train went over with pack mules but did help bury.

Capt. Ball of 2nd Cavalry made a scout up the Little Big Horn and men of this command told Lynch found many dead warriors in a coulee. Smelled so bad did not count them.

October 1908 Comanche stood on Custer hill (Later Lynch said Comanche found down near river: See note February 8, 1909) near where monument is with head drooped. Shot 5 times. He recognized his friends. When men came up and called him by name he nickered. Wounded — shot in chest and came out on left side. Shot just above hoof in one of his forefeet. Shot twice in neck. Shot through loins.

Lynch dressed his wounds the first time by orders of Nolan.[3] Dressed with zinc wash on 28th. That night started for boat. Comanche limped down to boat with the men carrying wounded men.

When Benteen was watering horses the pack train came up to him and he saw Sergeant Knipe ride up and speak to Benteen. McDougall then was in rear, but did not see anything more of him. Mules were pretty well together, never strung out more than 400 or 500 yards. Generally 3 or 4 abreast. Each loaded with about 300 lbs. Box hardtack on each side of the pack with box ammunition on top and between the hardtack boxes. In case of bacon it would be in sacks between two boxes of hardtack.

Frank Hunter, F troop private (Farrier). His horse ran away from Custer across Ford B and carried him through Hunkpapa camp up over Reno's battleground and onto hill and joined Reno about 4:00

---

3. Lieutenant Henry J. Nowlan, the regimental quartermaster, had been on the *Far West* from June 22 and came to the battlefield on June 27.

p.m. He was unhurt. Thinks . . . was nicknamed "Yankee" Herman or like name.

When [Reno was] corraled [on the hilltop] Lynch saw White Swan [the Crow Indian scout] at one time when Sioux making charge, drag himself out [to the firing line] by grabbing the grass with hands and pulling himself along with his gun to get a shot at Sioux. The men would then drag him back and in little while would find him trying again to get out to skirmish line to fire at Sioux. He was wounded 5 or 6 times and legs so badly wounded that could not use them.

The farrier is the veterinary of the co. Infantrymen are called "dough boys" because they tramp through the mud. Lynch from vicinity of Calhoun saw 7th Inf. men over at the gully and someone said "Let's go over and see what those dough boys are doing." He found them carrying dead bodies up the south side of gully and already had 7 of them laid on the bank.[4]

Lynch dressed Comanche's wounds first down at steamer. Lynch demonstrated that wound in breast and on side were made by same bullet by blowing in one with quill and discharge came out of wound in side.

Lynch, February 8, 1909, says Comanche was found down near mouth of deep gully a little way back from river. Dave Heaton, who was with Lieut. Bradley, says Comanche was the first signs of Custer fight they saw.

Lynch was with Custer 1 year in Civil War and 10 years fighting Indians and never knew him to use profanity. He neither drank, smoked nor chewed tobacco.

---

4. The following quotation is from a letter written by W. R. Logan at Fort Belknap Agency on May 17, 1909, to Walter Camp:

I was a member of the Little Big Horn expedition in 1876, and have the honor of being the first white man on the Custer battlefield after the fight, having arrived there on the morning of the 27th of June. You say that you have been told that the Seventh Infantry buried the dead in a deep coulee on the battlefield, this coulee lying about six or seven hundred yards over the ridge from where the body of the General was found; that your information is that a squadron of men under Sergeant Heaton carried these men's bodies out of the coulee and buried them in the vicinity. Your information on that point is not correct. The bodies were buried where found. The men were killed in bunches, principally each company by itself, and in some cases in company formation, i.e. skirmish formation. We buried the bodies, as I have said, about where they fell. We had no picks and shovels, the graves were dug out with knives and broken plates and other sharp utensils we could obtain. In some cases very little dirt and sage brush were put over the bodies. I was to the battlefield some ten or fifteen days after the burial, and a great many of the bodies had become exposed by the coyotes digging them out of their shallow graves.

(In Walter Camp Collection, box 4, folder 12, BYU Library.)

Interview with John Sivertsen, Washington, D.C.[1]

Sivertsen left in timber with Herendeen. Could not find his horse. Two days after got his horse unhurt with blouse hanging to saddle where he had put when he went into fight on p.m. of 25th. Horse was in bottoms. In woods he was with Serg. White, five men of G troop and scout Herendeen. . . .[2] Says shortly after got out of timber Indians set fire to it in several places. . . . McCormick[3] must have been one of the G troop men left in the timber as McIntosh took his horse. . . . After left timber and got across river he found a dead Indian with a soldier carbine and a whip. The Indian had been scalped. He does not know whether it was a Ree or a Sioux. This might be the Indian scalped by Corpl. Wallace,[4] whom O'Neill told about. He was the first man to wade through river going back about 4:30 p.m. Was fired on getting to river. He was first man to wade through river and first man up bluff. . . . When he got up, the first man he saw was French, his own captain. French held out his hand and said, "I am glad to see you, Sivertsen. I have got you down on the

---

1. Walter Camp field notes, folder 89, BYU Library.

   Sivertsen born in Norway in 1841. Came to U.S. in 1870. Enlisted in 7th Cav. June 19, 1873. 5'11" tall. Service: Genl. Stanley's Yellowstone campaign 1873. Custer's Black Hills Expedition 1874. Little Bighorn campaign 1876. Gen. Miles' Nez Perce campaign 1877. Battle of Canon Creek, September 13, 1877. Reenlisted in Company D, 2nd Artillery. Was on guard over Guiteau who shot Garfield. Came to Soldiers' Home in 1904. He was a farmer in Douglas County, Wisconsin 18 or 20 years and had family at Lake Nebagamon, 35 miles east of Superior. (Ibid.)

2. See account of George Herendeen.

3. Private Samuel McCormick of Company G gave his horse to Lieutenant Donald McIntosh in the retreat from the valley fight. He rejoined the command on the hilltop with George Herendeen.

4. John W. Wallace was a private in Company G and was in the valley and hilltop fights. He was promoted to corporal effective June 25, 1876.

dead list already."[5] On Reno hill a bullet passed through French's hat and French said: "Boys, that's a pretty close shave, and I guess it's about time I should make a move."[6]

---

5. John Sivertsen was a private in Company M and was in the valley and hilltop fights. He died August 30, 1925, at the National Soldiers' Home, Washington, D.C. His "Story of the Little Bighorn" is in *The Tepee Book,* 1916, p. 33, and 1926, pp. 45–47.

6. The following is a quotation from a letter written by W. O. Taylor at Orange, Mass., on December 12, 1909, to Walter Camp:

After twilight had come on the evening of the 25th and the fire of the Indians had slackened or ceased altogether, the men moved about quite freely, and were naturally rather anxious to know what our next move would be, the First Sergeant of my company had been wounded and his duties fell upon Sergeant Fehler, an elderly German, of a rather placid nature, our company was considerably scattered and when I saw the Sergeant (Fehler) near the lower end of the herded horses and pack mules, I approached and asked him "What are we going to do, stay here all night, or try to move away?" Major Reno was then standing quite near and heard my question, he turned at once with the remark, "I would like to know how the Hell we are going to move away." I was quite surprised, but as I had certain ideas in my mind I continued to Sergeant Fehler, that "if we are going to remain here we ought to be making some kind of barricade, for the Indians would be at us, the first thing in the morning." Major Reno again spoke up saying, "Yes, Sergeant, that is a good idea, set all the men you can at work at once"; Sergeant Fehler then began to order men to take boxes of hard-tack, pack-saddles, sides of bacon and anything they could use, and make a barricade across the lower end of the depression, this was finally done after a good deal of urging by the Sergeant, for many of the men showed but little interest in the work, it proved of great service the next day, commanding as it did, I think, the only feasible approach for a mounted charge against our lines.

(In Walter Camp Collection, box 6, folder 2, BYU Library.)

Interview with
Edward D. Pigford[1]

Says Sgt. O'Hara was hit on the skirmish line and not killed. When Pigford left the skirmish line O'Hara called to Pigford "For God's sake don't leave me." Pigford says the skirmish line was no sooner formed than it broke up. He personally fired only 4 or 5 shots. Says O'Hara was killed about 40 or 50 yds. from timber.

Says Bill Meyer was killed by an Indian on a horse who had followed to the east side. At this time there were several Indians who had followed to west side but did not cross the river after Reno's retreating soldiers. Pigford turned to fire at this Indian, but he got behind a rock and was taking aim at him (Pigford).

Says Co. M (Capt. French) went all way to Edgerly peaks, from which could look down in direction of Custer Ridge. Says at first when looked over toward Custer ridge the Indians were firing from a big circle, but it gradually closed until they seemed to converge into a large black mass on the side hill toward the river and all along the ridge. He thinks what they saw was the last stages of the fight. His description of what took place at Edgerly Hills while Co. M was there seems reliable.

Among other things he said the appearance of Indians coming from Custer Ridge toward Weir hills looked as thick as grasshoppers

---

1. Walter Camp field notes, folder 47, BYU Library. Edward D. Pigford, born in Allegheny County, Pennsylvania, enlisted on September 13, 1875. He was wounded in the right hip in the retreat from the valley fight on June 25, was slightly wounded in the right forearm by a small caliber bullet on June 26, and was discharged on October 15, 1876. His story, "Fighting With Custer," as told to Earle Forrest, appeared in the *Washington, Pennsylvania Morning Observer*, October 3–19, 1932. Pigford died on December 6, 1932, and was buried at Dravosberg, Pennsylvania.

in a harvest field. Capt. French's nickname among enlisted men was "Tucker."

Pigford says the Indian killed near Co. H line was one who had charged up and stopped there. The soldiers had fled to north end of Benteen's line. Every little while this Indian would rise up and fire. Once when he rose up he exposed the upper half of his body, and Pigford taking deliberate aim, killed him.

Says one ruse the Indians got up to draw fire of soldiers on Reno hill was a stuffed dummy in buckskin tied on a pony and the pony lashed up and driven over the ridge toward the soldiers and then turned loose. As the pony ran around, the soldiers for quite a while poured shots at him and his rider at long range.

Says that while men were getting water on p.m. June 26, he with others was guarding the route and saw an Indian in a tree on west side of river. He put up his sights and fired at him and saw him fall. On June 27 they found this Indian with a wound in his thigh and his neck broken. He had fallen out of the tree when shot and apparently had landed on his head and died there. Apparently none of the Indians had found him.

Interview with Ferdinand Widmayer, October 7, 1910[1]

Says heard Trumpeter Fisher[2] say that he helped Hodgson across river in Reno's retreat. Sure Sterland[3] left at Powder River. Slept with him in wagon there on rainy night. Sure mules — swings and leaders — taken for packs. Wheelers kept at Powder River. Says Bloody Knife went with Reno's scout. He recalls this well because after Reno had gone the boys said did not see how Custer could go anywhere without Bloody Knife.

Says Sgt. Carey[4] was not left in timber when Reno retreated. Says there were three. Says might have been Trumpeter Weaver.[5] Geo. Weaver called "Cully" Weaver. Geo. Weaver died at Ft. Meade. Thinks Trumpeter Weaver left in timber.

Sure David Ackison, Co. E, left at Powder. Sure Jerry Woodruff, Co. E, left at Powder. Says Hiram E. Brown of F went with packs. Widmayer had to turn over 2 mules to him which he took with the

---

1. Walter Camp field notes, folder 43, BYU Library. Ferdinand Widmayer, born in Germany, enlisted on September 26, 1873. At the time of the Little Bighorn River fight he was on detached service from Company M at Yellowstone Depot on the Powder River. He retired as color sergeant and resided in Philadelphia, Pennsylvania.

2. Charles Fischer was a trumpeter in Company M.

3. Walter Scott Sterland was a private in Company M and was on detached service at Yellowstone Depot on the Powder River. He died on August 27, 1922, at Dickinson, North Dakota.

4. Sergeant Patrick Carey of Company M was wounded in the right hip in the hilltop fight on June 26 and was taken to Fort A. Lincoln on the steamer *Far West*.

5. Henry C. Weaver was a trumpeter in Company M.

command for packs. Says Rooney with troop at Little Bighorn.[6]

Saw Nathan Short. Heard that a dead soldier was found and went to see him. Bones of man and horse and carbine were found. Sling belt still on the skeleton. Says was near the Rosebud. Body lay out in open space near some brush but not in brush. No log near the remains. A good many went to see it. Sure this was before met Crook. Sure the bones of a horse also there. Says body had been dead a long time and clothing rotted. If this is correct could not have been Short, but he says the talk at the time was that it was supposed to have been one of Custer's men who got away. Says the remains of the man were buried there.

----

6. David Ackison was a private in Company E and was absent because of illness at Yellowstone Depot; and Jerry Woodruff, also a private in Company E, was on detached service at Fort A. Lincoln. Hiram E. Brown, a private in Company F, was on detached duty in the Quartermaster Department, and James M. Rooney, a private in Company F, was with the pack train on June 25.

Interview with John Foley[1]

John Foley, Troop K, buried Cooke and found note in his left hand regarding "Whoever finds this note give it to Capt. Nolan." The note read: "Capt. Nolan, you may have everything belonging to me." (The above is doubtful.) Foley saw no scalped men in group around Custer. . . . John Foley found Francis T. Hughes, private, L troop, near Custer. In village John Foley found head of corporal of G troop under an overturned kettle. This corporal had red hair. Don't know name.[2]

John Foley, Rott and Rafter[3] went for water. Foley carried kettles and rushed for water. Before going Benteen told him he would have his troop fire some volleys to keep the Indians in check on west bank of river. When he heard the firing he rushed for water, but not all Indians were silenced as he heard plenty of bullets whistle around him. He got 2 kettles and back in safety.

---

1. Walter Camp field notes, folder 101, BYU Library.

John Foley born in Ireland 1839. . . . Enlisted April 20, 1861 in Co. F 22nd Ohio. Served 4 months and discharged. Reenlisted Co. A 1st Ohio Cavalry. In battle Cedar Mountain July 10 and 11, 1862. . . . wounded severely twice in face and leg. Next enlistment Co. B 2nd Ohio Heavy Artillery. Served 3 years 10 months in Rebellion. Enlisted in 7th Cavalry K troop, Capt. West, August 1866. Reenlisted in 7th Cavalry K troop, Capt. West, August 1871. Reenlisted in 7th Cavalry K troop, Capt. West, September 1876. Was in Washita. Was in Yellowstone campaign. Was in Black Hills. Was in Nez Perce in 1877. Horse killed and rolled on him. Living at Soldiers' Home.

(Ibid.)

2. James Martin and Otto Hagemann were corporals in Company G, and both were killed in the fight. Martin was killed in the retreat from the valley fight on June 25. Both had brown hair.

3. Sergeants John Rafter and Louis Rott of Company K.

Interview with
James Wilber[1]

Was one of 10 men with Serg. John Ryan. When John Ryan and 10 men forded river, Cooke sat on bank on his horse.

We were galloping fast, and just as we got to river Cooke called out: "For God's sake men, don't run those horses like that; you will need them in a few minutes."

Wilber saw Cooke but did not see Keogh. On far side of ford went through considerable timber.

John Ryan and 10 men actually went to Uncapapa tepees, and Rutten was among the tepees and from here his horse ran away, ditto John H. Meyer. Says Rutten's horse got farther into village than Meyer. Both got back to skirmish line after horse cut a circle with them. That is to say, Ryan and 10 men got a good ways ahead of skirmish line. Sergeant O'Hara was killed near the tepees and was first man killed in battle. Wilber says Hodgson grabbed stirrup of Trumpeter Fisher of M troop in crossing river in retreat. Lieut. Bradley and an orderly discovered Custer's body as Terry's column was passing up river on a.m. of June 27.

Howard, the milk peddler at Ft. Lincoln, was one of the scouts but did not get to river on June 25. He lingered behind somewhere and first got up to column a few minutes after DeRudio and Tom O'Neill

---

1. Walter Camp field notes, folder 89, BYU Library. James Wilber (James W. Darcy), born in Baltimore, Maryland, enlisted in the 7th Cavalry in 1875. He was wounded in the left leg on the water party on June 26, 1876, in the Little Bighorn River fight, was discharged for disability on November 1, 1876, and retired to the National Soldiers' Home in Washington, D.C. His "Story of the Little Big Horn" is found in *The Tepee Book* (Sheridan, Wyoming: The Mills Co., 1916), p. 45. He died on July 13, 1920, at the Soldiers' Home.

came in on morning of June 27. Wilber thinks he has a ranch some-where near Ft. Lincoln now.

Wilber says Dick Hanley told him that a C troop man left Custer later than Trumpeter Martin. Wilber says 4 Crows were with Reno on hill two days. Wilber says he saw four Crows on hill with Reno during the two days. Wilber says that on Reno's march down to ford, M troop was ahead, A next and G last and that when he forded, Adjt. Cooke was on the river bank. Custer wanted to take band beyond Powder River, but Terry would not consent to it.

Interview with Patrick Corcoran, Washington, D.C.[1]

Saw Knipe ride up and speak to Benteen when Benteen just got through watering horses. Next came to burning tepee quite near watering place. Benteen got to bluff before Reno did and about an hour before McDougall got up with packs.

Before Benteen charged, about half of his men had run over toward hospital. Benteen called to men "Where are you running to, men? Come on back and we will drive them off. You might as well be killed out there as in here." This corroborates what Knipe said about Benteen's men coming half way over at one time. Remembers distinctly of hearing volleys toward Custer late in evening.

Corcoran was wounded on hill early on morning of 26th. Reno came around and asked him how he was getting along. At this time he saw Reno[2] have a quart bottle of whisky[3] and saw him take a big drink out of it in hospital on morning of 26th. . . .

---

1. Walter Camp field notes, folder 38, BYU Library. Patrick Corcoran stated in his enlistment that he was born in Cattaraugus County, New York. He told Walter Camp he was born in Canada in March, 1844. He enlisted in Company K, 7th Cavalry, in St. Louis in July, 1867, and again in August, 1872. He was wounded in the right shoulder in the hilltop fight on June 26, 1876, and taken to Fort A. Lincoln on the steamer *Far West*. He was discharged for disability in 1877 and usually resided at the National Soldiers' Home in Washington, D.C.

2. DeRudio saw him drinking at Ford A and 20 minutes later Gerard says he saw him finish the bottle at the skirmish line fight, and that at that time Reno was intoxicated, etc.

(Camp MSS field notes, unclassified miscellaneous IV, Lilly Library.)

3. The following information is taken from Taylor's letter to Camp (See fn. 6, p. 142):

As to Major Reno's condition during the fight in the valley, I do not know that I can give you any new information. You tell me that "Reno admitted he had liquor in his possession at 9 P.M. on June 25th" (is there any chance for a mistake in someone's writing P.M. for A.M.) . . .

150

I will say, that on June 25th, and, as near as I can estimate the time, about one o'clock P.M. or a little later, we were nearing the Indian skirmishes on our ride toward their village, the Indians were firing and shouting their defiance, and we had been ordered to charge and some of the men began to cheer when Major Reno shouted out "Stop that noise." And once again came the command, "Charge." Charrrage, was the way it sounded to me, and it came in such a tone that I turned my head and glanced backward. The Major and Lieut. Hodgson were riding side by side in the rear of my company (A) perhaps 30 or 40 feet away, possibly more but certainly a very short distance. As I looked back Major Reno was just taking a bottle from his lips and passed it to Lieut. Hodgson. In appearance I should say it was a quart flask, about one half or two thirds full.

(In Walter Camp Collection, box 6, folder 2, BYU Library.)

151

Interview with Hugh McGonigle, October, 1908[1]

Was in timber with Lattman and Andrew J. Moore and 3 others[2] whom he cannot remember. Was in brush about an hour. In going out saw some young Indians dressed in white men's clothes and exchanged shots. In going across river three men went first and 3 men covered them and then those three covered while remaining three crossed.

They got over and Moore was killed June 26 on Reno hill. McGonigle[3] cautioned Moore to kneel when he was taking aim to fire, but Moore said he could not take good aim in that way. Accordingly he became careless and would rise up to fire and soon was shot through the body and killed.

---

1. Walter Camp field notes, folder 88, BYU Library. Hugh McGonigle, born in Philadelphia, Pennsylvania, enlisted for the third time on July 22, 1872. He was discharged on June 25, 1877, at the camp on Sunday Creek, Montana.

2. It occurs to me that McGonigle might have been with Herendeen and 14 others and that Moore was one of those that Herendeen said would not go out of timber with him.

(Note of February 7, 1909, in Walter Camp field notes, folder 88, BYU Library.)

3. Gerard says McGonigle . . . stepson of Reno.

(Walter Camp field notes, folder 94, BYU Library.)

Interviews
With
Indian
Scouts

Curley

Goes Ahead

Hairy Moccasin

White Man Runs Him

Little Sioux

Strike Two

Soldier

Young Hawk

Red Bear and Young Hawk

Interview with Curley,
September 18, 1908[1]

On September 18, 1908, the Crow Curley, scout with Custer on
July 25, 1876, accompanied me on a visit to the vicinity of the burning
tepee and from there back over Custer's route to the battlefield. On
this day he, with three other Crows (Hairy Moccasin, Goes Ahead, and
White Man Runs Him) were with Mitch Bouyer. Two other Crow
scouts, White Swan and Half Yellow Face, were with Gerard. At this
time Curley was 20 years old.

He directed me to the site of the big Sioux camp, all of which,
with the exception of the lone tepee covering a dead warrior, had been
moved in advance of Custer's arrival. This was located on the north

---

1. Walter Camp field notes, folder 27, BYU Library. Curley was a Crow
Indian born about 1856 on the Little Rosebud. He enlisted in the 7th Infantry
on April 10, 1876, at the Crow Agency as a scout and was attached to the 7th
Cavalry on June 21. He was with the Custer column on June 25, witnessed the
fight of the Custer column, and carried the news of the fight to the steamer *Far
West*. He was mustered out on September 30, 1876. He died of pneumonia on
May 21, 1923, at his ranch near the Crow Agency and was buried in the Custer
Battlefield National Cemetery. "Curley's Narrative" as told to Lieutenant
Charles F. Roe with Thomas LeForge interpreting is in the *Army and Navy
Journal*, Washington, D.C., March 25, 1882, 19:34, p. 761. The *New Northwest*
(Deer Lodge, Mont.) for July 21, 1876, and July 21, 1907, has the "Story of
Curley the Scout." Copies are in the Montana State Historical Society Library.
His account is found also in Joseph Dixon's *The Vanishing Race* (Garden City,
New Jersey: Doubleday, Page & Co., 1925), pp. 140–45, 159–64 and in John
Finerty's *Warpath and Bivouac* (Chicago: M. A. Donohue & Co., 1890). "Curley
The Crow Scout Once More" is found in *Winners Of The West* (St. Joseph,
Missouri: National Indian Wars Veterans), July, 1924, 1:8, 1–2, and the "State-
ment of Curley The Scout" is found in *The Tepee Book*, June 1916, and June
1926. There are innumerable accounts attributed to Curley in newspapers
beginning from 1876.

side of Benteen Creek,[2] about 4 miles from the Little Bighorn, on a wide and smooth piece of ground gently sloping toward the creek. When we arrived on this ground, Curley drew my attention to rotten pieces of wood lying about, which he said had been carried there by the Sioux for their camp fires. Buffalo heads and joint bones were also strewn over the ground, and these he also said were still good evidence of an Indian camp which evidently had extended about ½ mile.

The site of the burning tepee he could not locate exactly, ("Heap Sioux tepee here," said Curley) but said it was on one side or the other of a gulch running through the camping ground. Pointing his finger, he said: "Mebby so here, mebby so there," meaning that he was not sure on which side of the ravine it was standing. His means of identifying the locality was a high rocky bluff, from which he, with Mitch Bouyer and three other Crow scouts, had been watching the Sioux with field glasses all that forenoon before the arrival of Custer's command. Curley said the tepee stood just opposite the bluff, and as the troops came along, the tepee was set on fire by the soldiers.

From this point he went with Custer's battalion as it came along, and when Custer diverged from Reno's trail, about 1¼ miles from the river, Bouyer and his four Crows went with Custer. Custer's route from this point was directly across the country, on the crest of a long ridge, running to the bluffs and coming out at a point about 500 ft. north of the Reno corral. From here Custer passed along the crest of the bluffs for fully ¾ mile, in full view of the river and of the valley over across it. Custer hurried his men, going at a gallop most of the time. Reno and his command were plainly seen by Custer's whole command while marching this ¾ mile. On the first line of bluffs back from the river there are two high peaks marked "A" on the map,[3] now called Reno peaks. For some distance south of these there is a high ridge running parallel with the river, but not so high as the peaks. Custer's command passed into the valley of a tributary of Reno Creek[4]

---

2. Walter Camp also identifies Benteen Creek as Reno Creek. It is identified by Indians as Ash Creek and by Lieutenant Godfrey as Sundance Creek.

3. Walter Camp prepared several maps pertaining to the Little Bighorn River fight, one of which is a large table-size map in several sections. The identifications in this Curley narrative are not shown in the Camp map illustrated in this book. Camp uses the terms Reno peaks, Edgerley peaks, and Weir peaks interchangeably.

4. This reference to Reno Creek and later references are confusing and misleading. Camp almost undoubtedly was referring to Cedar Coulee as the tributary, and by Reno Creek he was referring to Medicine Tail Coulee.

just behind this ridge and the peaks and went down it, going in a direction directly north and coming out into the bed of Reno Creek about a mile from its mouth at Ford B. From the moment Custer's command commenced to descend this tributary of Reno Creek, it passed out of view of Reno's battalion, but Bouyer and his four scouts kept to the left of Custer, on the crest of the high ridge and peaks, and at all times could command a view of the river and the bottoms beyond. Before Bouyer got to the peaks, he left three of his Crow scouts behind, with orders to watch the Indian camp in the valley opposite and any movements of Indians in Custer's rear. Taking Curley with him, he passed on and over the peaks, and then on a course parallel with that of Custer (directly north) until they came down into the bed of Reno Creek, where they met Custer about ½ mile from the river. When they got to the top of the first of these peaks, they looked across and observed that Reno's command was fighting. At the sight of this, Bouyer could hardly restrain himself and shouted and waved his hat excitedly for some little time. Undoubtedly Bouyer is the man seen by some in Reno's command to wave his hat, for Custer never went to the peaks or high ridge; and when the hat was waved, Custer was entirely out of sight from Reno's position and must have been so for several minutes.

After Bouyer and Curley joined Custer, the command passed rapidly down to Ford B. As soon as the soldiers came in sight of the village, the Sioux gave voice to a "heap big yell, like dog," as Curley expressed it, and when Custer's soldiers got closer, there was "heap shoot, bang! bang! bang!" The troops did not dismount here, and some of them rode into the river before stopping and turning back. Curley saw one soldier[5] gallop across the river just below the ford at great speed, pass up the bank, through the Sioux posted along it, and come out into full view on the open ground beyond the ford. The Sioux defending the ford he observed to be all dismounted. He afterwards learned that these were men who did not have time to get their ponies, which were grazing back on the hills west of the village.

When Custer withdrew from the ford, he proceeded down the

---

5. The direct quotation in this footnote is from the July 1908 letter of Daniel Knipe to Walter Camp. This soldier that crossed the river may have been Sergeant James Bustard of Company I.

Sergeant of I Troop was lying, he and his horse, across the ford in the Indian village or camp. He was not mutilated; his horse was some twenty or thirty steps from him.

(In Walter Camp Collection, box 5, folder 7, BYU Library.)

river for some distance and then struck out for higher ground in columns of fours, going direct to the point where markers are found at the southeast point of the battlefield ([at] Sergeant Finley's marker).[6] Before they got to this point, Mitch Bouyer lost his horse. Indians were now in front and in the ravines on both sides, and a strong force of Indians were coming up in the rear. Curley says the command was being driven like a herd of horses, and the only thing that could be done was to charge the enemy in the direction that was thought to be most advantageous to go and then only to have them close in on all sides. The front was driving the Indians and the rear was being driven. In ascending to the elevation now marked by slabs for Calhoun and Crittenden, an attempt was made to cover the retreat until some kind of a stand could be made. Men were left at the Finley marker, and some of the troops dismounted just beyond this, Curley staking his horse with the rest. The dismounted men then tried to drive the Indians from the gulch ahead, but the men left in the rear were quickly killed, and the advance of the Indians from that direction was hardly checked at all.

Custer stopped at this point for a brief space of time, and what was decided upon had to be done in great haste. There was a hurried conference of officers, and Bouyer told Curley that the subject of conversation was to the effect that if the command could make a stand somewhere, the remainder of the regiment would probably soon come up and relieve them. Personally, Bouyer did not expect that relief would come, as he thought the other commands had been scared out. Bouyer thought the orders would be to charge straight ahead, drive the Indians from the ravine, and try to find more favorable ground. For a moment or two the fire of the Indians slackened in this direction, and it was thought the plan could be carried out, when a large force of warriors swept around that corner as if in anticipation of the intentions of the soldiers, and the scheme had to be given up. There was then "heap shoot, shoot, shoot" (Curley clapping his hands after the manner of the sign language to indicate the rapidity of the firing). It was now plain that no advance could be made in the intended direction, and Custer struck out westward, it being understood that some of the soldiers (probably Calhoun's troop) would try to hold the ground at this corner. Curley says, however, that the men would not stand, all who could do so either going for their horses or running in the direc-

6. Sergeant Jeremiah Finley of Company C.

158

tion of the general retreat, which was headed for the highest ground, now occupied by the monument. In doing this they had to run the gauntlet of a fire from a ravine full of warriors to the northward and a large force of Indians shooting over the long ridge extending westerly to the monument. Curley said that while on the way to where the Calhoun marker now stands, a few men had started in the direction of the monument along the southside of the ridge, but as the Indians charged up from the direction of the river these men were driven over the crest and fell in with the line of retreat.

Most of the men able to do so had now followed the line of retreat down the gully and diagonally up the slope toward the monument. In this the men with the gray horses appeared to be keeping well together, but it seemed to him that the other companies were getting badly mixed up.

Mitch Bouyer now turned to Curley, saying that Tom Custer had suggested that the scouts had better save themselves if they could. Bouyer advised Curley to try it, and Curley said he told Bouyer he would do so if he (Bouyer) also would try it. Bouyer declined by saying that he was too badly wounded, and he would have to stay to fight it out, although he believed they would all be killed. Curley now decided to stay no longer. He turned around to look for his horse, and there he found a hand-to-hand encounter. As for him the Sioux were a little too quick, and he saw a warrior running off with his horse at the end of the lariat. Just then a mounted Indian was shot off his pony. Catching the warrior's horse and taking his Winchester and belt of cartridge to replace his own weapon which was dirty and working badly, he mounted and rode out. The mass of Indians had now charged around on the flanks of the retreating soldiers, and Curley, by riding around the corner as though one of the charging Indians and giving voice to the Sioux yell or war cry, passed out without being recognized and was soon in a ravine, out of sight. He went up the right-hand ravine (to the right of Godfrey's spring), and stopped to look back only twice. He estimates that his last look at the battlefield must have been ½ hour after leaving, and the soldiers were still fighting, although he could not discern anything as to the formation. He traveled on a wide circuit and met the steamer *Far West* lying at the mouth of the Little Bighorn, where he got aboard and remained for several days.

According to the account of Grant Marsh, captain of the steamer, Curley came through the brush on the river's bank, naked, armed and riding an Indian pony.[7] They at once saw that something was wrong with the Indian, but no Crow interpreter was around, and Curley was having difficulty in making his audience understand. He would grab his hair, pull it straight up, groan, and then make a motion to indicate scalping, but this was not definite enough, and he was pressed for further explanation. Finally he grabbed up a piece of paper and pencil and undertook the graphics method. He first drew a small circle and within it made dots, which he intended to represent soldiers. He next drew a much larger circle surrounding the first and between them drew a large number of dots, saying, as he dotted them down, "Heap Sioux, heap Sioux." This made matters clearer to the dull people, for they now understood that the soldiers had been surrounded.

---

7. See also the account of James Sipes.

Interview with Curley, August 3–4, 1909, Russell White Bear, Interpreter[1]

Curley interview August 3 on battlefield, August 4 on divide.

Curley was born on Rosebud River. *Before 1876 I had had experience in three battles with Sioux. . . .* What do the Crows call Little Bighorn? *Little Bighorn.*[2] Also Big Horn River? *Big Horn.* Before 1876 what was considered eastern boundary of Crow country? *Tongue.* The Crow country extended to the Tongue.

Curley: *Shi shi' esh;* Half Yellow Face: *Ischu shi dish;* White Swan: *Be da'chish;* Hairy Moccasin: *Isape eshish;* Goes Ahead: *Ba suck osh;* White Man: *Ba chida crush* (long u).

Curley said Mitch Bouyer and 4 Crows, including himself, lay on rocky hill all forenoon watching the Sioux, and lone tepee in Indian camp was down under them, to left. When soldiers came along they set the tepee on fire. Here they joined Custer. While with Custer did he hear Reno's firing, and where was Curley then? *No, after came down off bluff too much excitement and not paying attention to matters in that direction.* While Reno's fight was still in progress when he left the bluffs south of Ford B, he heard nothing of it after passing Dry Creek, *as the excitement in our front was too great.* After Custer had sighted the village and was moving toward it, did Mitch Bouyer say what movement he thought Custer was about to make? Did he think Custer was going to charge the village? *Yes, thought Custer would charge.*

Escape of Hairy Moccasin, Goes Ahead, and White Man Runs Him:

---

1. Walter Camp field notes, folder 77, BYU Library.

2. Ask Curley if river at Reno's skirmish line has changed much since 1876. *Yes, a good deal. Also same applies north of Ford B.*

(Ibid.)

These three Crows were with Bouyer and me as far as the bluff at the cut bank just south of Ford B and about 1500 ft. from that ford. While we were here, Custer's command hove in sight, galloping right down the coulee toward the river. Bouyer now said he would cut across and meet it, and he started down off the east slope of the bluff and I with him. Here Hairy Moccasin, Goes Ahead, and White Man Runs Him turned tail and put back up the river following our trail along the bluffs. Hairy Moccasin, White Man, and Goes Ahead got away when Mitch Bouyer went down to see what Custer intended to do, as Custer was coming down Dry Creek.[3] Then the 3 Crows shipped out without leave and went south along bluffs. This was the last I saw of them until I met them on the Yellowstone some weeks later, but they have told me that they retreated as far as Sundance Creek,[4] went up the trail we came in on, and then cut a wide circuit over to the vicinity of the mouth of the Little Bighorn where the next day they yelled over to Gibbon's Crows the information of Custer's defeat, of which they saw only the part in which Reno participated.

Custer's route according to Curley: Custer left coulee of Dry Creek 900 ft. east of its mouth and struck the river 1,000 ft. downstream from its mouth. It is about 900 ft. further to the first high cut bank. It appeared to Curley here that Custer would charge across into the village, but the west bank was thick with dismounted Sioux, and back in the village hundreds of mounted ones were coming up. Good many soldiers got nearly into water and one got across and was killed in village. He was some noncommissioned officer. The hot fire then impressed Curley with the idea that it would be necessary for Custer to retreat, and he did so, going in a direction downstream and quartering back upon the high ridge.

While Custer's firing at the cut bank was in progress I saw no large body of Indians fording, but as soon as we began to retreat they must have swarmed across both above and below us, for we had not proceeded one-third of the way to the ridge before the Sioux were thick upon both our right and left flanks firing into us heavily. I do not know whether or not any one was killed on the way to the ridge but the firing was so heavy that I do not see how the command made the ridge without some loss. Going up from river, Sioux on all sides except front. Mitch Bouyer told me to keep out of the skirmish as

---

3. Camp often refers to Medicine Tail Coulee as Dry Creek.
4. (Also Ash Creek, Benteen Creek, and Reno Creek.)

much as possible, as they might wish to send me with a dispatch to the other troops.

When Custer retreated up from the river, did he stop anywhere to fight? *Did not stop but did some firing.* When got up to about where fence is they began dismounting, and dismounted men were on flanks of horseholders to protect them.

After we made the ridge just west of where Calhoun's marker is placed, we were twice ordered to load and fire together. It occurred to me at the time that this must be some signal. Does not know whether or not it was a signal, but there seemed to be some understanding or system about it.

The apparent line of men between C and H Curley says were men who charged Indians. Other Indians charged in behind them and cut them off and most of them were killed.

I escaped by riding to the right and front, through dust and powder smoke, pulling over my head a cape made by cutting up blankets, which I had tied to my saddle.[5] The Sioux appeared not to discover my identity. I was dressed in shirt and leggins, abut the same as the Sioux, most of whom had their faces and clothing painted in striking colors. As nearly as I can recollect I went straight east or south of east, turning the point of the hill [where Sergeant Butler was found]. *As I did this, I passed a dead Sioux who had been killed by the fire of our soldiers on their retreat up from the river. I dismounted quickly and seized his gun[6] and cartridge belt. Further on, and on the north slope of the coulee of Dry Creek, rather out of view from the battle in progress, I caught up with a loose Sioux pony which I led along with me until I came to the steamer.[7]*

After I left the Custer battlefield, I went east and crossed the divide to the Rosebud and went down it to its mouth, where the steamer had ferried us across the Yellowstone before we started up the Rosebud. Here I found no one but found Gibbon's trail up the Yel-

---

5. Curley did not lose his own horse but took one on way after got away. Picked up a Sioux blanket separately. Curley got out and came south nearly to Dry Creek.

(Ibid.)

6. What kind of a gun did he take from the dead Sioux and what did he do with his own? *Took Winchester. Threw his own away.*

(Ibid.)

7. When he got to the boat did he have more than one horse, and where did he pick up the extra ones? *Yes, had two. Picked up the extra one near Dry Creek.*

(Ibid.)

163

lowstone and followed it. I did not overtake Gibbon, but when I got onto the divide east of the Big Horn, I saw the steamer and went to it at the junction of Little Bighorn and the Big Horn. I arrived at the steamer about the middle of the forenoon of the third day [June 28] *having been three nights on the way.*

Ask him what Crows took news to Terry and how they got there. *Went on a wide circle over toward Rosebud.* Inquire particularly of Curley whether he met other Crows or troops before he got to steamer and whether he crossed Little Bighorn or Big Horn to west side. *Did not meet any one. He was all while on east side of Little Bighorn. The boat was in Big Horn just at mouth of Little Bighorn.* Ask Curley if he met troops on way to steamer Far West. *No.* What route Curley took to steamer and particularly whether he yelled across river to Gibbon's Crows on p.m. June 26 and told of Custer defeat. *No. Hairy Moccasin, Goes Ahead, and White Man did this and then went on to Yellowstone.* The way Curley communicated the news of the Custer defeat.

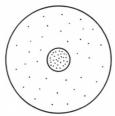

Within the smaller circle: "soldiers." Between the two circumference lines: "Heap Sioux."

After got to boat was sent back to battlefield with a message and then returned to boat. *We cut hay bedding for the wounded soldiers on the boat.*

Curley's story explains why troopers found dead were so mixed up, members of troop C being found on all parts of the field. This was a puzzle to Knipe[8] until he heard this story.

Curley's story has been both believed and disbelieved. As to the disbelief, I have never heard or seen in print the least particle of reliable evidence to prove that he was not in the beginning of the fight, as he states. His story throughout agrees with other authentic accounts. *The story about my going to Custer on the battlefield and trying to persuade him to try to escape after the men were nearly all killed is*

---

8. Daniel Knipe, who had carried a message from Custer to McDougall, was with Walter Camp on the battlefield.

untrue. I never told it. The fact that I could speak no English and Custer not a word of Crow shows how ridiculous the story is. The familiar story to the effect that Curley went to Custer late in the battle and offered to pilot him out and that Custer disdainfully refused to go is not true. Curley did not talk with General Custer on the battlefield at all, nor at any other time, because he could speak no English. He talked only with Mitch Bouyer, who could interpret Crow. Curley left early in the battle, from the point where Calhoun fell, which was ¾ mile from where Custer fell. And far from Curley suggesting to Custer a means of escape, it was Tom Custer who suggested to Bouyer and Curley how they could get away, and but for which, and the advice of Bouyer, Curley would probably never have attempted to leave the battlefield in the way he did.

Says W. M. Camp is the first man who seemed to take down his interview carefully and ask questions about particular things in a careful and persistent manner.

Interview with Curley,
July 19, 1910,
Fred Old Horn,
Interpreter[1]

Curley is a Mountain Crow. Agency at Sweetwater. Get as much as I can of his early history. Had he ever fought the Sioux before 1876? *Yes I helped to steal some of Sioux horses, and some of our men were killed. In some of these trips we got into tight places and had narrow escapes.*

Crows called Custer Young Star, Gibbon No Hip, Terry Morning Star. Did ever see photo of Half Yellow Face and where? *No. Never saw his photo. Died soon after fight.*

When Custer separated from Reno he took Mitch Bouyer and 6 Crows. Was Billy Cross or other scout there? *No. No scouts but Bouyer and Crows.* Why not all six Crows? *Custer had told Half Yellow Face and White Swan to go up on hill and take a look around, and instead of doing this they went with Reno. They were afraid and did not want to do as Custer ordered them. This was some little time after we had parted from Reno.* These two Crows met Reno's soldiers at Ford A.

Bouyer and the Crows were ahead of Custer's command. Custer did not see Reno's fight. Mitch Bouyer and myself did. When Reno fighting no one but Mitch Bouyer with me. Before got to Crow Hill, Bouyer waved hat to Custer from here. Saw Reno fighting from Edgerly peaks.

How much of Reno's battle did Curley see? Did he see Reno's retreat? *Yes, saw retreat and Bouyer then gave signal to Custer. Custer and Tom Custer returned signal by waving hats, and men cheered. Bouyer probably told Custer Reno had been defeated, for Bouyer did a whole lot of talking to Custer when he joined him and kept talking while they were riding side by side.*

---

1. Walter Camp field notes, folder 6, BYU Library.

Get from him a more definite statement as to where 3 Crows left Bouyer. Get it on the ground if possible. Hairy Moccasin, White Man, and Goes Ahead must have left Bouyer before Reno's battle ended because while Reno was retreating they were down near Ford A.[2] I therefore think that Curley and Bouyer were on Weir hill alone. See what Goes Ahead says.

When he and Bouyer, on Bouyer hill, saw Custer's command up Medicine Tail Coulee, was the command standing still or coming down the coulee? *Coming.* When he and Bouyer went from bluff down into Medicine Tail Coulee to meet Custer did Custer remain there any length of time? *No, kept going right on.* Also whether Custer stopped in Medicine Tail coulee any considerable length of time. What he was doing there etc., or why he was waiting? *Did not stop.*

In retreating up from river what was the formation — column or skirmish line? What officer did he see on this retreat and where was he, in front or rear? What was Custer doing down at the river and how long did he wait down there? *No time at all.* Did he see any soldiers on top of Greasy Grass hill while he was on the flat or at any other time? *Yet, 10 or 15 went up and along the ridge, probably guides or flankers. When whole command was at Finley the volleys were fired, and they were fired at the Sioux who were closing in.*

Curley got away to 4 markers at extreme southeast. While here the Indians were killing soldiers over by Finley, and all soldiers halted here. Sioux were on all sides shooting. Soldiers were dismounted and leading horses and firing at Sioux the best they could. Sioux were all along on Custer Ridge. Mitch Bouyer said, "You had better leave now for we will all be cleaned out."[3] *Bouyer told me to ride out through*

---

2. Camp undoubtedly meant Ford B. See interviews with Goes Ahead, Hairy Moccasin, and White Man Runs Him.

3. The following quotation is from the letter written by W. R. Logan in May 1909 to Walter Camp:

You ask whether the body of Mitch Bouyer, the scout, was ever found, and at what point. I found the body of Mitch Bouyer on the ridge something over half way between where Custer fell and where Reno made his stand on the high butte. The body was lying on the east slope of the ridge, pretty well down towards the bottom of the coulee. In my opinion Mitch had tried to get from the Custer fight over to Reno, and I firmly believe he was carrying a message at the time from Custer to Reno. I know that the general opinion is that Mitch's body was never found, and I doubt very much whether it was ever buried. I remember very distinctly the finding of Mitch's body, as we were warm friends, and when I returned to the camp, I mentioned the fact to my father, and he said he would take steps to see that the body was buried, but . . . I think it was neglected.

(In Walter Camp Collection, box 4, folder 12, BYU Library.)

the coulee over to east. Bouyer had just been talking with General Custer and Custer's brother Tom, and then he came and told me this.

Little Face *(Eeseeuh Kahty)* was the Crow who told the tale of the 3 Crows who escaped from battle Little Bighorn, across Big Horn on morning June 26. Look him up and see what the 3 reported of Curley that morning. *Yes, White Man, Hairy Moccasin, and Goes Ahead told soldiers at mouth of Little Bighorn that Half Yellow Face, White Swan, and I were dead. And when they got home they told the same story, and the people of us three tortured themselves over the news before they learned that I had escaped. They crossed river and cried and told such a bad news that all the other scouts ran away.* The three Crows, in reporting to Bradley's Crows, pretended to be telling of Custer's defeat, when in fact, they had seen only Reno's battle. Had they told the truth as they very well knew it, they would have had to tell of deserting Custer and Bouyer. So they reported Curley "missing and probably killed" and in this way gave no intimation of their own actions. The fact is that the battalion which they had good reason to think was annihilated was safe (except for heavy loss) while the battalion which they reported as lost they knew nothing whatever about, having left it an hour or nearly an hour before it became engaged. By reporting Custer's battalion lost they justified their presence at mouth of Little Bighorn at that time.

From where Curley left at the 4 markers, the bearing to coulee up which rode is N81 deg. E or 9 deg. north of east natural bearings. When he was escaping as before, did he see anything of the 5 men of Co. F? No. *When I rode out, there were no Sioux in front. I had a cape and cap made of a blanket and threw it over my head and rode out in disguise. The Sioux gave chase, but my horse was too fast, and they did not pursue far and I soon got away from them. Not sure that they knew me to be a Crow. I rode up the coulee to the head of it and over the distant ridge. I had my own gun, a Winchester, and leggin's on.*

About Fenton Campbell's interpretation concerning Curley getting the Winchester from dead Sioux etc. *Soldiers killed this Sioux, and I took his gun and threw mine away. Had fired away all my ammunition. I had only thirty shells, and the soldiers shells would not fit mine; so I took that of the Sioux.*

What route to steamer? *To Tullock to Rosebud and then across to Big Horn. After leaving Custer, went beyond high point close to Tullock's fork and next morning went to Rosebud and back to Big Horn. Did not go to mouth of Rosebud. Started west because my*

168

home in that direction. Intended to go to north of Big Horn where I thought there would be a camp (and there was such). Ask again whether he went to the mouth of the Rosebud after leaving Little Bighorn and before he came to the boat. *No, went to Rosebud but not to mouth.*

In *Bismarck Tribune* July 12, 1876, Grant Marsh reports that Curley came to boat on morning of June 27, and "before Terry had found remains of the Custer command." Says Curley captured 2 horses from Sioux. Says Curley then told (as soon as interpreter could be had) about changing the dress of his hair in getting out of Custer fight. . . . It occurs to me after reading Marsh's story that Curley must have got to the boat on the 27.[4] He would not therefore have time to go to mouth of Rosebud but may have started for there and saw the smoke of the steamer from high ground.

Ask him if he remembers drawing the two circles to indicate that Custer was surrounded and destroyed. *At the steamer I told of Custer's defeat by sticking little sticks in the ground and then sweeping them away with my hand. I also pointed at the sticks and made motions like scalping by pulling at my own hair and groaning, but the soldiers were dull and did not appear to understand me. I also did this on top of a box.*

He also continually repeated "Absaroke. Absaroke." What did he mean by this? He meant that he was a Crow and that the other scouts had run away and soldiers killed. One of the things Curley did to convey information of who he was to beat upon his breast and say "Absaroke. Absaroke." Some of the scholarly men about Washington and elsewhere are still studying the archives to find out what Curley meant. What Curley was trying to make them understand was simply: "I am a Crow." It occurred to Curley that if they could . . . be

---

4. There is this to say about the date of his arrival at the steamer, however. It was before Terry had sent word to steamer that Custer had been defeated, for Curley's information was the first that the steamer had had.

(Walter Camp field notes, folder 6, BYU Library.)

made to know that he was a Crow, they might surmise where he had come from (Custer). When I told Curley in 1910 that the historians were still doubtful as to the translation of the word Absaroke, he had a hearty laugh.

New York Herald 7/11/76 col. 2: Capt. E. W. Smith told the correspondent (Lounsberry) that the map of the battlefield drawn by Curley at the steamboat is absolutely correct. See account of an officer of 7th Inf. (evidently) in *New York Herald* 7/13/76, col. 1, where he says the Crows reported 3 of their number killed. Curley's story to Gen. Roe 3/8/81 (*Army and Navy Journal* 3/25/1882, p. 761), La Forge interpreter (probably made up a good deal of it or the interview was not on the ground but at Ft. Custer).

Curley on June 28[5] carried a message from *Far West* to battlefield and saw some of the dead buried. The dead were then partly buried. This was the next day after he got to the steamer.

I was then given another message and sent back to steamer[6] which was tied up right where ice house of Ft. Custer was afterward built. Soldiers on steamer put grass in steamer to put wounded on. That night carried wounded soldiers down and put on steamer and next morning went to Yellowstone river, and Half Yellow Face and I camped with the soldiers.

Late in p.m. we got to Pease bottom where the steamer was. There we were ferried across Yellowstone by steamer, I and my horse were the first to go on board. We had Tom LaForge[7] on steamer, a good interpreter. The soldiers knew that I had been with Custer and talked with me much. I have always told the same story but there have been different interpreters.

Next morning went to No Hip and among the infantry troops that walked there was an officer with a white mustache. I was barefoot and wished I had a pair of shoes. I had got my moccasins wet and torn them and was in bad shape. I talked to Gibbon and this officer and

---

5. The statement that he took message to battlefield on June 28, the day after arriving at steamer, may be an error of interpretation.

(Ibid.)

6. *The note which I carried up Little Bighorn on June 28 was to Custer battlefield. From there I took a message to camp on flat where Half Yellow Face and White Swan were and from there took a message to steamer.*

(Ibid.)

7. The story of Thomas H. LeForge, a white man who lived with the Crow Indians, is told by Thomas Bailey Marquis in *Memoirs of A White Crow Indian* (Century Co.: New York, 1928).

said: "You enlisted us to fight the Sioux and then went and sold us 6 Crows to Custer for $600. I was told this by Bouyer. I don't like this and I want to go home. You have not used us for the purpose for which we enlisted, and you have got me nearly killed. I want to go home." Gibbon said: "Well, you have nearly lost your life and you may go." Gibbon gave me meat and sugar and hardtack and let me go home. Left the soldiers seven days after the fight and went home. White Swan, who was shot in thigh and wrist stayed at Pease Bottom and doctor with him until his folks came after him. White Swan's horse was hit three times. White Swan was shot in the retreat of the Rees out of bottom.

About finding of body of Nathan Short. What does he remember about it? *Nothing. Was not there.* Did he and [Half Yellow] Face accompany detail that took away bodies of officers in 1877? Get him to tell me something about it. *Yes, I was there, but Half Yellow Face not. We looked for Bouyer's body for eight days and never found it. We found his saddle and horse in village but not the body.*

171

Interview with Curley, September 30, 1913, Thomas Le Forge, Interpreter[1]

The reason White Swan and Half Yellow Face went with Reno was that at about the time Custer left the divide, he ordered these two Crows to go to a certain high point on a butte and take a look. They did this, and instead of coming back to Custer and reporting, they went over to Reno's battalion and remained with him. The other four Crows remained with Custer until we got to ridge south of Medicine Tail coulee. Here Hairy Moccasin, White Man Runs Him, and Goes Ahead left us, and Mitch and I went on. We joined Custer on Medicine Tail Coulee as he was advancing toward the village. He did not halt after we joined him. He had all the bugles blowing for some time, the purpose of which I did not understand [perhaps he was having them play Garry Owen — WMC].

I had seen Reno defeated in the bottom and discussed it with Mitch. I saw Mitch say something to General Custer when we met him and presumed that he must have informed him about Reno's situation.

On the battlefield, near Calhoun marker, I saw Mitch talking with the general. Mitch said that Custer told him the command would very likely all be wiped out and he (Custer) wanted the scouts to get out if they could. I was riding my own horse. I found a dead Sioux and exchanged my Winchester for his Sharps rifle and belt of cartridges.[2] On my saddle I had a coat made of a blanket with holes cut out for arms, and a hood over my head. In this fashion I rode out.

I first went over to Lookout Point and remained at the summit, on back side, until sundown. From there I could see soldiers gathered

---

1. Camp MSS, field notes, unclassified envelope 71, Lilly Library.

2. There is a variance in Curley's statements about the rifle he obtained from the Sioux Indian. In the 1908, 1909, and 1910 interviews it was a Winchester. It may be an error of interpretation here that the rifle was a Sharps.

on Reno hill. I went on and got to Tullock's fork by dark. There I halted and next went to Sarpy Creek and down it to Yellowstone and up it, on south side, and saw camp over in Pease bottom. In that vicinity I shot and killed a bull (buffalo) and roasted some of the meat, which was the first thing I had to eat since leaving the soldiers.

I went on upstream and picked up Gibbon's trail and followed it to the steamer. On this trail I found fragments of hardtack to eat. After I got to the boat, a white man was going up to the battlefield and I went with him. When I got there the dead had not all been buried. I was sent back to the boat with a message and slept on the boat that night, June 28. I had only one horse[3] when I arrived at the boat.

---

3. In the interview in August 1909 Curley stated that he had captured a Sioux pony in the fight and picked up another pony near Medicine Tail Coulee.

Interview with Goes Ahead, August 5, 1909, Russell White Bear, Interpreter[1]

Is 56 years old. After separating from Reno 4 Crows went with Custer.[2] With him when he turned to right off Reno's trail. *As to whether Curley left us and went back I decline to answer. I prefer that White Man or Hairy Moccasin answer this question.* Went to bluff with Mitch Bouyer beyond point where Custer turned down coulee to right. Before this Custer had said that scouts had taken him

---

1. Walter Camp field notes, folder 59, BYU Library. Goes Ahead was a Crow scout with the Custer column on June 25. He was born about 1852 on the Platte River and enlisted on April 10, 1876, in Lieutenant James Bradley's Detachment of Indian Scouts for service with the 7th Infantry. He was on detached service from June 21 with the 7th Cavalry. He withdrew from the Custer column about 3:15 p.m. and eventually returned to Crow Agency with White Man Runs Him and Hairy Moccasin. He died on May 29, 1919, and was buried in the Custer Battlefield National Cemetery. His account "Reminiscences of an Indian Scout for Custer" was published in *The Tepee Book,* November 1916, 2:11, pp. 16–21. Another account is found in Joseph Dixon's *The Vanishing Race* (Garden City, N.Y.: Doubleday, Page & Co., 1913), and another is found in *The Billings Gazette* June 21, 1953: "Crow Agency Man Relates Custer Scout's Story of Battle of Little Bighorn."

2. The following is an excerpt from a letter written by Walter Camp on February 28, 1910, at 7740 Union Avenue, Chicago, Illinois, to General Charles A. Woodruff, Veterans Home, California:

Goes Ahead told me nothing that disputed Curley's story in the least. Goes Ahead said that no one of the three Crows went as far as Medicine Tail coulee, so could not have been with Custer's command in that coulee, and that no one of the three saw or heard any part of Custer's fight — says they turned back on the bluff and went southward too early to have seen any of Custer's movements in the vicinity of Medicine Tail coulee. He admits that they told Bradley's Crows the next morning that Custer's men were all being killed, but explains that after they saw Reno's men being chased out of the valley and shot down as they ran, they concluded that all the regiment would meet with the same fate. He says that they had seen the full size of the village and knew that there were too many Sioux, etc.

(Copy in Walter Camp Collection, box 9, folder 11, BYU Library.)

to the enemy and need not go into the fight. Three Crows (Hairy Moccasin, Goes Ahead, and White Man Runs Him) turned back.

We saw Reno's battle and went back south along bluff and met Benteen's command. We three Crows did not see Custer after he turned down the coulee to right. Did not see Custer fight. Did not see beginning of it or any part of it. Do not know whether Custer went to river. We turned back too early to see where Custer went north of Dry Creek.

We three Crows made a circle to the east and came back to Little Bighorn and went on and swam the Big Horn to west side and next day yelled across to Gibbon's Crows information of Custer's defeat, although did not know positively about all being killed but supposed they must be.

Half Yellow Face and White Swan went into the valley with Reno and had not got out when we left. White Swan was wounded in Reno's valley fight. All six Crows were on Crows Nest at daylight June 25.

Interview with Hairy Moccasin at Lodgegrass, Montana, February 23, 1911, Eli Black Hawk, Interpreter[1]

I am a Mountain Crow 57 years old. The Mountain Crows and the River Crows had one agency at Stillwater. Gibbon was known as No Hip, which in Crow is Isshushumdate. *Custer was known as* Ihcke Deikdagua *which means, literally, Morning Star Sun, or perhaps, better, Morning Star.*

Before we had left the mouth of the Rosebud, I and two other Crows had been sent up the north bank of the Yellowstone, along with a company of cavalry, to scout the country and look for Sioux. We went as far as where Junction City is now [mouth of Big Horn, but verify], *remained there one night and returned to mouth of Rosebud before Custer left there. We found no Sioux.*

On the night of June 24 the officer in charge of the scouts took five Crows and Mitch Bouyer and went to a high place in Wolf Mountains. As soon as it came daylight enough to see, we saw smoke and dust in the valley of the Little Bighorn. The smoke indicated a village and the dust a pony herd. Half Yellow Face was not with us. I do not know where he was unless he remained back with the soldiers.

While up there we saw two Sioux with three horses, who traveled off toward the Little Bighorn.

When Custer separated from Reno he took four Crows, and Reno

1. Walter Camp field notes, folders 15 and 26, BYU Library. Hairy Moccasin was enlisted in Lieutenant James Bradley's Detachment of Indian Scouts on April 10, 1876, for service with the 7th Infantry. He was on detached service with the 7th Cavalry from June 21. He withdrew from the Custer column about 3:15 p.m. on June 25 and eventually returned to Crow Agency. He died on October 9, 1922, at Lodgegrass, Montana. His account is also in *The Tepee Book,* 1916, p. 54; 1926, p. 67 and in Joseph Dixon's *The Vanishing Race,* pp. 138–40.

two. The idea in sending two with Reno was Crows were better informed of the country. Besides Bouyer and the four Crows there was no other scout or guide, either white, red or half-breed. Hairy Moccasin was positive and emphatic about this.

Custer's command as well as Bouyer and the 4 Crows saw Reno's fight in the valley. Then Custer and command turned down south coulee into Medicine Tail Coulee and went down toward river and out onto flat. Two men were killed here, and the Sioux told me five years afterward that a single soldier rode his horse across the river into camp and was killed in the camp.

Here the soldiers got into the coulee which comes down from Custer ridge, and Mitch Bouyer told us we could go. Curley had left us at Weir peaks and cleared out of the country, and we did not see him again for about fourteen sleeps (two weeks).

We went back on the trail up Medicine Tail and south coulees and along bluffs past Reno hill and on up nearly to Ford A, where we met the pack train (Here undoubtedly means . . . Benteen, because the pack train did not come that way).

As we came along the bluffs a short distance north of the DeWolf marker, we met a dismounted soldier who had come up the bluffs, and he went along with us until we met the pack train.[2] *We supposed this soldier had been in Reno's fight in the bottom. From a high point* (he was not clear as to whether it was Weir peaks or Sharpshooter hill) *we watched the fight on Custer Ridge quite a while and satisfied ourselves that the soldiers over there were whipped and killed.* (Says this was before they met the packs, and here he is probably indulging in fiction.)

Says that while going along the bluffs after leaving Custer they saw nothing of Reno's command whatever (very strange).

Stayed around until Reno was surrounded and then started to get out of the country. *We went back toward Tullock's fork and struck a tributary of Little Bighorn or Big Horn running northwest and went down it to Little Bighorn or Big Horn and next morning yelled across to Gibbon's Crows that Custer's command was surrounded and all killed.*

Never heard anything of finding Nathan Short's body and horse.

---

2. On way to Benteen, after leaving Custer did [you] meet a dismounted man with horse broken down and did you try to overtake him and did he threaten to shoot? Meaning Thompson. (*No.*) They met a dismounted man but says this man went along with them. On way to pack train from Custer met only one soldier, and from what he says he could not have been Thompson.

(Walter Camp field notes, folders 15 and 26, BYU Library.)

177

Interview with
White Man Runs Him[1]

Ba-tsida-crush (as pronounced by himself), *54 years old. Four Crows went with Custer after separating from Reno. Went with Custer all way to mouth Dry Creek and Custer's fight started about 500 ft. downstream from there* (pointing out distance to me as he talked). *Custer sat on bluff and saw all of Reno's valley fight.*[2]

---

1. Walter Camp field notes, folder 59, BYU Library. White Man Runs Him was a Crow Indian enlisted in Lieutenant James Bradley's Detachment of Indian Scouts on April 10, 1876, for service with the 7th Infantry. He was on detached service with the 7th Cavalry from June 21 but withdrew from the Custer column about 3:15 p.m. on June 25 and eventually returned to the Crow Agency. He died on June 2, 1929, near Lodgegrass, Montana, and was buried in the Custer Battlefield National Cemetery. His account is in *The Tepee Book,* 1916, p. 52; 1926, p. 65 and in Joseph Dixon's *The Vanishing Race.* His account, as told to Colonel Tim McCoy, is in William Graham's *The Custer Myth,* pp. 20–24.

2. The following quotation is from the Walter Camp letter to General Charles A. Woodruff in February, 1910:

> White Man told me quite a different story, saying that Custer saw Reno's battle from the bluffs (which is entirely preposterous) and that the three Crows then went as far as Medicine Tail Coulee with Custer and then were given permission to go back, etc. Goes Ahead's statement not only disagrees with this but also says that Custer had gone out of sight behind the bluff quite some time before Reno's fight began. Curley says that Reno's fight started just as he and Bouyer got to the high point, which is almost a mile, the way a horse will travel, from the point where Custer disappeared from view of Reno, and a little more than a mile from the DeWolf marker. In regard to Benteen's statement about meeting the Crows, he is very clear as to time and place, and is corroborated by Godfrey and several of the enlisted men — and by Goes Ahead and *White Man Runs Him, himself.* Benteen met the three Crows on the first rise of the bluffs north of the mouth of Sundance Creek. This is 1600 or 1800 feet north of Ford A, and about 1⅛ miles, in an airline, south of Reno Hill (where Reno was corraled two days). Godfrey stated to me personally that they (Godfrey being with Benteen) met the Crows here and that he, personally, rode up to one of the Crows and tried to talk to him. He says there could be no mistake about these men meeting Benteen's command on the bluff at this place; in fact White Man goes into details about it. He could not be mistaken about the identity of the command, because there was no other command than Benteen's in the vicinity.

(In Walter Camp Collection, box 9, folder 11, BYU Library.)

Mitch Bouyer told us we need not stay and fight but to go and get to Reno if possible. Bouyer said he would stay with the soldiers and fight with them. Sioux began crossing at Ford B and below and soon were getting on all sides of Custer. There was much excitement among the soldiers.

We went back and met Benteen and had some talk through some soldier who could talk a little of Crow. Half Yellow Face and White Swan had not yet come out of the valley when we left. Then we cut a big circle over toward east and early next morning saw soldiers on Big Horn at mouth of Little Big Horn. Thought they were Sioux and swam across and later yelled over to Gibbon's Crows and told them of Custer's fight. We supposed they must all be killed, and we accordingly told Gibbon's men this.

Interview with
Little Sioux[1]

*On Crows Nest: Red Star,[2] Bull, Black Fox (Don't remember
others). One Feather, Strikes Two, Red Star, Whole Buffalo (Tonhechi Tu), Boy Chief, Little Sioux were up ahead after horses. We
saw three Sioux squaws and two boys leaving village and we got after
them. Squaws were on east side of river opposite timber. All six got
after squaws, but One Feather and Tonhechi Tu took after two Sioux
horses. We pursued on after squaws and ran upon a big bunch of
horses and took after them and let women go. These horses were on
east side opposite point of timber. We did not drive Sioux horses to
west side but kept them on east side and ran them across the flat and
went up through hills with them. As we were going up hill the soldiers
fired on us and wounded Boy Chief's horse. The Sioux were tight
after us and followed up into hills.* (These Indians were probably the
ones who killed DeWolf.)

Among these soldiers was Stabbed, who took off his hat and waved

---

1. Walter Camp field notes, folder 54, BYU Library. Little Sioux was an
Arikara Indian born at Fort Clark, Dakota. He enlisted for the fifth time on
November 18, 1873, at Fort A. Lincoln. After crossing the Little Bighorn he
turned to the right to capture some Sioux ponies and drive them across the river
to the ridgetop. He returned to Yellowstone Depot on the Powder River. He
was also known as Sioux and One Wolf. For accounts by the Ree scouts, see
also Orin G. Libbey's "The Arikara Narrative of the Campaign Against the
Hostile Dakotas, June 1876" in North Dakota *Historical Collections*, (Bismarck:
Torch Press, 1920), 6:1–209. Although there are errors of interpretation, this is
one of the indispensable classics of the Little Bighorn River fight.

2. The story of Red Star is in Libbey's "Arikara Narrative . . ." pp. 71–93,
118–21. Red Star was named Strike Bear or Strikes Bear, or Strikes the Bear at
the time of the Little Bighorn River fight, and his name was changed later to
Red Star.

it to stop the soldiers firing. These soldiers were on top of hill. They were the rear of a body of soldiers going downstream on top of the hills. There were a few straggling shots fired at us. Possibly this was Weir's troop, as Edgerly spoke of one of the men waving a hat after he (Edgerly) had fired at him. However, the Rees with captured horses must have gone up the bluffs long before Weir got there.
(This is important. The horses were driven across flat on east side and up hills.) *Drove horses back a ways and then returned to river and found Reno's men on top of ridge. Soldiers were straggling up out of the bottom, some wounded.*

Sioux village. There were groups of tepees in all the bends of the river. After awhile the pack train arrived. I went back to where the captured horses were tied. We had been instructed by Custer to capture all the Sioux horses we could and get them back out of the way. Went back to captured horses. A few of our Ree scouts had straggled behind, and they came to the captured horses. I and Boy Chief, Watokshu, Caroo, Red Bear, Strikes Two. The pack train fortified, and we were separated from it. We rounded up the captured horses and started for Rosebud back on trail. Red Wolf, Bull, One Feather, Strike the Lodge, and others took captured horses to Rosebud. Pack train was attacked and Sioux got after us, and we started for Rosebud and Sioux got in our front twice, trying to head us off. This was after dark. The party that had captured horses had been attacked by Sioux who got horses back. This recovery of horses by Sioux was in the night.

We got to Rosebud in the night. We traveled all night and got to Rosebud and followed it all next day and eventually got to Yellow-stone. Going down Rosebud we got nothing to eat until we got to the old camp at mouth of Rosebud, and here we found moldy hardtack. We traveled two days two nights and half a day. On the way down Rosebud we picked up a Sioux pony, black with white legs. Near mouth of Rosebud we lost this horse and a buckskin one. They strayed off. Scouts from Powder later picked up these horses. We followed Yellowstone down to camp at mouth of Powder. A halfbreed scout (Billy Cross) went back with us. Chakawo (the drummer) *Chahcawo.*

I had an army gun — infantry gun with 2 bands.[3] *We had army saddles that Custer had issued to us at Ft. Lincoln; at least those of us who had no saddles took cavalry saddles. One of our scouts had a*

---

3. See John S. du Mont *Custer Battle Guns* (Fort Collins, Colorado: Old Army Press, 1974). This is the best analytical study of the weapons used in the Little Bighorn River fight.

cavalry horse, but the rest of us had our own horses. In the captured
herd were two mules. After staying at mouth of Powder awhile we
went back and camped at mouth of Rosebud. . . . There were a lot of
Crows there with their women. We had been out a long time and were
hard up for women.

Horn in Front discharge papers signed by W. P. Carlin, Lt. Col. 6th Inf. and by John C. Carland, 1st Lt. 6th Inf. Dated October 1, 1873. Horn in Front was father of Young Hawk. Young Hawk was a scout with Custer on Black Hills expedition. Horn in Front, his father, was also there.

Did Baker and Young Hawk go out and meet Bradley morning June 27? No, says Forked Horn and Young Hawk did this.

Arickaree Sahnish *in own language. The Mandans call the Rees* Arikara. *Gros Ventres call us* Arikaraho. Arickaree names for:

Missouri River	Holy Water	*Tswarukti Hukuhanu*
Little Missouri River	Forked River	*Nahuka Chitowi*
Yellowstone River	Elk River	*Wa Hukahanu*
Powder River Powder Horn	Ashes River	*Htkanatusa Hukahanu*
Tongue River	Tongue	*Hatu Hukahanu*
Rosebud River	Roseberry or Tomato	*Paht Hukahanu*
Little Bighorn River	Little Goat River	*Arikisu Hukuha Chripos*
Bighorn River	Horn	*Miy Arikau Hukuhanu*
Creek		*Hshanu*
Heart River		*Wisu Hukahanu*

Interview with Strike Two, July 23, 1912[1]

Up the Rosebud we found trail and on morning of June 25 got word that Sioux camp had been located. At divide on June 25 Custer said, "There are other soldiers coming to attack the village, and I want to be there first so that we will get the honor of fighting the Sioux. I want you to charge the camp first and capture all the horses you can."

At lone tepee Custer became impatient and said that we were slow and if he had to urge us again to go forward he would take our guns and horses and put us afoot. We now started out fast and forded Little Bighorn and soon overtook a bunch of horses herded by two Sioux. We followed horses and soon saw the village, and Sioux came out of village to help the two herders.

The village was not stirred up and Forked Horn, Red Foolish Bear, Little Brave, Watoksha,[2] Caroo,[3] Machpiya Sha,[4] Bobtail Bull and Strikes Two . . . had a little skirmish, and Bobtail said, "Look for a means of escape if the soldiers were to retreat, as there are more people here than we thought. . . ." *All this was while the soldiers were deploy-*

---

1. Walter Camp field notes, folder 54, BYU Library. Strike Two was an Arikara scout born at Fort Clark, Dakota. He had been enlisted in 1873, 1874, and 1876. His fourth enlistment was on May 9, 1876, at Fort A. Lincoln. After crossing the Little Bighorn he aided in capturing a herd of Sioux ponies and driving them across the river to the ridgetop. He returned to Yellowstone Depot on the Powder River. He died on September 8, 1922, at Elbowood, North Dakota.

2. *Watoksha,* also spelled *Watokshu* by Camp, was a Dakota Sioux scout also known as Ring Cloud, Spotted Horn Cloud, and Round Wooden Cloud.

3. *Caroo,* also spelled *Karu* by Camp, was a Dakota Sioux scout also known as Bear Running In The Timber.

4. *Machpiya Sha,* also spelled *Mahcpiya Ska* by Camp, was a Dakota Sioux scout also known as White Cloud.

ing and before their fight began. *In this skirmish I killed one Sioux and saw a little bunch of Sioux horses come out of the brush just ahead of soldiers, and Bloody Knife said, "Take these horses and drive them to the rear." We all had infantry rifles with two bands. All of us had those guns except Stabbed who had his own gun — a repeater. While I stood on edge of bank clearing my gun, the soldiers began firing. I looked behind and saw three Rees coming: Boy Chief, Red Star, and Bull in Water. Some one turned and saw three more coming — Little Sioux, One Feather, and The Whole Buffalo* (Sioux).

The Sioux horses captured by Bloody Knife now stampeded and crossed the river, and we, I and above six, put in after them. My horse went in to his back, and I got my seat wet. Some of them ran back toward Sioux village, but we turned them and got the whole bunch together. I was driving twenty head and one suckling colt. Red Star had three, and Boy Chief (Black Calf) *had five. Red Star was named White Calf then.*

Of our party of seven, four were holding horses. While we were driving horses up hill from river, some soldiers passed by and fired on us by mistake (Custer's soldiers), *and one of the captured horses was killed. We drove the horses up high bank on east side and Stabbed now joined us, making eight in the party, and soon Strike the Lodge and Assiniboine* (Assiniboine was a nickname for one of the enlisted scouts; he did not explain which one) *came up, making ten, and we drove horses back and got them in a good position. Here a soldier with stripes on his arms came along* (probably Knipe) *and asked, "How goes it?" While we were going back we saw the pack train come along. Bull and Share were each leading a pack mule* (They were not in the fight in the bottom).

Here we distributed the horses, giving [them to] *Assiniboine, Soldier, Red Star, Good Face, Stab, Little Sioux. Each one now saddled up a fresh horse, and we followed the pack train to river, and soldiers were retreating out of bottom and soldiers all in confusion. The Sioux were pursuing soldiers up hill, and we charged them and drove them back to west side of river where soldiers had been killed. We could see bunches of Sioux all over the valley. While we were watching here, some soldiers came out of timber, having been left there when Reno retreated. Watokshu and Good Elk also escaped from the timber at this time. The pack train had now arrived on the bluff where we were standing and looking into the valley. We called*

184

Varnum Pointed Face.[5] *A white soldier was on Bobtail Bull's horse, Bobtail Bull having been killed, and we took his horse and put him among the pack mules. We also found Little Brave's horse and tied him among the pack mules. Bobtail Bull's horse had blood marks down his legs and on hoofs and saddle, so we concluded* [Bobtail Bull] *was wounded and killed after fording the river — that is on east side. Six of us left the bluff and went to where we could see the timber, and Young Hawk, Forked Horn, Foolish Red Bear, Goose, White Swan, and Half Yellow Face came out of the timber in the valley. From same point we could see that Custer was being defeated.*

We six went to where pack train was, and Stab and Soldier proposed that we water our horses, and the three Sioux scouts: Watokshu, White Cloud, and Karu joined us, making nine (He must have Karu confused with one of the other Sioux scouts), *and we went to water horses. A Sioux interpreter* (Billy Cross) *went with us, making ten in all. We watered, and on way back we stopped to smoke. I took a walk and saw seven men whom I supposed to be our scouts but found out they were Sioux who had surrounded the soldiers. Stab proposed that we hit for some timber and we did so, but found timber scattering and went on to a knoll and had a skirmish with pursuers. The Sioux interpreter* (Billy Cross, White Man) *went with us. Soldiers on bluff* [were] *surrounded and fighting at same time, and all of us fought until sundown. After dark we could see flashes of guns. We got on horses and fired guns and made a bluff at a charge and then started for Rosebud.*

Arrived at Rosebud at daylight. The others holding captured horses had started ahead of us. On Rosebud we found some abandoned hardtack, some moldy. On Rosebud Black Fox came up from front and joined us, having started back on trail ahead of us. He had a mare and colt. I was thirty-two years old then. We camped on Rosebud to rest, and two of my horses got away from me and went on ahead, and they were caught by Indian scouts coming toward us from mouth of Powder. Next morning some of us went out looking for these horses and ran upon track of a shod horse (soldier coming with dispatch). *Stab had extra horse and loaned it to me and we went on to Tongue River. We camped there and then went on to Powder River.*

The interpreter (white man Billy Cross) *was still with us all the way, and when got to Powder River, all the soldiers crowded around*

---

5. Lieutenant Charles Varnum was commanding the Detachment of Indian Scouts, 7th Cavalry. The scouts also called him Peaked Face.

185

him to hear what had happened. After we got there we saw the Rees who had captured horses. They had ridden captured Sioux horses and left their own horses that were played out. We came back on the same trail that we went up with Custer. Later we returned to Rosebud where whole command camped. The Crows were here visiting and had their women with them (Terry's camp in early August). *Never heard of dead soldier or dead horse being found near mouth of Rosebud.*

Interview with Soldier[1]

On way to Little Bighorn we camped third night on abandoned Indian camp and found a stone with two bulls drawn on it. On one bull was drawn a bullet and on the other a lance. The two bulls were charging toward each other. Custer asked Bloody Knife to translate it, and Bloody Knife said it meant a hard battle would occur if an enemy came that way.

Reno's scout, William Baker, Forked Horn, Young Hawk, One Feather went up Powder and across to Tongue. On this we discovered an abandoned Sioux camp, and Forked Horn advised Reno that Sioux too many. . . . We went up the Rosebud just beyond site of Bozeman fight and then turned back . . . and met Custer. Custer sent five back to Powder River with dispatches. I wanted to go back to Powder with dispatches because my father Horns in Front was sick then, and I wanted to see him, but Custer would not let me go.[2]

I had a good looking horse but he was lazy. Starting at the lone tepee we began the charge. My horse was slow and I was left behind. I have always been sorry that I did not get an opportunity to fire a shot in that battle.

---

1. Walter Camp field notes, folder 54, BYU Library. Soldier was an Arikara Indian born in 1831. He enlisted for the thirteenth time on April 26, 1876, at Fort A. Lincoln. He was with the Reno column on June 25 but was left behind on the march because his pony was in poor condition. He did not cross the river into the valley fight, but returned to Yellowstone Depot.

2. Peter Beauchamp says that when Custer was negotiating to enlist the Ree Scouts, there was opposition on the part of the societies among the Rees. This opposition was because of a dislike which the societies entertained for the chief, Son of the Star. The opposition of the societies was so strong that the men who went to Ft. Lincoln to enlist had to steal themselves away when they left the reservation.

(Walter Camp field notes, folder 54, BYU Library.)

A messenger[3] met the general, and Custer took off his buckskin coat and tied it on behind his saddle. Custer rode up and down the column talking to the soldiers. The soldiers cheered and some tied handkerchiefs around their heads and threw hats away. They gave a big cheer and went ahead, but my lazy old horse straggled behind. I saw where we had crossed the river, and I was long way behind the soldiers. There were other stragglers between me and Custer. The ones nearest to me were White Eagle and Bull. Stabbed was behind, came up behind me and explained that he had been out with a message to soldiers over to east (Benteen). *Stabbed had a lot of Winchester cartridges in a feed bag, which he gave me to take along. He said there were many Sioux and there would be a big fight, and if he came back he would stay with me and we would make a stand. Stabbed had a Winchester. I had a long infantry gun with two bands.*

I, White Eagle, and Bull followed Custer and five companies. We came upon a white soldier[4] whose horse had given out, and he was kicking the horse and striking him with his fist and saying "Me go Custer. Me go Custer." As we went up a little dip we looked over and saw the valley full of Sioux tepees, and I would estimate that there were eight or nine big circles. The first (Hunkpapa) camp was breaking up. If I had had a good horse, I probably would have kept up to Custer and been killed with him. I soon came across a second soldier whose horse was down, overcome by heat, and he could not get him up and was swearing and calling him a son of a bitch and kicking him.

Just after this I saw Ree scouts who had captured horses come up the ridge and Strikes Two said: "Leader, I will give you this spotted horse that is leading the herd." Where they came up the river ran right along the foot of the bluff. Strikes Two said, "Don't take him out. We will drive the whole herd together back to lone tepee." We started back and saw the pack mules coming along by lone tepee. Again my horse could not keep up, and Red Star came up behind me and said, "Uncle, do you see that mouse-colored horse with a white belly? I captured him and you may have him, so take care of him." I took him and brought him back to our reservation, and he lived many years on

---

3. This may have been one of the two messengers from Reno. The first messenger was Private Archibald McIlhargey and the second was Private John Mitchell, both of Company I. Both were killed with Custer.

4. Notice that in Soldier's story he says nothing about the first soldier's horse being down — merely that he could not get him along.

(Walter Camp field notes, folder 54, BYU Library.)

Ft. Berthold reservation. I was following the herd back toward lone tepee. We came to the two soldiers whose horses had given out. They were together and on foot on the side of the hill. Five Sioux came up, following us. These two soldiers became separated and the Sioux circled them and we supposed killed them both. We drove the horses back and met the packs. I was still behind. When I got up to them, all of the Rees had picked fresh horses and changed, and Red Star was riding the big horse that Strikes Two wanted me to ride. I then picked a spotted one, and when I got saddled up, I followed back to bluff over river.

When got there could not see any fighting going on and thought that fighting must all be stopped. Soon we saw survivors of valley fight coming up the ridge. Little Brave's spotted horse came up with the rest. Red Bear came straggling up without any shoes, and the boys picked the prickly pear prongs out of his feet. I soon recognized Bobtail Bull's horse. Strikes Two remarked that Bobtail Bull must have been killed in the fight. Horse had bridle, saddle, and blanket tied to horn of saddle. I went to Gerard and showed him Bobtail Bull's horse, and Gerard [must have been some one besides Gerard] *told us to catch him. I went and took the blanket and said I would keep it. Horse had a curbed bit and fancy trimmings. Stab took the bridle. Horse had no picket rope. Stab proposed that we follow the ridge toward where Custer had gone. We did so. Sioux were coming and getting around us before we got to end of ridge. A group of soldiers stood on the ridge behind us. The party was Stab, Strikes Two, Boy Chief, Strike Lodge, Little Sioux, Soldier, Karu, Watoksha, Mahcpiya Sha, and Cross. The Sioux now attacked us and drove us and the soldiers, and we went back beyond the lone tepee. Stab was riding one of the two captured mules, and his own horse was put in the captured herd.*

A band of Sioux pressed us hard, and one of them painted red, riding a bay horse with bald face, nearly caught up with us. Piece of yellow cloth tied on his hair. We agreed to go ahead aways and turn around and fight. I took a shot at him, and he dodged. That was all the damage I did him. He was so close that others of us shot at him, and Stab claimed he had hit him, as he acted as if hit. This Sioux now turned and rode back on the trail we had come. Years afterward, a Sioux, Plenty Crow, from Cheyenne River Reservation, verified the fact that this was Cheyenne and that we had hit him. From this point we started toward the Powder late in p.m. but before sundown. Struck Rosebud before dark.

Mahcpiya Sha *caught a black Sioux horse just before we reached the Rosebud. This was an intelligent horse, smelled of the ground often, and he followed the back trail well. We traveled all night to site of old Sioux Sundance (mouth of Lamedeer Creek near where agency now is) and got there (mouth of Lamedeer Creek) at daylight June 26. We did not stop here but kept on. We stopped once and shot sage hens and cooked them. This was the only time our horses grazed until we got to mouth of Rosebud. There we got old moldy crackers.*

The party that brought the captured herd from Little Bighorn were Share, White Eagle, Whole Buffalo, Bull, Bull Water, Red Bear, Red Star, One Feather, and Red Wolf. There were eight with the horses and ten in our party on way back to Powder.

When we were eating this hardtack (early in morning) at mouth of Rosebud, Black Fox overtook us, leading a horse. He had run away with the Crows and left them and overtook us. The Crows told him how to get to mouth Rosebud. We now had eleven in our party (including Black Fox), as follows: Soldier, Stabbed, Strikes Two, Boy Chief, Strike Lodge, Little Sioux, Karu, Watoksha, Mahcpiya Sha, Black Fox, and Billy Cross, called "Ieska," [who] rode a buckskin.

The party of eleven got to Powder River first. Billy Cross, Watoksha and Tonhechi Tu[5] *left us at mouth Rosebud and beat us a little in reaching Powder River camp ... The remaining eight stopped at Tongue and camped. We got to Powder a little after noon. Never heard of a horse playing out in either the party of eleven or party of eight while on way back to Powder.*

Four or five days after we got to Powder, steamboat arrived with wounded soldiers. Goose (Ree) *was among these wounded. My eyes went on the bum and Stabbed gave me a lump of alum. I applied it and it nearly burned my eyes out but they improved right along. Major Moore,[6] in command of this camp, the Rees called White Hat* [Chiskoku Taka].

A party of us were detailed to carry mail to mouth Rosebud to meet remnants of Custer's command. We met a party of our own Rees carrying messages in opposite direction, and Chakawo was in this party. When we got to camp at mouth Rosebud, we found our Rees all

---

5. *Tonhechi Tu* was a Blackfoot Sioux Indian scout, also known as Bear Come Out (Appearing Bear), and The Whole Buffalo (Buffalo Body, Buffalo Ancestor).

6. Orlando H. Moore, major, 6th Infantry, was in command of Yellowstone Depot on the Powder River.

in rags, their clothing all worn out. Crows and Crow women were here. After some days the whole camp moved up the Rosebud opposite the gap and were told Sioux were coming, and we were all ready to fight when soldiers came and met us.

At the end of this interview I was showing Soldier pictures of officers. He recognized nearly all of them and commented on recollections of several of them. When I showed Soldier picture of Lieutenant Cooke, he kissed it, saying that he was a lovable man, his very breath being nothing but kindness.

Interview with
Young Hawk[1]

I was the scout who ripped open the lone tepee when we came along marching toward Little Bighorn June 25. Bloody Knife was killed in the timber. Bobtail Bull was in my party when we retreated out of the bottom. We followed on Reno's line retreat but turned to left and got across the river lower down than Reno. The Sioux on east side of river a little below where Reno crossed headed us off. We saw Bobtail Bull chased into river a little above us. We got into brush on east side of river.

Little Brave and Isaiah killed[2] where marked on map between timber and river on line of retreat. White Swan and Half Yellow Face were with our party of Ree scouts in Reno's fight in bottom, and I helped get Goose and White Swan up out of bottom after they were wounded. When White Swan was wounded he was just outside the brush. I dragged him in and saved him from the Sioux. At camp at Pease bottom a Crow Indian who wore a belt of buffalo hide taken from chin of buffalo where hair longest told me that the Ree who wore the two rabbit ears (Black Fox) was the one whom "we picked up after the Custer fight. When we left Little Bighorn we saw a man going away off and we chased him and found out he was a Ree. I told the Ree that I had captured five head of horses and gave a black horse to Black Fox." This is the horse that Black Fox rode when he overtook

---

1. Walter Camp field notes, folder 54, BYU Library. Young Hawk, also known as Striped Horn or Crazy Head, was born in 1859, the son of Forked Horn. His fourth enlistment was on May 9, 1876, at Fort A. Lincoln. He was in the valley and hilltop fights on the Little Bighorn River. He died on January 16, 1915, at Elbowood, North Dakota.

2. Isaiah Dorman, the Negro interpreter from Fort Rice, and Little Brave (also known as Little Soldier) were both killed in the retreat in the valley fight.

the other Rees at mouth of Rosebud. When we arrived at the Rosebud I found Black Fox there and the black horse identical with the description given me by the Crow, which proves that Black Fox was with the Crows after leaving Little Bighorn after battle.

Did Baker and Young Hawk go out and meet Bradley on morning June 27? No, says Forked Horn and Young Hawk did this.

Young Hawk says that at Powder River Bill Jackson[3] was sent out on some errand and came back with a great story about being chased by Sioux. *He had wounded his horse slightly and had a scalp which he said he had taken from a Sioux. When we examined it closely, we found he had stuck hair onto a piece of leather and this gave him away. Had it not been for this discovery we would have believed his story.*

Bob Jackson[4] punished at Little Missouri for riding through camp and firing off his gun and showing what he would do to the Sioux. He had to stand with one foot on a barrel. Young Hawk says Bob Jackson was in camp at mouth of Powder River after battle of Little Bighorn but was not in the battle.

---

3. William Jackson was a Pikuni Blackfoot Indian, the son of Thomas and Emilea A. Jackson. He was the younger brother of Robert Jackson. He enlisted as a scout for the third time on December 24, 1875, and was in the valley and hilltop fights on the Little Bighorn River. He died on December 30, 1899, at his homestead on Cutbank Creek, Blackfeet Indian Reservation, Montana. His story, told by James Willard Schultz, *William Jackson Indian Scout* (Houghton Mifflin Co.: Boston, 1926), is a useful account. A typescript *Account of the Battle of the Little Big Horn by a Scout* as told to Jack Monroe is in the Montana Historical Society Collection. "The Story of Scout Wm. Jackson" is in the *Dupuyer Acantha* [Montana], July 6, 1899 (copy in the Montana State Historical Society Library).

4. Robert Jackson was a Pikuni Blackfoot Indian who enlisted as a scout in the 7th Cavalry on December 24, 1875. He was born on August 27, 1856, at Fort Benton, Montana Territory. He was in the Yellowstone expedition in 1873, the Black Hills expedition in 1874, and the Sioux campaign in 1876 and was discharged at Fort A. Lincoln on June 25, 1876. He later resided at Pryor, Montana, joined a wild west show in 1895, and resided in Colorado Springs in 1899.

Interview with Red Bear and Young Hawk, July 22, 1912[1]

Scouts at Crow Nest: Red Star, Black Fox, Bull, Forked Horn, Strikes The Lodge, [and] *Foolish Red Bear says Strike Two. We were camped on both sides of creek where Cheyennes now live. Bobtail Bull saddled up and went out ahead, having seen two ponies. When he got up, he saw two Sioux come and take them. All the rest above saddled up and started out to find Bobtail Bull but he came in after they had left; they did not meet him. This was the party that went to Crow's Nest. Bobtail Bull came in and reported what he had seen.*

Red Bear took One Horn's place. At first Custer would not let him go, as his mare was heavy with foal. But One Horn's horse gave out. I and _____ went with mail, and my horse gave out beyond Heart River. We arrived at Custer's camp, and Custer said he appreciated what I had done very much. He said he had heard I had lost a horse, and if he lived long enough he would see that I got pay for it. I arrived three days before the big snow storm; scouts Left Hand, and Scabby Wolf sent back to Ft. Lincoln in this snowstorm.

---

1. Walter Camp field notes, folder 54, BYU Library. Red Bear, also known as Good Elk or Handsome Elk, was an Arikara Indian enlisted for the third time on May 13, 1876. He was on the skirmish line in the valley fight, then joined other Ree scouts, and returned to Yellowstone Depot on the Powder River. He died on May 7, 1934, at Nishu, North Dakota.

Interviews
with
Indians
Who
Fought
Custer

Foolish Elk

Turtle Rib

Black Bear

He Dog

Flying By

White Bull

Tall Bull

Standing Bear

Interview with Foolish Elk, September 22, 1908, Louis Roubideaux of Rosebud and Mr. Shaw of Valentine, Nebraska, Interpreters Simultaneously[1]

Foolish Elk said he was an Ogalalla Sioux 54 years old, and on the day of the Custer battle fought with Crazy Horse. He appeared to be the opposite of what his name might imply, as I found him to be a man of more than average intelligence. At one time he was chief of police at the Rosebud Agency. He is a man of genial disposition and has a general reputation for honesty and truthfulness. Mr. S. B. Weston, at one time chief clerk at Rosebud, said that Foolish Elk's statements could always be relied upon. He talked without hesitation, seeming to have his recollections well in mind, and apparently he had no fear of telling all he knew. He talked on only one point of information at a time, sometimes at considerable length in a connected sort of way, and then would stop and wait for another question. He appeared to be indifferent to any opinion I might have as to his fund of information, and said he would tell me only what he saw or knew to be fact, and when he did not know he said so frankly and without hesitating.

He said he was in the fight against Crook on the Rosebud about a week before the Custer battle. Before the battle of the Rosebud started, they were in doubt as to the intentions of the soldiers, not knowing whether they wished to fight or make a treaty. The Indians therefore got all ready to fight and waited to see what the soldiers would do. As the soldiers started the firing, the Indians concluded that they desired to fight, and so they gave them what they appeared to want. In this fight the Indians thought they had won a victory, but it was understood that other troops were in the Indian country, and they concluded to go to the big village with Sitting Bull on the Greasy Grass Creek (Little Bighorn) without further loss of men and ammunition.

---

1. Walter Camp field notes, folder 106, BYU Library.

They therefore withdrew and went over the divide to the Little Big-horn. He could not describe the exact route traveled, but did not think Custer's command could have followed any part of their trail except for a few miles before striking the village.

They arrived at the village the day before the battle (June 24). There was then some kind of vague report that soldiers were coming, but they did not know whether it was the command of their recent enemy, Crook (Lone Star), or Custer whom they knew as "Long Yellow Hair." In the village there were representatives of seven tribes of the Sioux.[2] There was not much concern about the soldiers, as the Indians thought they had enough men to whip any force that would come against them, seeing that the Indians were all together for once — all the different tribes.

On June 25 the fighting started at the Uncapapa tepees (by Reno at south end of village). On the part of the Indians there was no or-ganized resistance, but men from all the tribes who happened to have their horses grabbed up their guns and went up the river to join in the fight. The fight did not last long, and before the larger part of the Indians could get there, they had chased the soldiers out of the river valley and up into the bluffs. The soldiers retreated across the river at the nearest point they could reach and seemed to be in too much of a hurry to take their back track to the ford where they had come into the valley.

Before the Indians had decided what they would do with these soldiers who made the first attack, a force of soldiers was seen coming from the east (Custer). These men sat on their horses and fired across the river into the village, without getting into it. He afterward heard that one man[3] rode his horse over into the village and was killed, but he did not see him.

The Indians were now getting their horses in from the hills and soon came up in large numbers. Some crossed the stream farther down and others crossed the ford and followed on after Custer in overwhelm-ing numbers. They could not see how such a small force of soldiers had any chance to stand against them. The Indians were between Custer and the river and all the time coming up and getting around to the east of him, passing around both his front and rear. Custer was following the ridges, and the Indians were keeping abreast of him in

---

2. The tribes of the Siouan Teton family were the Hunkpapa, Brule, Sans Arc, Minneconjou, Blackfeet, Ogalalla, and Two Kettles.

3. Sergeant James Bustard of Company I may have been this man.

the hollows and ravines. Personally, he was with the Indians to the east, or on Custer's right. Custer charged the Indians twice (probably at Calhoun and at monument[4] or in gully toward river from monument) but could not drive them away, and then the battle became furious. It did not appear to him that a stand was made by Custer's men anywhere except at the monument. He was in the gully and saw the soldiers killed on the side hill (Keogh) as they "marched" toward the high ground at end of ridge (monument). They made no stand here, but all were going toward the high ground at end of ridge. The gray horses went up in a body; then came bay horses and men on foot all mixed together. The men on the horses did not stop to fight, but went ahead as fast as they could go. The men on foot, however, were shooting as they passed along. When the horses got to the top of the ridge the gray ones and bays became mingled, and the soldiers with them were all in confusion. The Indians were so numerous that the soldiers could not go any further, and they knew that they had to die.

He saw no man get away but had heard four different eye witnesses tell of one soldier[5] who rode through the Indians on a very swift horse which they could not catch. They told that after chasing him for about a mile or two the soldier drew his pistol and killed himself. This they could not understand, because the man's horse was swifter than theirs and was continually getting farther away from the pursuers.

The Indians captured many horses that were not wounded, and they got much ammunition out of the saddles and out of the belts of the killed and wounded. Many squaws followed the course of the battle and stripped the dead. He did not remain to see any of the wounded soldiers killed, but thought most of them must have been killed before the general firing stopped. He did not know whether or not any of the dead soldiers were scalped. No soldiers, dead or alive, were taken into the village. He wanted to know why I inquired on this point. I told him that it might be supposed that some of the soldiers were taken alive and tortured. He then laughed and said that had I seen the amount of firing that was done on the battlefield I would never suppose that any of the soldiers could come out alive. I then asked him how he could account for some 18 bodies that could not be

---

4. Lieutenant James Calhoun commanded Company L in the fight and held the southeast end of Custer ridge. The monument mentioned is the present monument at the northwest end of Custer ridge.

5. This may have been Lieutenant Henry M. Harrington of Company C.

found. He said he could give no explanation, but felt sure that all would have been found had those in search of them looked far enough.

On the day of the battle no Indian recognized Custer, either alive or dead. They had remembered him as a man with long hair, but his hair was cut. On the next day one of the Uncapapa men who knew him recognized him from his features, and later his horse was recognized among the captured animals. This was the sorrel horse "Dandy" with white face and white feet.

Interview with Turtle Rib, September 22, 1908; Valentine, Nebraska[1]

Now 60 years old, a member of Minneconjou Sioux. He fought under Lamedeer. He was not in the battle with Crook. They came into the village from the direction of the Rosebud, arriving on the day before the battle. The soldiers were following their trail. Three days before this their men had engaged a considerable band of Crows. The village was arranged in camps of the different tribes in the following order, down the river: Uncapapa, Blackfeet (under Black Moon), Minneconjou, Sans Arc, Ogalalla, Northern Cheyenne, Brule (these last two should probably be reversed).

The fighting (Reno) started against the camp of the Uncapapas. He (Turtle Rib) was asleep when the soldiers were first reported in the valley but got in before the fighting stopped and killed one of the Rees. He saw other Rees getting away with a drove of Sioux ponies. The fighting against Reno did not last long. He could not say how many minutes, but only a few.

He did not see the fighting at Ford B, but when he passed back through the village to go against the soldiers on the high ground across the river (Custer) the women were stampeded and the children were crying. They said soldiers had come over the hill from the east and had been driven back. When he got up with the soldiers, there was a running fight with some of the soldiers on foot. Those who kept their horses seemed to be stampeded. Some were going toward the monument, and some were trying to ride back the way they came. Those on foot seemed to be the coolest and fought the hardest. No stand was made except at the end of the long ridge (where Custer fell), and here the bay and gray horses were all mixed together. There was a big dust, and the Indians were running all around the locality much excited

---

1. Walter Camp field notes, folder 105, BYU Library.

and shooting into the soldiers. He saw one soldier ride across a hollow and try to get away. He was the third Indian to give chase. The soldier rode like the wind and appeared to be getting away from them, when he killed himself. He could not recall the direction in which this soldier went.

When he returned, the fight was nearly over. The Indians were up close, and the soldiers were shooting with pistols. He saw some of the soldiers shoot each other. The Indians were all around. Some of them shot arrows and in the smoke and big dust hit their own men. His own nephew was killed here by a soldier's bullet. The Indians had many killed and more wounded. It took a good many to bring water up from river to the wounded Indians. He never heard the number of Indians killed.

They captured many horses and got much ammunition from them. They took no soldiers off the battlefield alive. He supposed them all killed where they lay. The Indians were so busy caring for their own wounded and going off to fight Reno that they did not stop to scalp or mutilate soldiers. What the squaws did after this he did not know, as scalping of dead or mutilation would be nothing uncommon with Indians. The Indians did not recognize Custer fighting or afterward among the dead.

Interview with Black Bear, July 18, 1911; Philip Wells, Interpreter[1]

In 1876 I was on the reservation at Red Cloud Agency and lost some horses. Following their trail, I concluded that they had been stolen by some of the Indians going out to join the hostiles under Crazy Horse and Sitting Bull, or perhaps by some of the raiders from the hostile camp. I therefore formed a party and went out to the hostile camp. We found our horses and left the Indian camp on the Greasy Grass Creek.[2] While crossing the divide early on the morning of 6/25/76, we discovered soldiers marching toward the village. We ran into the high hills and watched them, holding bunches of grass in front of our heads as a disguise.

While here, three Cheyennes came up to us and said they had been following the soldiers all the way from Powder River. That morning they had come upon a box of bread lost by the soldiers and were in the act of opening it when soldiers appeared and they (the Cheyennes) had run off. After the soldiers marched, the Cheyennes left us and followed the soldiers toward the Little Bighorn.

We did not go to warn the village. As we were not hostiles we continued on toward the agency. Our party consisted of the following Indians besides myself: Owl Bull, Knife and his wife, Medicine Bird (now dead), Blue Cloud (now dead), Kills Enemy in Winter (now dead). In other words, our party consisted of six men and one squaw, the wife of Knife.

I have heard about the old man and the boy who were hunting lost horses and discovered the soldiers the same morning that we did. I have heard that the old man went in and warned the village but that

---

1. Walter Camp field notes, folder 108, BYU Library.
2. Greasy Grass Creek was an Indian name for the Little Bighorn River.

the boy was killed by the soldiers on the way to the river. There was also an Indian who had killed a buffalo who was surprised by the soldiers on their way to the village. This man ran off and returned to the village by a roundabout route, so that he did not reach the village until after the soldiers did.

Interview with He Dog,
July 13, 1910;
William Berger,
Interpreter[1]

Sunka Bloka ... *70 years old. I was on reservation before 1876 on the Platte. We* (Ogalallas) *wintered on the Tongue. Battle March 17, 1876, with Crook (Three Star —* Wicokpi Yammi) *against Cheyennes, but I was there with a few Sioux. This was a Cheyenne camp under Little Wolf. When fought Crook, Ogalalla village was on Sundance Creek[2] not far from Little Bighorn. A bluff with pines on it near by* (this must have been at lone tepee). *I lost seven horses in this scrap. The next night we camped on Lodgepole Creek and sent men who got some of these horses back.*

Indian in lone tepee was a Sans Arc, a brother of Turning Bear. He was shot through bowels in Crook fight.[3] We started out to fight Crook the second time but did not see Crows around and afraid Crows would get at our village, and we turned back. The reason did not pursue Crook was that we were too far from our villages which were not only a long distance off but were strung out over much country. Did not pursue Crook because afraid Crows and Shoshones would get at our village. We saw Crook had a good many Indians. We knew that we had defeated him because he turned back.

Moved to Little Bighorn third day after Crook fight. Sioux did not want to fight and so when got away off at Little Bighorn thought would have no more fighting. We had our wives and children with us and had to get buffalo meat for them and wished to be let alone.

It has always been an argument among Sioux whether second or third day after we moved camp to Little Bighorn that Sioux party of

---

1. Walter Camp field notes, folder 55, BYU Library.

2. Also Ash Creek, Reno Creek and Benteen Creek.

3. He Dog is here referring to the fight with Crook on the Rosebud on June 17.

seven Sioux saw Custer's dust. These Indians did not come back and warn village but made a circle around the soldiers and went on southeast to the agencies. Fast Horn was the Indian whom Varnum saw from Crows Nest and he got back to village only a short time before Reno appeared. Of the seven scouts who discovered Custer, Black Bear and Dirt Kettle were among them. They saw Custer's dust and Custer coming so fast doubted whether they could beat him to village — so took a look at soldiers and went on toward agencies.

Ogalallas were not on Little Bighorn June 25 but back from river northwest of Hunkpapa. Did not expect to fight here as Crook had gone away, and so forth. Brules not on Little Bighorn in village June 25 but over by Ogalalla. Good many Brules there. More than twenty lodges was reported to me. Flying Chaser — Wakuya Kinyan *was the head man of Brules but not a big chief. More Hunkpapas than any other tribe. Minneconjou next. Hunk and Blackfeet together had 600 or 700 lodges. Thirty or forty lodges of Santees.* Inkpaluta,[4] *their chief, was there. Just two Arapahoes.* (Thinks 1,800 lodges in whole village about right.) *Did not see any white man among Sioux. In my camp there was a Canadian half breed who spoke very good English as well as Sioux.*

When Reno approached, the Hunks went out ahead, mostly on foot, and I was slow in getting my horse. The Hunks went up to point of timber and held the soldiers back. I was on hill to west of Reno's skirmish line, and Indians were getting ready for word to charge in a body on soldiers at timber. Sioux had not all got there yet, but Indians from all tribes — all that could get horses and get there. Just as we charged, the soldiers left the timber in two bunches on their horses as fast as they could ride up the river. Chased Indian scouts from timber to river also and killed some of them. Saw Benteen coming and quit pursuing Reno.

I went back to Hunkpapas camp, and then we looked and saw other soldiers coming on the big hill right over east. They kept right on down the river and crossed Medicine Tail coulee and onto little rise. (The first rise above flat south of mouth of Medicine Tail) (where Foley found). Pointed distance as same from his office to tank so that it agrees with my map exactly (about 600 ft.).

Here Custer's line was scattered all along parallel with river from Foley and Butler. When Custer passed near to Ford B, he was moving

---

4. *Inkpaluta,* or more commonly *Inkpaduta,* was a Santee Sioux noted for his depredations in Iowa, Minnesota, and Dakota in the 1860s.

as though to reach the lower end of our camp. (It is my opinion that the 5 men killed on hill by cut bank opposite the village were at the head of the column and were met by Indians moving up the river.) *The Indians had left the camp over west to get ready. There was no fighting while Custer down near river but a few shots down there. No general fighting; fifteen or twenty Sioux on east side of river, and some of soldiers replied, but not much shooting there. Did not hear Custer fire any volleys.*

Says location of Foley is right and he the one who shot himself. *Before fight started, we drove him up a slope to a ridge (Keogh) and over to other side of it. Soldiers mounted all time and kept going right along. All together all time. Did not fight by companies. Indians all along Custer ridge, and Custer went down along hollow by Keogh.*

At this time Indians all around. At first gray horses all together but after got on hill mixed up with other horses. Fighting started at Finley and kept up all along. At Keogh is where Crazy Horse charged and broke through and split up soldiers into two bunches. Horses stampeded toward river, getting away from soldiers. There was no charge by Custer's [men] on ridge during fight. Custer's men at end of ridge. Did not run out of ammunition. Found ammunition on dead soldiers.

When the men rushed from Custer's last stand toward river, the dismounted ones took to the gully, and the mounted ones tried to get away to south toward Finley. Line H to C mounted soldiers trying to get away when they ran toward gully. Foley rode out of fight from H.

(Corroborates twenty-eight dead men in gully.)

Fight with Custer did not last much more than an hour, as nearly as I can estimate it. Did not know were fighting Custer. Did not know what soldiers they were. Cheyennes were very brave in this fight and took a leading part. The bloodthirsty ones got tired of scalping before came to Custer group. Never knew about Bustard killed in village.[5]

He knew a Santee who was always with the soldiers. Mitch Bouyer (might also have been Bloody Knife). He was killed, and Sioux recognized his body as a Sioux.

After killing all of Pecushi's[6] *soldiers, we attacked the other*

---

5. Sergeant James Bustard of Company I may have crossed the Little Bighorn at Ford B. It was later claimed that his body was found in the village after the fight.

6. *Peoushi* — a Sioux name for Lieutenant Colonel George Custer, meaning Long Hair.

207

soldiers and had them cut off and surrounded on the high bluffs, where we shot at them as they rushed for water. Did not have time to do Reno and Benteen up before Terry came. Had not assistance come to them, we would have worn them out in a few days.

Had plenty of ammunition left after June 26. We had ways of getting more, and the ammunition taken from Custer's men we used against the other soldiers. Many had Winchesters, but we had all kinds of guns. The number of Indians killed at Little Bighorn was between thirty and forty. Many more than this were wounded, and some of these died later.

After fight, all tribes went up river near to big hills (Big Horn Mts.). All remained together until got to Slim Buttes and there split up, Sitting Bull setting out for Canada. I was in Slim Buttes fight. After camp broken up, Ogalallas, Sans Arc, Minneconjou, and Cheyennes stopped near there, but Hunkpapas went on. The tribe massacred there were Minneconjou, who were out deer hunting. No chief was killed here. The man wounded in bowels and died here was not a chief. He was a Sans Arc relative of mine. There were never two American horses to my knowledge.

Low Dog was an Ogalalla. Big Foot was a Minneconjou. Black Twins not in fight. Died in 1875. Kicking Bear was not a subchief. Crazy Horse and Big Road the principal chiefs. Red Cloud was an Ogalalla born.

Interview with Flying By, May 21, 1907; William S. Claymore, Interpreter[1]

Keya Heyi, Minneconjou . . . 57 years old. Son of Lamedeer.[2]
Lamedeer is Ta-ak-cha-ooshta. *Our village the winter before was on Tongue River. Lamedeer had between 600 and 800 tepees. Few Santees there. I was a hostile. Was in fight with Crook. Rode all night before got to this battle.[3] Was in village two or three days before battle.[4]*

Some Sioux who had lost horses came in and reported Custer coming on trail, and Custer showed up not long after Custer's soldiers got there. (They called Custer *Peoushi* [Long Hair]) *Some of Indians thought it might be Custer. Had not been looking for soldiers in that direction.*

Soldiers attacked Hunkpapa tepees first. All Indians that had ponies went out to help Hunkpapa fight Reno, and some were dismounted. Battle with Reno lasted only short time, and my horse shot. Soldiers went through timber and retreated to river. My horse shot, and I went back to village for another horse. Hunkpapas and Minne squaws had been taking down tepees during Reno fight.

As soon as Reno retreated, more soldiers (Custer) *were in sight from village farther down the stream. The soldiers had four or five flags. Custer acted as though would cross and attack village.*

When I got to Custer, Indians had been fighting quite awhile. Some of the soldiers let horses go early in fight. Soldiers did not charge

1. Walter Camp field notes, folder 108, BYU Library.

2. Lamedeer was a leader of the Minneconjou Sioux and was killed by soldiers under Colonel Nelson Miles in May 1877.

3. It is not clear as to whether Flying By is here referring to the fight with Crook on March 17, 1876, or June 17, 1876.

4. Flying By is here referring to the Little Bighorn River fight on June 25.

after I got there. We crossed over at all points along river as quick as we could and found Custer already fighting Indians and driving Indians back toward river, but when we got over in great numbers, Custer was soon surrounded. The soldiers then got off horses and some let them go, and we captured a lot of them. I captured one myself. I took some of the horses to village before battle was over and then came back. Got ammunition from saddles of horses. After came back from taking horses to village, I came to gully east of long ridge and many soldiers already killed.

Flying By did not understand my map but took pencil and paper and drew one very similar to it. Says Custer's soldiers kept together all the time and were killed moving along toward camp. Killed all way along. Some soldiers still had horses at this time. During fight, gray horses and others much mixed up. Did not make any stand except in one place where Custer killed at end of long ridge.

Soldiers had plenty of ammunition when killed. Indians closed in, and at last part of battle soldiers were running through Indian lines trying to get away. Only four soldiers got into gully toward river. Battle against Custer alone lasted about half the afternoon. Did not recognize Custer until some time after the battle and all soldiers killed. Soldiers excited and shot wild. *We lost only a few men.* Four Minneconjou killed.

After Custer fight we went over the fought soldiers with the pack mules until Indians reported other soldiers coming under officer called the Bear Coat.

Moved toward Big Horn mountains and then back to Rosebud and down that stream. When moved away had considerable ammunition. I had a Winchester rifle with fourteen shots. Many of Indians had pump guns.

Heresay: afterward found two soldiers on Rosebud nearly starved to death. Heard of man who had been eating frogs. Hump died last spring. Greasy Grass Creek in Sioux is *Pa-zees-la-wak-pa.* Gall is *Pizi* (Pezee).

Interview with White Bull, July 23, 1910; Thaddeus Redwater, Interpreter[1]

White Bull (75 years old) . . . was in fight of 3/17/76. Cheyenne camp under Willow Brushes only a few Sioux. Wintered on Tongue until towards spring when moved to Powder. Camp at time of Crook fight was near Second Fork of Reno Creek. There were some white rocky bluffs there. His horses gave out, and he did not get to Crook fight but saw it at a distance. Did not pursue Crook because ponies worn out. One Cheyenne was killed and another wounded in this fight.

Did not learn of approach of soldiers until Reno attacked. Did not get into Custer fight until it was nearly over. Says (and so does Tall Bull) that many of Custer's soldiers acted like men intoxicated or beside themselves, as they fired into the air without taking aim. Did not try to crush Reno because thought could starve him out and in this way not lose men recklessly charging the fortifications which protected the soldiers, and did not know how many soldiers were there. When Terry approached thought had better retire. Says the Cheyennes had about 200 tepees and about 3,000 people.

---

1. Walter Camp field notes, folder 58, BYU Library. See also White Bull's note in the appendix about numbers of Indians killed in the Little Bighorn River fight. White Bull, a very important member of the Northern Cheyennes, was sometimes referred to as Ice or Ice Bear. His name should not be confused with that of White Bull of the Minneconjou Sioux, whose story is told by Stanley Vestal in *Warpath: True Story of the Fighting Sioux* (New York: Houghton Mifflin Co., 1932).

Interview with Tall Bull, July 22, 1910; Thaddeus Redwater, Interpreter, Lamedeer, Montana[1]

Hotuga Kastatche . . . *Tall Bull, 57 years old. Crook's fight 3/17/76 was with Cheyenne camp. Only few Sioux lodges. Most of Cheyennes wintered 75/76 Lower Powder — down near Yellowstone. When fought Crook 6/17/76 our camp was at lone tepee.*[2]

When heard soldiers to south we left the women and children in camp and traveled all night and reached headwaters Rosebud about daylight next morning. Did not follow up Crook because thought had done enough for one day and did not know Crook in such a bad fix. Did not expect soldiers would follow us as far as Little Bighorn.

Cheyenne call Little Bighorn [the] Goat River. Cheyenne village at north end of camp just as I have it. Tall Bull says there were 3,000 population in Cheyenne village. Head chiefs Little Bighorn: Two Moons, White Bull, and Lame White Man, who was killed. Only part of Cheyennes and Sioux got into Reno fight in bottoms. Cheyennes did not learn soldiers coming until Reno attacked. The Sioux must have known of approach of soldiers but Cheyennes did not.

After returning from Reno, women going over east to get on high ground to overlook Reno fight discovered Custer coming. Custer got onto flat near Ford B within easy gunshot of village, and Indians drove him back.

---

1. Walter Camp field notes, folder 58, BYU Library.

2. On June 20, 1876, Capt. Pollock telegraphed the Dept. Commander from Ft. Laramie that "Jordan under date of June 19 says Little Wolf, chief of Northern Cheyennes, left the agency Thursday (June 15) with 1,000 of his people, including 200 warriors for the north. All other Indians have gone to Ash Creek to attend the grand sundance commencing today." (It occurs to me that [the name] Sundance Creek for this stream may have arisen from the fact that a sundance was held there beginning June 20 and that Ash Creek was the real name Godfrey may have meant in calling it this, merely that it was the creek on which the sundance was held.)"

(Camp MSS, field notes, unclassified miscellaneous VI, Lilly Library.)

By time I got there [Indians] had driven soldiers to first rise (where Foley lay), and they were going up the ridge to right of Custer coulee and Indians driving them.

The men who had not horses to go to Reno first began the attack on Custer, and I did not see the first of it. Soldiers did not make any charge on Indians during the Custer fight. He is very clear that Custer was driven farther and farther back from river. Soldiers fell back from river. Some mounted and some on foot and not in very good order. Heard the volleys. The first was at the beginning of fight at C (Finley marker). The last was at G. Gray horses all mixed up with bays.

I was near H[3] and heard a big war whoop that soldiers were coming. Soldiers came on foot and ran right through us into deep gully, and this was the last of the fight, and the men were killed in this gully. Tall Bull says that some of the men who ran from the edge of the ridge to the gully were firing their guns at random. Tall Bull has been several times on battlefield in recent years and knows ground well and is apparently honest in his statements.

After Little Bighorn went up Little Bighorn to near Sheridan and across to Rosebud and down Rosebud and across to point about 18 miles below Lamedeer and across to Tongue and down Powder to near mouth and then to north side of Black Hills and then crossed Little Missouri and went back to Powder and up Crazy Woman's Fork and then broke up, some of Indians going north. The Slim Buttes fight was with a small party of Sioux who were detached from the main Indian camp, and they were out deer hunting. At that time there were ten or a dozen small detached parties of Indians out hunting. The soldiers struck this camp and massacred the people. *Some ran to us, and we attacked the soldiers and fought most of the day.*

---

3. See Walter Camp's map, page 36.

Interview with Standing Bear, July 12, 1910, at Manderson, South Dakota[1]

Says Black Bear and several others early in morning of June 25 were up on divide going off on a visit, and as they proceeded they crossed the trail of the Sioux leading into valley of Little Bighorn. This trail was then several days old and there was something about it that attracted their attention, and upon closer inspection, they discovered a fresh trail of shod horse tracks on the older trail. Having fought soldiers (Crook) only a few days before, their suspicions were at once aroused, and one of them proposed that they ride back to the top of the divide and take a look around, which they quickly did. From this point they could see the smoke of Custer's camp to their left, and away off to their right, high up among some trees, a small party of men, apparently scouts (Varnum's party). From this I take it that the shod horse tracks on the old trail which they discovered was the trail of Varnum in advance of Custer. They then retraced their steps to high ground, and here it was that Varnum saw them.

Says that Custer's dust was seen approaching the village over low ground to the east, down a kind of dry coulee. As soon as the soldiers came in sight they halted and apparently were preparing for a charge. All this time the Ogalallas were getting ready. Finally the soldiers advanced very near to the river, but before they could cross were engaged by the Indians and forced back to the ridge where the main fight took place.

Says as soon as Custer came in sight and halted, some of the Indians crossed over, but he advanced against this resistance nearly to the river before it became strong enough to check him.

Says that the Indians first prepared to fight were the ones camped

---

1. Walter Camp field notes, folders 20 and 55, BYU Library.

farthest from the river. While Reno's battle was going on, Crazy Horse was getting his warriors ready, and before they were ready the other soldiers (Custer) appeared. Crazy Horse, however, took time to consult the medicine man and invoke the spirits. This he did very coolly, and he delayed so long that many of his warriors became impatient.

Was on bluffs (where Knipe saw Indians), and Custer went down coulee into Medicine Tail and crossed over to Custer ridge in full view of village. Custer's soldiers did not fire into village. On my map I should change places with Minneconjou and Sans Arc camps. Ogalallas were not on river at all but over toward bluffs to west of Brule and Sans Arc. Custer's men did not fight by companies but all were together all the time. Could not make him say different. His recollection clear on this point. The gray horses mixed in with rest and but few horses got beyond Keogh. Nearly all killed or captured before got farther than this.

Keogh is the first place where any of the soldiers stopped to fight. Those between Custer and river were soldiers running toward river on foot. Between Calhoun and monument there were Indians both sides of river as soldiers went along. The soldiers killed between Custer and river were men on foot trying to make the river, and they were killed in the deep ravine.

Standing Bear took a buckskin shirt from one of the dead men and gave it to his mother, and she kept it many years and finally cut it up. At the time he supposed this to be the only buckskin shirt that was found, and he therefore for some years supposed he had Custer's shirt, whom he (after the battle) was told wore such a shirt. In talking with other Indians, however, he found it was claimed that other buckskin shirts were found among the dead.

At the time of the battle and while in the vicinity, no Indian recognized Custer's body, nor even supposed they had been fighting *Peoushi*. He saw the three Indian scouts killed with Reno and one of these they took to be Sioux (This must have been Bloody Knife, who was part Sioux).

Interviews
with
Members
of the
Sioux
Campaign
and
Others

George Herendeen

Frederic F. Gerard

James M. Sipes

Frederick E. Server

Bernard Prevo

Richard E. Thompson

Charles F. Roe

Samuel Burkhardt, Jr.

Herbert J. Slocum

Interview with
George Herendeen[1]

For the most part the statements which I here make are taken
from very full notes of the Little Big Horn expedition made in 1877
when all of the details were fresh in my mind. I am not, therefore,
depending on memory for more than these thirty three years. Herendeen 64 years old in 1909.

With 149 civilians crossed Yellowstone March 24, 1874, at mouth
Porcupine Creek and started for Rosebud and had fight at big bend of

---

1. Walter Camp field notes, folder 98, BYU Library. George Herendeen
was born on November 28, 1846, in Parkman Township, Geauga County, Ohio.
After service during the Civil War he went west and was in Denver, Colorado, in
1868. He probably worked as a cowboy in New Mexico and then followed the
cattle trails into Montana about 1869. In 1874 he was with the Yellowstone
Wagonroad and Prospecting Expedition, and in 1875 he helped Fellows Pease
build the Fort Pease stockade on the north bank of the Yellowstone River near
the mouth of the Bighorn River. He joined Custer's column on June 22 and
was in the valley and hilltop fights. He was engaged in the Nez Perce campaign
in 1877. In later years he resided in Bozeman, Lewistown, and Great Falls and
moved to Harlem, Montana, in 1889, where he was employed on the Fort
Belknap Indian Reservation under W. R. Logan. He died on June 17, 1918,
and was buried in Harlem Cemetery. More biographical information is found in
Barry Johnson's "George Herendeen, Montana Scout," *The English Westerners'
Brand Book* (London: The English Westerners Society), 2:3, April 1960, and
2:4, July 1960. "Custer Vindicated — A Scout's Story of the Battle of the Little
Big Horn" — was published in the *New York Times* and *New York Herald*,
January 22, 1878, and reprinted in William A. Graham's *The Custer Myth*
(Harrisburg, Pa.: The Stackpole Co., 1953), pp. 261-65. A copy of a letter from
Herendeen to his wife, dated January 4, 1878, concerning details of the Little
Bighorn River fight is in the Library of Congress. A statement dated July 1,
1876, by Herendeen concerning the fight was published in *The Army and Navy
Journal*, July 15, 1876. "Herendeen's Story" sent by telegraph from Bismarck
July 7, 1876, was published in the *New York Times* on July 8, 1876. Page four

Rosebud about half way from mouth to where Custer left and crossed divide. When Custer came along June 23 or 24, 1876, I showed him where we had fought this battle. Fight 4/5/74 on big bend Rosebud about half way from mouth to where Custer left it to cross divide. Took seven scalps, and Indians claimed we killed 200 of them. These were Sitting Bull's Indians and Cheyennes. We had 149 men, civilians. We estimated there were 500 or 600 Indians. Second fight foot of Wolf Mountains farther up the Rosebud. Third fight near Rotten Grass Creek on Big Horn.[2] All three hard fights. In this last fight we fought 1,400 Indians. In the whole expedition we lost one man killed (Zachary Yates) and two wounded. All these three fights within ten days. We were prospecting along the Rosebud. The purpose of our expedition was to prospect it and explore.

In 1875 we made another expedition with twenty-nine men and had a series of skirmishes with the Indians. Five of these were killed and thirteen wounded by the end of the season in our different fights. Our expeditions forced the government to open the country, and in 1876 the war started.

In the winter of 1875–76 I lived at Baker's Battlefield, Montana, most of the time alone and had accumulated a large number of skins. In February Major Brisbin[3] came down the Yellowstone, clearing the valley of settlers in anticipation of the Sioux war. It had been decided to make war on the Sioux, and it was desired to have the settlers out of the way. When he came to me, I at first refused to move, but he finally prevailed on me to do so and agreed to transport my skins for me and did so and took me on down the river as far as mouth of Big Horn. We then returned up river, and I went to Bozeman with my stuff.

Gibbon soon after this started down the Yellowstone to join

---

is reprinted in Graham's *The Custer Myth,* pp. 257–60. General Scott's notes on Herendeen's story in the *Times* and the *Herald* were collected by William J. Ghent, and a copy is in the Dustin Collection, Custer Battlefield National Monument. The Dustin Collection also has Albert W. Johnson's *Notes On George Herendeen* in a letter to Theo. W. Goldin. A. J. Noyes's *In The Land of Chinook, the Story of Blaine County* has a biography and photograph of Herendeen.

2. Says he had been in battles against Indians with citizens — one only about 15 miles from Little Bighorn battle, another about 50 miles and another about 12 miles. One of these was on Rosebud. *When Custer was marching up the Rosebud, I showed him where this fight had been.*

(Walter Camp field notes, folder 98, BYU Library.)

3. James Sanks Brisbin, major, 2nd Cavalry.

Terry, and about two weeks later, I followed and overtook his com-
mand.

How long was he with Gibbon at Ft. Ellis? *Since April 1876.*

When we got to Pease Bottom (mouth of Big Horn) *there were*
some half dozen or more boats (skiffs) *there to which I fell heir. Gib-*
bon said he wished to borrow these for his men to scout the river with,
and I loaned them to him. I scouted ahead in a boat, and when I got
far beyond Pompey's Pillar, I went on ahead two or three days' march
and at Wolf Rapids met the Far West *coming up with General Terry*
and staff aboard and took some dispatches and from Terry that night
went back and met Gibbon.

I was present on the boat the same day Custer started from the
mouth of the Rosebud, [as were] *Generals Terry, Gibbon, and*
Custer and Major Brisbin of the 2nd Cavalry. I was called in, and
Custer asked me if I knew where the head of Tullock's fork was, and I
said "Yes, I have been there." And Custer said: "All right, then, he is
the man I want." This is how I came to go with Custer.

When it was decided that I was to go with Custer from the mouth
of the Rosebud, I had a saddle but no horse. Custer then had one of
the enlisted men of 7th Cavalry give his horse up to me, and this young
fellow[4] *went on the steamer. His term of enlistment was about to run*
out, but he afterward told me that my taking his horse had saved his
life, as if he had gone with Custer he thought he would have been in
the fight with the five companies.

Early on June 25 I told Custer that Tullock's Creek was just over
the divide, but Custer replied rather impatiently to the effect that
there was now no occasion for sending me there as the Indians were
known to be in his front, and that his command had been discovered by
them. He said the only thing for him (Custer) to do was therefore to
charge their village as soon as possible. It was also my opinion that
Custer wished to fight the Indians with the 7th Cavalry alone, and he
was clearly making every effort to do this. It appeared to me at the
time that Custer was right and that there was really no use in scouting
Tullock's fork.[5]

---

4. At mouth of Rosebud on June 22 a scout was dismounted and Custer gave him his
choice of horses ridden by about 20 men of headquarters detail. The choice fell on the horse of
Dennis Lynch. Lynch hesitated to give him up, but finally consented, and Custer told him to
get on the boat and look after his luggage, which Lynch did and afterward said that this act of
Custer's saved his life.

(Walter Camp Collection, Herendeen envelope, box 1, BYU Library.)

5. *Early on June 25 we lay in camp in the hollow east of the divide. I said to Custer:*

When the column started to cross the divide,[6] he [Herendeen] was a little in advance and saw an Indian up a dry ravine, and Bouyer came in and told him he had seen two more driving two loose horses some time before this.

When on way to skirmish line did he see Custer's command on bluffs? *No.* What did he see of Rees in valley? Says he had two or three Crows with him after crossing Little Bighorn with Reno and one was with him when skirmish line was formed. Ask him why Bouyer and other Crows happened to go with Custer, seeing that Custer told Reno to take the scouts along.[7] Draw him out all I can as to just what scouts he saw with Reno before forming skirmish line. Where did he see Bob Jackson and Billy Cross last and how did they get out? *Bob Jackson was not on the Little Bighorn June 25 or June 26; he was back at Powder River. I do not remember seeing Billy Cross in Reno's valley fight at all or at any point after Reno separated from Custer until I met him coming down the bluff as I went up after coming out of timber.*

Says after tying his horse he went out, and the skirmish line was still firing.[8] Soldiers fired about 15 min. altogether and about 20 minutes from time deployed until retreat. Says that he remained in timber, and Indians began coming around on south side of it. The firing of soldiers had ceased, and when he went to look for soldiers,

---

"*General, the head of Tullock's Creek lies just over those hills yonder.*" *He replied rather impatiently:* "*Yes, but there are no Indians in that direction — they are all in our front, and besides they have discovered us. It will be of no use to send you down Tullock's Creek. The only thing to do is to push ahead and attack the camp as soon as possible.*"

(Walter Camp field notes, folder 98, BYU Library.)

6. About 1856 Sir Geo. Gore camped near point where Custer left Rosebud and passed over divide. Gore was an English adventurer and trapper.

(Ibid.)

7. Herendeen says Bouyer was acquainted with the country and this is why Custer wanted Bouyer with the 5 companies. Says Bouyer was a half-breed from the same country as himself. . . . Herendeen says Mitch Bouyer was a man with a very dark skin. He was ¾ Sioux. I noticed the same of his son, James LaForge, of Crow Agency, Montana.

(Ibid.)

8. Says when Reno formed skirmish line, he (Herendeen) was on the extreme left of it, but a little in rear, in a little swale. At this time there were no Indians within range but some sitting on horses over on bluffs to left. When soldiers dismounted, Indians began to work up closer. Says Reynolds and Gerard were with him and Crow Indian. (He could therefore not have been on the left of skirmish line. This must have been typographical error.) But says soon took horses to timber and after this he lost sight of the others and was alone and on south side of timber. The soldiers were on west side of timber facing bluffs. How long did firing on skirmish line last? *About 5 min. or less.*

(Ibid.)

222

found all horses gone but his own.[9] He mounted and rode down to a little park in the timber and here saw a company drawn up facing the east, or the left of the line was toward the village. Reno was there sitting on his horse. The Indians now fired a volley into timber from south, and Bloody Knife and a private soldier were hit. Bloody Knife was killed by shot from east by Indians who had gone into brush from south — by Indians not more than 50 yds. away. Reno immediately ordered his men to dismount and then quickly to mount, and everybody left the timber on the run, going out by numerous trails through the thick brush.[10] He went out with the men and got about 150 yds. out of timber when his horse was shot down and he went back to the timber.[11] Everybody was going as fast as the horses could go. There was a thick dust, and about 20 Sioux who were pursuing the soldiers nearly ran over him [Herendeen].

When he got back to the timber, soldiers were still leaving it, but he found a small party — seven or eight mounted and some dismounted (found 13 men in timber with 5 or 6 horses), and he advised them all to remain in the timber as there was no chance of getting away by running. Made men take ammunition from saddle pockets and turn horses loose. Remained here 2 hours and were not molested by Indians. . . . Isaiah killed soon after getting out of timber not far from Charley Reynolds.

I saw Reynolds come out of timber, and said: "Charley, don't try to ride out. We can't get away from this timber." Reynolds was then trying to mount his horse. He finally mounted and got about 150 yds. when he was shot, and Isaiah fell near him, and while I was in the timber, I saw Indians shooting at Isaiah and squaws pounding him with stone hammers. His legs below the knees were shot full of bullets

---

9. *After I tied my horse, I saw Indians getting around to the south side of the timber, and I shot at one at close range, and he and his horse went down. I then wondered where the men could be and why they did not come in and help stand off these Indians. When I went to investigate, I found the men with Reno mounting. I then ran down and got on my horse.*

(Ibid.)

10. Thinks there were 1800 lodges and about 3500 warriors. Thinks Reno could have held the timber easily.

(Ibid.)

11. *When I got out of the timber, my horse was shot and went down, and I went back on foot. Reynolds was then trying to mount, and I called to him and said: "You can't make it,"* etc. What front of woods was Charlie Reynolds killed, south or west? *South.*

(Ibid.)

223

only an inch or two apart.[12] *Most of the men with me in the timber were a badly scared lot of fellows, and they were already as good as whipped. They appeared to be without experience as soldiers.* Could he give names of any of the men in the timber? *No.* How about the two men who would not leave the timber with him? Who were they and what became of them? Did not know what became of the two men who would not go out of timber but supposed they must have been killed. There were two men who would not go out of timber who were said to have money cached in there somewhere. Was told later they had good deal of money cached and did not wish to leave it.

About ½ hour after troops had retreated from timber, firing began down the river. The volleys were in early part of Custer's firing. This firing down the river consisted of a great many volleys, with scattering shots between the volleys, and after the volleys ceased there were a great many scattering shots. (These volleys must have been Custer stopping to fire as he retreated from the river, and the scattering shots were probably the Indians returning the fire. The great many scattering shots were probably Custer's and the Indians' shooting after Custer's men were broken up.) Thinks Custer's battle did not last an hour.

Once in awhile while in the timber, I would go to the edge and look, and finally seeing only a few Indians, I told the men we would go out and that we must walk and not run and go across the open flat. There was a wounded corporal or sergeant.[13] *On the way out of the timber only one shot was exchanged with these Indians. I told the men not to shoot unless necessary, that I did not wish to stir up a general engagement with them*[14] — *not to run but to go in skirmish order,*

---

12. Isaiah Dorman, the interpreter at Ft. Rice, was a man of considerable intelligence and a man who enjoyed the respect and confidence of the soldiers in spite of his color. Isaiah was killed about 30 ft. from Charley Reynolds. Isaiah Dorman was killed and ripped open. The coffee pot and cup which he carried were filled with blood. What devilish purpose the Indians had in catching this blood he did not know.

(Walter Camp field notes, folder 94, BYU Library. See also Ronald C. McConnell's "Isaiah Dorman and the Custer Expedition" in *The Journal of Negro History* (Philadelphia: United Publishers Corp.), July 1948, 33:344–52.)

13. *When Custer's firing had stopped, I told the men it was time to get out of the timber and began to make arrangements to go out. Looking out through the brush I saw only a few Indians, apparently on picket. Late in the afternoon he and 12 men left the timber.*

(Walter Camp field notes, folder 98, BYU Library.)

14. *After leaving the timber we crossed the open flat, as I had satisfied myself that the only Indians around were the few we saw on picket and the squaws robbing and mutilating the dead. As we emerged from the timber these few Indians ran off.*

(Ibid.)

*take it cool, and we would get out. I told them I had been in just such
scrapes before and knew we could get out if we kept cool. I told them
I could get out alone, and if they would do what I told them I could
get them out also. The wounded sergeant then spoke up and said:
"They will do what you want, for I will compel them to obey. I will
shoot the first man who starts to run or to disobey orders." This
wounded sergeant* (He must have been Chas White) *helped me out in
good shape. When we got to the river, the water was rather deep
where we forded. This sergeant and I remained on the west bank
while the balance forded, and we told them when they would get over
to protect us while we forded, and they did so.*

*We forded the river some distance below where Reno did and
went up the bluff farther north than where Reno retreated up. This
was farther north than where DeWolf was killed. The Indians were
now coming up the valley to attack Reno.*

Did Edgerly shoot at him as he was getting across river after coming out of timber? No.

*On the way up the bluff we came upon a dead Sioux, whose gun
lay beside him with a cartridge stuck fast in it. We did not stop, but as
we neared the top of the bluff I met Billy Cross coming down. I told
him that if he wanted a scalp he would find a dead Sioux farther down.
He lead Rees with him, and they were all mounted. They went on
down, and I did not see them again on the Little Bighorn. Cross afterward told me that when the Sioux charged Reno that evening, they
were cut off and had to cut around and went back to the Powder River.*
(This corroborates Adam Carrier's story.)

*When we got to the top of the bluff, we met Reno's advance
toward Custer just as they stopped and fell back. Had we been twenty
minutes later, we never would have been able to join Reno.*[15] *I found
that my horse had jumped up after being shot in the bottom and had
followed along in the retreat and was on top of the bluff when I got
there. After we were corraled on Reno hill, my horse was killed, and
he was one of the dead horses piled up on Moylan's line. I lay behind
him on June 26, and he was bloated up with gas, and two or three times
when the body was struck, I could hear the hiss of escaping gas.*

*On June 27 we moved down off the bluff and camped in the
bottom, and the wounded also were taken down there. In hunting*

---

15. Gives great praise to Benteen, who stood up amid a hail of bullets.
(Ibid.)

around for dead bodies, we found a dead horse in the middle of the river just below where Reno had crossed in retreat. This horse lay in water too shallow to float him off. The horse was much bloated, and upon investigation we found a dead soldier under him. Whether he had been drowned by being caught under the horse when the latter fell, or whether he had been killed simultaneously with the horse I do not know.[16]

Captain (or Lieutenant) Doane made the stretchers to transport the wounded men to the Far West. Some wounded horses were condemned and killed, and these freshly killed horses were skinned to make the stretchers.

Ask him what became of two Crows. Did they go into fight with Reno in valley? Were they Half Yellow Face and White Swan and where was White Swan wounded? When I got out of the timber and got up to Reno on the bluff, White Swan and Half Yellow Face were already there, having gone up in Reno's retreat or shortly afterward. White Swan was wounded in Reno's valley fight, and Half Yellow Face had got him out. Half Yellow Face took White Swan to the steamer on a travois of his own getup.[17]

Nathan Short was found over on the Rosebud, pretty well down toward its mouth. His recollection of the camp talk about it corroborates Henley's account. Ask about John or Jos. Wilkinson. Was he along on expedition? He was not with Custer at all. He was on the steamer with Terry. Also Jack Omahundro (Texas Jack). He was with Bill Cody with Crook. Recollections of Crow scouts, and of Curley and what he thinks of Curley's story. Believes it.

On June 25, 1877, I went to the battlefield with Captain Nowlan and took away the remains of ten officers.[18] I was ordered to do so by General Sherman, who was at Ft. Keogh reviewing the troops. We went overland with Captain Nowlan with his troop. We went to the

---

16. He saw no dead soldiers in village while destroying tepees on June 27.
(Ibid.)
17. Did you go on boat with wounded? Yes, as far as the mouth of the Big Horn.
(Ibid.)
18. John Baronett and Herendeen were with Nowlan in 1877 to take away remains of officers. Herendeen says these two were the only civilians who accompanied Nowlan's troop from Ft. Keogh. At Ft. Custer some civilian teamsters were taken along to transport the coffins. Herendeen (8/5/11) says that out of the grave where Custer was buried not more than a double handful of small bones were picked up. The body had been dragged out and torn to pieces by coyotes and bones scattered about.

(Walter Camp field notes, folder 37, BYU Library.)

mouth of the Little Horn where the officer who built Ft. Custer had preceded us three or four days. We here made rough boxes and went to the Custer battlefield and got the remains, and when we got back to the mouth of the Little Bighorn, we found the steamer Fletcher waiting for the remains. We then marched back 'to Ft. Keogh overland. When Custer was buried, there were stakes marked VI and VII for Custer and Tom Custer, and but for me they would have made a mistake and got other remains than Custer's. Already had other remains. I identified Custer's remains.

Interviews with Frederic F. Gerard, January 22 and April 3, 1909[1]

Born in St. Louis November 14, 1829. Educated at Xavier College, where he remained 4 years. Made first trip up Missouri with Honore Picotte on September 28, 1848. Hired out as clerk to American Fur Co. at Ft. Pierre S. Dak. and here known by Indians as Swift Buffalo. In spring of 1849 went to Fort Clark at a salary of $500. The American Fur Co.'s post there was built in 1831. In 1855 in company with Honore Picotte he went to Ft. Berthold.

On December 25, 1863, Ft. Berthold was attacked by 600 Yankton Sioux belonging to Two Bear's band, and they fought from 9:00 a.m. to 4:00 p.m. and tried to set the block houses on fire. The fort was defended by Gerard and 17 other men, and they killed about 40 of the Sioux and wounded about 100. The Sioux were driven off by Assiniboines, and the white men deserted Gerard, who for 10 days held the place alone and made ready to blow up the place with gunpowder should the Sioux return to attack it. Years later Sioux used to return and try to take Gerard's life for their severe punishment at time of attack, but he was always on his guard.

On July 6, 1872, he was hired as post interpreter at Ft. A. Lincoln and located a farm on present site of Mandan. In 1873 he saved Gen. Rosser and a surveying party from being cut off by Indians. . . . Gerard was post interpreter at Ft. Lincoln from July 10, 1872, to July 1, 1883.

I did not go out on either Yellowstone or Black Hills expeditions,

---

1. Walter Camp field notes, folder 94, BYU Library. An account of Frederic Francis Gerard is also in Frances C. Holley's *Once Their Home* . . . , pp. 262–66, and in *North Dakota Historical Collections* (Bismarck, N.D.: Torch Press, 1906), 1:347–48 and 1920, 6:171–75, reprinted in William Graham's *The Custer Myth*, pp. 250–51. See also *Interview with F. F. Gerard's Daughter*, Library of St. Benedict's Academy, St. Joseph, Minnesota.

as I was not supposed to leave the post. I went to Ft. Berthold in 1850, about two years after the post had started. The hand-to-hand combat with Sitting Bull was in the trading post at Ft. Berthold several years before the Battle of the Little Bighorn, probably about 1868. The cause was a dispute about the price of some Iroquois shells. Sitting Bull got them in his possession and was going to set his own price upon them, after turning over to me some buffalo hides. The result was that I took the shells from him forcibly. He pulled up his double-barrelled gun, and I seized him and the gun being cocked, I slipped the caps off with my thumb. Son of the Star was the Ree who stepped up and proposed to kill him, but there being a large camp of hostile Sioux just across the river, I wished to avoid trouble.

After the scrap with Sitting Bull, he went away and sent word by Bloody Knife that he had an arrow in his quiver for me. I sent word back that I had a rifle that could speak true, and if he ever came back he would hear it speak. Four or five years after this he sent in two horses, two Indians, and pipes and wanted to make peace and come in trade with the Rees. I consulted the Rees and smoked and let him come in. I gave the Rees one horse and the Gros Ventres the other. According to Indian custom I then owed Sitting Bull two horses, and he remembered it for some years after the Battle of the Little Big Horn; he once happened to see a black stallion of mine (the same one I rode at Little Bighorn) with Mr. Parkin, my partner in business, and took it, saying: "Now I have one of the horses that Gerard owes me."

I had a conversation with Custer one night before we reached Yellowstone. Custer said he would have some Gatlings along, and if he got within range of a village he would make short work of it. I told him "General, don't you be deceived in believing you can get Indians to stand while you grind out shots with a Gatling. I would advise you to leave Gatlings behind and take a twelve-pounder that will throw shells. Then if you get within a mile or two of an Indian camp, you can make them scatter pretty lively."

Before we had proceeded far in the expedition, General Terry called me into consultation regarding the Indians and asked me how many I expected to encounter. I told him that a good many Indians had left the reservations and that if all these united with the hostiles in one band, they would probably have a force of 4,000 warriors; that they were hard fighters, well armed and well supplied with ammunition and provisions and would undoubtedly show fight if overtaken. These Indians had scouts and lookouts passing to and from the agencies as often as every week and kept the hostiles informed of all *that was going on at the army posts. I told him that if met by a column of soldiers strong enough to defeat them they would scatter, rendezvous on the Powder, and probably make a break for the British possessions. The conversation lasted for some time, and every little while the General would interrupt with the searching inquiry: "How do you know these things?" in reply to which I would give my reasons in some detail, etc.*

Going up Rosebud sometimes in bed of stream and sometimes to right of it. Trail turned up a branch of Rosebud. At the forks they could see there had been a gathering of Indians and a tepee, and other signs of ceremonial performances were still in evidence. The grass had been eaten off for long distances round about.[2] The main trail led west toward the divide between the Rosebud and the Little Big Horn, but there was another trail into this point from the south. *I have since heard that here or near this point was the site of the village from which the warriors sallied forth and fought Gen. Crook on the same stream thirty miles farther south just one week previous to our arrival (June 17), but we were then entirely ignorant of that fact or of any of Crook's movements in the country south of us.*

On night of June 24 Custer said Crow scouts knew of high mountain on divide from which could overlook valley of Little Bighorn. The scouts would reach this during the night, and he wished to have the command in the neighborhood before daylight, where it would be concealed during the following day while the scouts would push forward and discover the exact location of the village.

When we went into camp early on the morning of June 25 in the woods, in sort of a narrow valley some miles east of the divide, I threw myself on the ground and soon fell asleep. I had not slept long, however, before General Custer came up and touched me with his foot, waking me up and saying: "Gerard, get up. Some of the scouts have come in from the high point, and I think we should go up there." General Custer now told his brother Tom not to move the command from where it was until further orders. We went up to the high

---

2. He says of habits of Indians when traveling in hostile country, they would start early in p.m. and go 30 miles and camp and for fear of being discovered by foes, would build no fires. When not allowed to cook they ate raw liver, raw kidney and raw gristle from behind ears of buffalo. The next morning they would kill more buffalo, but build no fires, and in p.m. move on.

(Walter Camp field notes, folder 94, BYU Library.)

mountain peak, which was about thirteen miles east of the Little Big-horn, and through my glasses I made out a pony herd on the hills or table land beyond that stream. I could distinctly see a large dark spot, or mass, and could even see dust rising, from which I concluded that I was looking at a herd of ponies that were being driven. This was now some hours after daylight, and the light was strong and the atmosphere very clear. I have heard General Custer criticized for not sending Herendeen to scout Tullock's fork. General Custer did not overlook this, and the subject came up for discussion while we were on the divide. From the Crow's Nest we had a good view of the valley of Tullock's Creek, which takes its rise not far from where we were. We could see all over that part of the country, and as no trail led that way we concluded there were no Indians in that part of the country. Not long after this General Custer, finding that the Indian scouts had dis-covered us, decided to attack the camp that day, and I presume that he saw the futility of sending a scout through a valley where we knew there were no Indians to inform General Terry of that fact after he (Custer) would have made the attack.

Soon after we had passed the divide, in the morning Mark Kel-logg, reporter of the New York Herald *came pushing ahead to the scouts. He was riding a mule that was a little slow, and coming up to me, asked if I would lend him my spurs. As I was not using them, I consented and handed them over to him with the remark that he had better not put them on, as I would advise him to fall back to the com-mand and stay with it. He replied that he was expecting interesting developments, and he wished to keep up with the scouts and report everything he could see out ahead. . . . When we got within two or three miles of Ford A, we could see a big dust over in the valley of Little Bighorn, there being a north wind, and this gave the impression that the Indians were fleeing north.* Gerard thinks the Indians knew Custer was coming but had not counted on his night march.

After Gerard got across the river, one of the Indian scouts called out that the Sioux were coming up to meet Reno. Gerard exclaimed, "Hell, Custer ought to know this right away, for he thinks the Indians are running. He ought to know they are preparing to fight. I'll go back and inform him." And so he went back and met Cooke at the knoll ½ or ¾ mile east of the ford. It was probably 75 or 100 feet high, but right in the mouth of the valley. The trail passed to the right of it. When Cooke saw him coming up he said: "Well, Gerard, what is the matter now?"

I told him that Reno and his battalion had forded and that the Indians were coming up the valley to meet him, and I thought the General ought to know that the Indians were showing fight instead of running away. He said: "All right, Gerard, you go ahead, and I will go back and report." I turned and rode back toward the river, and before I reached it met a mounted soldier hurrying east (McIlhargey).

After fording went ahead and rode behind command with Charlie Reynolds. Ree scouts were up ahead of the line of soldiers and over to the left. When got up near point of timber the Rees espied a considerable herd of ponies over in the foothills to the left of the valley, perhaps ½ mile distant. They made for these and tried to drive off the whole herd, but a band of Sioux got there nearly as soon as the Rees so that the latter succeeded in getting away with only part of the herd, with the Sioux tight behind. After being chased up the valley some distance, the Rees let go part of their quarry, which the Sioux recovered but in doing this lost ground in the race so that the Rees made the ford safely and got over with their stolen property, continued back on the trail content to leave the Sioux with the soldiers.[3]

Reno now had arrived at the point of timber, and here he dismounted and threw out a skirmish line across the valley. The horses were led into the timber by the 'Number Fours.' Charlie Reynolds and I led our horses into the brush and tied them, went out and took station just in rear of the skirmish line, where it rested on the timber, to watch the firing, which lasted about five minutes. The Sioux began passing around the left line and turning to our rear, and the men soon broke from the line and went into the woods. As Major Reno left the line and passed into the timber, I saw him put a bottle of whisky to his mouth and drink the whole contents. The men ran into the timber pell mell, and all resistance to the Sioux had ceased.

In the timber all was confusion, and in trying to pick out their horses the language of some of the men was hasty and vigorous, to say the least. The Sioux had closed in and were firing into the timber more or less at random from the south and the northwest. Toward the west the bank or bench leading up to the level of the prairie rather protected the timber from firing from that direction, as no firing low

3. Young Hawk . . . [stated] . . . that Custer told Rees in event of meeting Sioux to cut out herd and get it to rear and keep out of way of soldiers. If Custer told the Rees this, it must have been communicated to them through Gerard. Gerard says he does not recollect this.

(Walter Camp field notes, folder 94, BYU Library.)

enough to be effective could be made on the timber from that direction without coming right up to the edge of the bank or within ten yards of the edge of the timber.

It occurred to me then, and I am still of the same opinion, that this timber was a splendid place for defense, and that Reno made a terrible blunder in not remaining right there. The Sioux were thick enough outside, mostly at long range, however; but had a little deter- mination been displayed in the way of defense, they would never have come into the brush to find the soldiers. It is certain that if Reno had held out against these Indians, hundreds of them would have remained to hold him in the timber, and Custer would have had a better show at the other end of the village.[4]

Benteen's command, now but two miles away and advancing toward the sound of the firing, would have made the issue still more interesting for all concerned. Reno, however, seeing no support from the rear, lost his head, if he had any, and suddenly decided to run the gauntlet of the Sioux. In less than five minutes after entering the timber the men began to bolt from it in disorder and spur their horses toward Ford A. Some left the timber from the south side and some up the bank at the west and then turned in the direction of the general retreat. . . .

I was joined by Bill Jackson and a little later by Lieutenant DeRudio and O'Neill. DeRudio's horse had broken away from him when the men left the timber, and O'Neill was dismounted. I was riding a stallion and Jackson a mare, and no sooner had we dismounted and tied them than the horses began to act badly, putting us in danger of being discovered by the noise they made. We finally improved the situation by tying their heads together. As my horse was very strong and swift, I was taken with the notion of throwing away the saddle, mounting him bare back, and trying to cut through the Sioux and rejoin the command. Upon mentioning my purpose, however, DeRudio protested strongly, saying that I would have no chance of escape in that manner and that if I wished to discover the rest of the

---

4. Gerard thinks there were entirely too many Indians there for Custer to handle. He estimated before starting that would find as many as 4,000 warriors and subsequent observa- tion and events have never induced him to lower the estimate. He thinks Custer would have been badly defeated had he charged the village with his whole regiment. The losses to the whole regiment would probably have been fully as much as they actually turned out to be had Custer tried to stampede the village, although he probably would not have lost several of the companies almost entire.

(Ibid.)

party to the Sioux, that would be a sure way to do it.[5] *His advice caused me to give up the idea, and to this day I am not regretting that I did so.*

About ½ hour after troops had retreated from timber firing began down the river. . . . Before this there had been some general firing and when heard volleys thought Custer must be coming nearer. . . . These shots seemed to be much nearer to them than the general firing, insomuch that he thought Custer or a detachment of Custer's battalion was making way through the village. Gerard says he heard the two volleys fired. . . . Says these were certainly fired down at river. . . . There were 30 or 40 shots, then straggling shots and in a little while another volley, apparently nearer to them. He finally exclaimed, "Let us leave here and go down that way: Custer is coming." To this DeRudio objected, saying: "We had better stay where we are. It will be time enough to join Custer when he gets here." In the light of later events, Gerard was convinced that the shots heard were fired at men trying to escape through the village. With the knowledge that Reno was in the valley before Custer's fight began, it would only be natural that men escaping from the Custer fight would try to go in the direction of Reno's fight.

After leaving the timber, DeRudio and Tom O'Neill followed, hanging to tails of horses. Went up the river and at place where he supposed Reno had forded on retreat and under bluff where he had heard battle with Reno in evening he looked across and saw someone strike a match and proceed to light a pipe. He yelled over and immediately the match was extinguished. He heard grunts and whispers and supposed Indians did not tarry for further investigation. Went up river and back again and finally along toward morning heard Indians talking and could see them against the sky.

Indians discovered our presence and called out saying in Sioux, "Where you going. Hold on, don't go away, we are Sioux." Here O'Neill and DeRudio fell flat on their faces, and he whispered to them that they had struck Indians. Gerard now thought the Sioux would fire a volley and so lay down on his horse and turned horses and got out and here left O'Neill and DeRudio.

We went up river again, and just before daylight found a place

---

5. According to report of *Chicago Tribune* it was DeRudio who proposed to go out of timber when heard Custer's firing and Gerard advised not to.

(Ibid.)

where we thought we could ford. My horse waded out some distance and suddenly plunged into deep water and had to swim, followed by Jackson's horse. He swam straight across and landed against a cut bank, and not being able to touch bottom, he immediately turned and swam back for the other shore. At about the middle of the stream he bumped against Jackson's horse, and a lively struggle ensued between the two animals, each trying to clamber over the other. We were both knocked out of the saddle and were glad to escape the melee by swimming ashore, Jackson taking to the left, or west, bank and I to the right. Unfortunately for us we both had been holding our carbines in our arms to keep them above water. In swimming ashore we found our clothing, boots, and accoutrements rather serious impediments, but we were not swimming for pleasure. The horses meantime had separated and gone ashore on Jackson's side, and I called over to him to catch them, which he soon succeeded in doing.

As soon as I reached land, I became aware that I had lost my pistol, in addition to my gun, and the only weapon of defense or offense which I now possessed was a knife. The outlook from henceforth was therefore not at all encouraging. However, I thought it important to join Jackson as soon as possible, and going up the river a piece we found shallower water, where Jackson forded with both horses. Finding here no way to get up the right bank, we crossed again to the left side and continued on up the river, passing by Ford A, as I subsequently discovered.

We soon heard Sioux talking and horses splashing in the river, and so we cut a circuit out into the valley and went past them cautiously. We then went into thick timber and brush and tied the horses where they could graze and withdrew apace and crawled under some willows that had been bent over by flood water and went to sleep, being exhausted. Slept until 10:00 a.m. This was about two miles or 2 1/2 miles from the Reno corral.

When we woke up, we could hear firing and see the flashing of guns all around Reno's position. We remained here all day. Along toward evening, June 26, we heard Indians talking and sound getting nearer. Crawling out to the edge of the timber, we discovered Sioux in a gully facing our position and quite near. Presumably they were there for some purpose, and we decided to remain quiet with the hope of remaining undiscovered. It soon appeared that they were acting as a flank guard for the village which was on the move up the valley. The great horde of warriors and ponies and squaws and children passed so near to us that we could plainly see wounded warriors on travois and dead warriors thrown across and tied to the backs of horses. Above all the noise and rattle and the hum of voices and cries of children we could hear the death chanting of the squaws.

As soon as darkness came on, we set out in the direction of the point where we had seen the fighting during the day, feeling certain that soldiers must be entrenched there. We forded the river and proceeded down the right side, along the bluffs. As we approached the supposed position, we could now and then hear men talking in the still night. The interpretation this time was sure, and the sound of English decidedly welcome in our ears. When we got near, I yelled out, "Hello, hello there" and instantly heard guns click all around and "Hello, hello, who are you?" I yelled back "Gerard." Then I heard men say all along, "Gerard is coming in, etc." Before we got up to them, we found a dead Indian. We reached the line at 11:00 p.m. We immediately enquired for DeRudio and O'Neill but were informed that nothing had been seen or heard of them. Later in the night, however, they both came in.

They brought cold coffee and hardtack, but my stomach revolted. Then I tried to eat some salt pork not cooked, but I went to sleep with a mouthful of this not swallowed. I was worn out and sleepy beyond my ability to express. They threw a blanket over me, and I went to sleep and slept until about 10:00 a.m. June 27. Soon after I awoke, I volunteered to assist Dr. Porter, who was having difficulty in administering chloroform, two men having fainted while holding the sponge over the face of wounded men who were being operated on.

On the next day, June 28, I accompanied the troops to the Custer battlefield, when the dead were buried. Major Reno instructed me to select some high point and keep a constant lookout for Indians in all directions to avoid any chance of surprise while the men were burying the dead. The men proceeded over the battlefield in formation much like a skirmish line, so as not to overlook any of the scattering dead. As they came to bodies, dirt and sod were thrown over them lightly as they lay. No graves were dug except for the corpse of General Custer. Identification of the bodies of enlisted men was not attempted, but a good deal of effort was made to find the bodies of all the officers, but there was not entire success in this.

I was present with the group of officers when the bodies of General Custer and Captain Custer were buried. The horror of sight and feeling over the bodies of all these brave men after lying in the hot sun for three days I will not attempt to describe. The eyes of surviving comrades were filled with tears, and throats were choked with grief unspeakable. The stench of dead men was nauseating.

Gerard says Custer's body lay on the side of the hill, and Tom Custer on highest point of ridge where was a little level place. Says General and Tom lay 20 ft. apart at farthest. . . . Tom Custer — they had smashed back of his head in with a stone or hammer and shot an arrow into top of his skull. The arrow point had penetrated his brain and point of it turned so could not be pulled out. Says Genl. Custer was shot through head back of temples, about halfway between ears and eyes and no powder marks.

Gerard has always been of the opinion that Indians fought the battle without any plan, and that the position of forces on both sides was purely accidental, the soldiers on the one hand proceeding to attack a village they had not seen, and the location of which was uncertain until they were almost within gun-shot range of it. On the other hand, the Indians came out and met the troops just where they happened to find them.

After the battle I wished to return to Ft. Lincoln on the Far West *with the wounded, but General Terry would not grant my request. I therefore remained in the field with the regiment until the end of the campaign in the fall.*

After we had got back to Ft. Lincoln and I had substituted a new suit of clothes for my well worn campaign dress, I went aboard the steamer to pay my respects to General Terry. His remarks were to some extent reminiscent, and as a parting word, he said, in the presence of several officers: "Mr. Gerard, I recall very well certain remarks of yours at the outset of the campaign, and particularly your estimate of the fighting strength of the Indians. Had I known you as well then as I do now, the operations of the campaign would have been conducted on a different plan." One of the officers who heard this took occasion later to say to me privately that he considered that a remarkable statement to be made by the commanding officer of an expedition, and that I ought to feel highly complimented.[6]

Gerard at Court of Inquiry: *When I got to Chicago, Reno sent for me and treated me very hospitably and had me talk with his lawyer. This fellow tried to pick out of me what I was going to testify to, but I*

---

6. Col. Chas. A. Varnum told me that he saw this same statement by Gen. Terry in writing. Said it was in a letter from Terry to Gerard.

(Ibid.)

talked only in general terms. After awhile Reno came in and Gilbert[7] said to him in an undertone: "This man is all right; he knows nothing that is damaging." After I got on the stand, I told some things that did not set very well with them, and Gilbert tried all manner of tricks, browbeating, etc., to get me to contradict myself, and at times our tilts at each other were rather bitter. I understood from inside sources at the time that much that passed between us was not going to be permitted to go on record.

After I came off the stand, a commissioned officer of the 7th Cavalry with whom I was on very friendly terms, who was at the Little Bighorn, took me aside, grasped my hand and said: "Gerard, I want to congratulate you for telling the truth so fearlessly and for maintaining your story unshaken. When I go on the stand I will tell them a few things that I know." I replied by saying: "I am wondering whether you will or not." He said: "Well, just wait until you see."

Shortly after this he and I were together when a porter came up with a note which he opened and later said: "An invitation to a champagne supper." I said: "Yes, and it will also be a blanket for you."

In due course he was called as a witness, and I heard his testimony, and upon meeting him later I said: "Well, I noticed that when they got you on the stand you were not as well informed as you intended to be," and he replied: "Well, Gerard, they have got the whip over us; they have some things in the pigeon holes that could be used to make me feel rather uncomfortable, and I thought there was no use trying to stand against the whole gang by myself."

Gerard said the general understanding among all whom he talked with confidentially was that any officer who made himself obnoxious to the defense would incur the wrath of certain officers in pretty high authority in certain department headquarters farther west than Washington and not as far west as St. Paul. There was much dining and wining all the time the trial was going on, and he knew the whole object was to compromise certain of the witnesses. Before the trial began he and Dr. Porter and certain of the officers were called into a room to talk over what information they could give on certain points. Dr. Porter admitted that he could testify thus and so in reference to certain pertinent questions but said he hoped he would not be called upon to do so.

---

7. Mr. Lyman D. Gilbert of Harrisburg, Pennsylvania, was legal counsel for Marcus Reno at the court of inquiry.

The trial had not proceeded far before it came to be known among the witnesses, including commissioned officers, some of whom were outspoken to me in confidence, that the way of the innocent and truthful could be made hard. It was amusing therefore to see how badly some of the memories had failed in the space of less than three years since the battle. It was made the business of certain ones active for the defense to get hold of all the doubtful witnesses before they were called and entertain them well. On such occasions they were cautiously sounded and discreetly primed.

Interview with
James M. Sipes,
May 22, 1909[1]

Far West[2] *left Yankton on p.m. May 5. Left Ft. A. Lincoln after 7th Cavalry did.* (Mr. Sipes was not an employee on the boat but was traveling on it as barber but mainly for pleasure and to see the country). *Met 7th first at point where Glendive now is. Camp at Powder River was on big flat just below mouth of Powder. At mouth of Rosebud ferried Gibbon's command to south side.*

Had pilot house fortified with boiler plate bent into semicircles on each side of it and head high with opening in front. Lower deck thus protected with sacks of grain and 4-ft. cordwood stood on end. Had to burn wood and would stop and cut driftwood. Proceeded up river slowly and did not see Gibbon's command after it started.

Went up Big Horn past mouth of Little Bighorn about 15 miles by mistake and then dropped back to mouth of Little Bighorn. In doing this ran her ashore once and struck a big cottonwood tree and split her bow open. Carpenters had to bulkhead her, and still she leaked so badly had to keep pumps working. One of Gibbon's sick soldiers on board had told us had passed mouth of Little Bighorn when

---

1. Walter Camp field notes, folder 72, BYU Library.

2. The *Far West* had been contracted for by the Department of Dakota for the campaign in 1876. It was intended that the *Far West* haul freight and soldiers. Other Missouri River steamboats were contracted later in the summer. Grant Marsh was the captain of the *Far West* in 1876, and his account is in Joseph Mills Hanson's *The Conquest of the Missouri* (Chicago: A. C. McClurg & Co., 1909 and later editions). See also Sergeant James E. Wilson's "Report of Trip of Steamer Far West Up The Big Horn River, June 24-29, 1876" in Appendix PP, *Report of the Chief of Engineers* for Fiscal Year Ending June 30, 1877, in *The Report of the Secretary of War*, 1877, Part 2, 1378-81, GPO, Washington, 1877.

we did so, and after we had gone 15 miles farther up, we began to believe him and turned back.

Was up river about a mile above boat fishing (on Tuesday morning) with Capt. Marsh and steward of boat named Riley and also I think a man named Burley.

We were fishing on left bank of Little Bighorn, and Curley rode into water on right bank just opposite us, through brush, and forded over to us. We were much surprised, and I suspect we exhibited some fear, for he held up his hands or gun and made a peace sign. Curley had three ponies and a red Sioux blanket, which he afterward told us he had taken from a dead Sioux. Said the extra ponies were stray ones which he had picked up as he had come along. He had a gun and had taken down his hair (pompadour). Might have been a carbine or Winchester — not sure.

Beds for wounded made by cutting grass. Carried 54 wounded, of whom 3 died on boat. One left at mouth Big Horn buried north bank Yellowstone (Geo. H. King). Another buried mouth Powder, probably William George, and other died near Ft. Lincoln and carried there (Bennett).[3]

On the way down with the wounded we tied up at an island just below the mouth of the Tongue to load on wood for fuel. On the way down with the wounded, the camp at Powder River was passed on July 4. Soldiers there had piled up wood for a big bonfire to celebrate, but when they heard the news, they gave up the idea.

Says Mitch Bouyer on this expedition wore a vest made of a calf skin tanned with hair on. Says James Pym[4] shot in back and killed by a "kid" cowboy in Miles City about 20 years ago.

---

3. Corporal George H. King of Company A died on July 2 on the *Far West* at Pease Bottom and was buried on the north bank of the Yellowstone River at the mouth of the Bighorn River. Private William George of Company H died on the *Far West* on July 3 and was buried on the river bank at the mouth of the Powder River. Private James C. Bennett of Company C died on July 5 and was taken to Fort A. Lincoln for burial.

4. Private James Pym of Company B was in the hilltop fight and received the Medal of Honor for obtaining water for the wounded. After his service in the cavalry he resided in Miles City, Montana, where he was killed by a young cowboy about 1890.

Interview with
Frederick E. Server,
July 17, 1910[1]

Server told me . . . that the horses of Co. F 2nd Cavalry were used to put the 7th Inf. across to west side of Little Bighorn near the mouth of that stream. On the night of June 26 the cavalry camped in the bend of the Little Bighorn where Crow Agency now is.

All the afternoon of June 26, he, Server, (First Sgt. Co. G 2nd Cavalry) and Old Crow, a Crow guide (not an enlisted scout), with Gibbon acted as left flankers, away out on the hills and in the advance of the march of the 2nd Cavalry. On evening of June 26 they saw Indians in large numbers off to east of where Crow Agency now stands and dared not go down to join command until after dark. Before dark they saw tepees still standing in the village on north and Indians around on the hills. Over to the west the Indians fired in the advance of the 2nd Cavalry, and the artillery threw a few shells after the Indians.

On the morning of June 27 he and Old Crow continued to act as left flankers, and these two were the first to discover the dead on the Custer battlefield.[2] As soon as they found the dead he wrote a note and sent it to Gen. Terry by Old Crow and Terry sent up E. W. Smith, his adjt. . . . who said: "This is awful, but where is the rest of the 7th Cavalry? This is not all of them?"

As soon as Terry was assured that not all of the 7th Cavalry were

---

1. Walter Camp field notes, folder 56, BYU Library.

2. For another account by a member of the 2nd Cavalry see John F. McBlain's "With Gibbon On The Sioux Campaign of 1876" in *The Cavalry Journal* June 1896, 9:139–48. McBlain was enlisted on October 7, 1872, to June 29, 1877, in Major Brisbin's troops in the 2nd Cavalry, and he describes the arrival of Colonel Gibbon's column on June 27 on the scene of the Little Bighorn River fight.

killed at this place he continued the march up the valley, and Server and Old Crow kept going as left flankers until they ran upon Reno's command on Reno hill. Server says Godfrey came out and met him. Server says that to the best of his recollection there were three dead on Greasy Grass hill opposite the village.

Interview with
Bernard Prevo,
February 23, 1911[1]

Is 68 years old. Was born in Germany. Served in Co. G, 2nd Missouri Light Artillery. Went among Crow Indians in 1865. In summer of 1876 was interpreter and guide for Bradley's enlisted Crow scouts.[2] He was employed by the Quartermaster and was not enlisted, commonly known as Bravo.

The Crows were put on foot by Sioux stealing their horses at Pease Bottom. Prevo had warned the Crows not to turn their horses loose at night, but they said their horses could not get fat if picketed in close to camp, and so they were in the habit of taking them farther out where the grass was better and turning them loose, and one night the Sioux slipped up and stole them. About Sioux stealing Crow horses at Ft. Pease about 6 miles below mouth of Big Horn, Prevo went to Sioux village at mouth Little Bighorn and got other horses. He went alone to Pompeys Pillar and there met wagon train coming to Gibbon, and two men from the train went with him to Crow camp.

Prevo was with Bradley on the scouting expedition when he discovered the big Sioux village on the Tongue in the spring. (Question: Was this not Crazy Horse's village?) The country all about was full of Indians hunting buffalo and other game, and they had to conceal themselves in daytime. At length they came in view of the Sioux village, and Bradley wanted to creep up on it at night and count the lodges, but Prevo says he advised him not to go closer, as they would surely be discovered.

Bradley even wanted to try to get closer in daytime, so as to try to

---

1. Walter Camp field notes, folder 22, BYU Library.

2. Lieutenant James H. Bradley was in command of the Detachment of Indian Scouts of the 7th Infantry.

get a count of the lodges. It was decided however to abandon this plan, and the party left the country. They were soon discovered by the Sioux and followed all the way to the Yellowstone in sight of Gibbon's camp. This was the time when Capt. Ball[3] drowned the horses in trying to swim the Yellowstone. Gibbon wanted to go over to fight the Sioux who had followed Bradley to the Yellowstone, and to slip up and attack their camp on the Tongue, and so Prevo always thought it was a lucky thing for the command that the horses were drowned. The Crows offered to swim the horses over, but Capt. Ball thought he knew a better way, and he tried it and drowned the horses. He had them tied in a string and headed them for the other shore by starting out in a boat with the head horse of the string. (I was told by some one else that the horses swam straight ahead until they struck the strong current, when the head horse turned to swim back and pulled the following horses under.)

When we met Custer he told me that his scouts were not familiar with that part of the country, and he therefore wanted six of the best of the Crows. Custer told Prevo to encourage these Crows by telling them that he (Custer) was commonly known as "Charge the Camp." He had cleaned up a village in the south country some years before that, and when he met the Sioux he would do the same thing, and the Crows would come in for a good share of the horses they would capture.

The night before leaving mouth of Rosebud, Mitch Bouyer[4] got drunk. Said he was going with Custer and was boasting as to how he (Bouyer) would slaughter the Sioux, etc.

On the march up the Big Horn with Gibbon and Terry they were set across the Yellowstone by the steamer and marched up to mouth of Tullock's fork and went into camp. The next day, June 25, they struck across the high and broken country between Tullock's fork and the Big Horn and that night camped on some high bluffs in a dry place and the men all day suffering much for lack of water. The next morning some officer inquired as to what river lay in sight in valley below them and some one said Little Bighorn, and he (Prevo) immediately corrected him by saying that it was the Big Horn instead of the Little Bighorn.

---

3. Captain Edward Ball, 2nd Cavalry.

4. Mitch Bouyer was killed with the Custer column on June 25. He was a half-blood Sioux interpreter for the Crow scouts attached to the 7th Cavalry on June 22. His father, Vital Bouyer, was a Frenchman, and his mother was a full-blooded Sioux.

Being badly in need of water they got down into the valley where the men could get water. The cavalry was ahead, and about 6 miles below mouth of Little Bighorn they saw horse tracks in the grass, and following a little way they saw across the Big Horn 3 Indians [and] on their own (east) side a horse that these Indians had let go in their haste to swim the river. This horse was one that had been captured from the Sioux or picked up.

Drawing closer they found these 3 Indians to be Crows, White Man Runs Him, Goes Ahead, and Hairy Moccasin. Prevo met 3 Crows about 6 miles below mouth of Little Horn, on the Big Horn. They told Prevo that Custer's and Reno's command all killed and that Half Yellow Face, White Swan, and Curley were all killed. Prevo thought that some bad luck had overtaken Custer, but was not satisfied that all were killed, so he asked the three: "How do you know the other three Crows killed, etc., and did you see them drop?" He finally concluded that they had no definite knowledge of the fighting and supposed that there had been a fight and were using that fact as an excuse to run away.

Here the cavalry halted until the infantry came up. They then hung around on the other side of the river and kept calling over and advising the other Crows not to go up to battlefield, and later in day all of the Crows turned back and went to their people who were on Pryor Creek. There had been a good deal of talk about the Crows not wishing to go up to the battlefield, and finally Lieut. Burnett, Gibbon's Adjt., told the Crows that if they were afraid to go up to the battlefield they could fall in behind. After being told this they all lit out for their own country, and Prevo followed. On the way to Pryor Creek they met a band of Crows, and supposing each other to be Sioux they had a fight for some time, but no one was hurt.

They told the relatives that Half Yellow Face, Curley, and White Swan were killed, and these relatives began to mourn and torture themselves.

These 3 Crows had cut around to the east toward Tullock's fork after leaving Custer on June 25. Gibbon was pretty wrathy because the Crows had run away from him, but Prevo told him that they had been out a long time, had become hard up for women and would be back. In a short while they returned, and additional Crows were enlisted.

Interview with
Richard E. Thompson,
February 14, 1911[1]

On way to Powder River man bitten by rattlesnake trying to pull out of hole. Dr. gave him whisky and put him in a wagon and he began to sing and got well. Col. Thompson says the men detailed to go with him went on boat and up the Big Horn.

Col. Thompson says . . . that on night of June 21, at mouth of Rosebud, a group of officers, including Custer and Benteen, sat discussing the possibilities of the campaign, and Benteen and Custer engaged in some personalities and recriminations. Benteen said that if they were to get into a fight he hoped he would be better supported than he was at the Battle of Washita. Custer then twitted Benteen of shooting an Indian boy in that battle, and Benteen went on to explain why he had to do so to defend his own life. Thompson says that the discussion of matters between Custer and Benteen . . . waxed rather warm at this time, and it was plain to be seen that Benteen hated Custer. E. B. Gibbs, 1st Lieut. 6th Inf., was aide de camp to Gen. Terry, was on field Little Bighorn June 27 and June 28. Ed. Smith, Adjt. Genl. to Gen. Terry. Hughes was aide-de-camp. Michaelis ordnance officer. Col. Thompson, Capt. Hughes 3rd Inf., Michaelis, Nowlan[2] went all over the battlefield to identify dead on June 27. These four officers went with Benteen and Co. H to Custer ridge.

End of ridge was a round hill as Roe told. It was higher than rest of ridge. Dead horses for a barricade on this hill. Tom Custer lay

1. Walter Camp field notes, folder 51, BYU Library. Richard E. Thompson was appointed second lieutenant, 6th Infantry, after graduating from the Military Academy on July 1, 1864. He was on the supply steamer *Far West* at the time of the Little Bighorn River fight. He was probably interviewed by Walter Camp at Fort Snelling, Minnesota.

2. Captain Robert P. Hughes, Captain Otho E. Michaelis, and Lieutenant Henry J. Nowlan.

nearest the peak of round hill. Col. Thompson says Tom Custer lay on his face with head all hacked up with a hatchet in face. The only way he could be identified was by initials tattooed on his arm. Says his abdomen had been cut and his bowels had come out. Dr. Lord[3] well identified by Col. R. E. Thompson and others. He lay 20 ft. southeast of Custer's body on side hill. Lord had on a blue shirt and lay near Custer. Only about 20 ft. from him. Identified Lord's body for sure. Where each officer buried a piece of tepee pole was driven in ground at his head and the name of officer marked thereon.

Verifies the fact that only 9 or 10 men between gully and Custer. Says many bodies in gully — thinks 34. Says Mark Kellogg[4] lay 3/4 mile from Custer down near river on side hill about 100 yds. from river. Was identified by peculiar shaped boots that he wore.

Found Porter's coat with 2 bullets through it and next Sturgis[5] drawers all bloody. This was in village in a.m. June 27 before Bradley had reported finding Custer. Counted 1,900 lodges and wickiups in village. 3 tepees in village. 11 dead Indians in one. 8 dead Indians in another. 3 dead Indians in another. All finely dressed.

Col. Thompson says he saw Hodgson's[6] body lying at top of bank of river, perhaps 20 ft. from water. Query: was not Hodgson's body buried night of June 26? How therefore could Thompson have seen it, as he did not arrive until June 27? Thompson says that he personally saw Nathan Short's horse and carbine but not body of man. They lay in some brush near Rosebud and Yellowstone, and at the time it was supposed that this man had escaped from the Custer fight. He cannot account for the fact that others saw the man's body. It is possible that by the time Thompson saw the horse, the remains of the man had been buried. Col. Thompson sent sketch of Custer battlefield to Harpers in 1876 and wrote supplement in Phil Sheridan's book about Custer fight.

---

3. Dr. George Edwin Lord was the assistant surgeon killed with the Custer column. Reno's and other reports indicated that Lord's remains were not identified after the fight. A typescript copy of Dr. Lord's last letter to his wife prior to his death is in the Benteen-Goldin letters in the Dustin Collection, Custer Battlefield National Monument.

4. Marcus Henry Kellogg, reporter for *The Bismarck Tribune* (Dakota) and the *New York Herald*.

5. Lieutenant James E. Porter of Company I and Lieutenant James G. Sturgis of Company M.

6. Lieutenant Benjamin H. Hodgson of Company B, who was killed in the retreat from the valley fight, was buried by Captain McDougall on the night of June 26.

Interview with
Charles F. Roe,
December 8, 1910[1]

Old Crow was along with Gibbon's command and guided the column up the Big Horn in the dark. Roe does not know whether he was a guide employed by the quartermaster or just a camp follower. Bradley's mounted detachment[2] was for scouting purposes.

Roe thinks that Custer's object in sending Benteen to left from divide was to keep Benteen out of the fight, as Benteen had the advance and should regularly have been with headquarters. This is the opinion of Benteen's friends, so Roe says. I (WMC.) think their view will bear criticism. Still Custer sent no surgeon with Benteen.

Roe says that when Terry came up on morning of June 27 the first thing Benteen said was to ask Gen. Terry if he knew where Custer had gone. Terry said: "To the best of my knowledge and belief he lies on this ridge about 4 miles below here with all of his command killed." Benteen said: "I can hardly believe it. I think he is somewhere down the Big Horn grazing his horses. At the Battle of the Washita he went off and left part of his command, and I think he would do it again." Gen. Terry said: "I think you are mistaken, and you will take your company and go down where the dead are lying and investigate for

---

1. Walter Camp field notes, folders 43 and 46, BYU Library. Charles F. Roe was a second lieutenant and regimental adjutant of the 2nd Cavalry in Colonel John Gibbon's Montana column. He was on the battlefield on June 27. He resigned from the service on January 31, 1888. During the Spanish-American War he was a brigadier general of volunteers. His account "Custer Battlefield Monument" appeared in *The Army and Navy Journal*, September 17, 1881, 19:7, 145, and contains a description of the erection of the battle monument. *Custer's Last Battle, Narrative of the Tragedy of the Little Bighorn* was published in 1927 in New York by Robert Bruce, Nat'l. Highway Association.

2. Lieutenant James H. Bradley had a detachment of the 7th Infantry mounted on mules for scouting duty.

yourself." Benteen did this, Capt. Weir going along. When Benteen came back he was pale, and looked troubled and said: "We found them, but I did not expect that we would."

The 2nd Cav. and 7th Inf. buried McIntosh and some of the soldiers killed with Reno in the bottom.

Mitch Bouyer's body was found west or northwest where the monument stands on flat ground near the river and the timber line. About where Herendeen and I ate dinner and packed up. Roe did not see Bouyer's body but at the time believed the report about finding it, as Bouyer[3] was known to Gibbon's command very well.

When buried remains around monument, did ridge rise to peak, and was wide level place formed at monument? *No, the ridge was level originally.* Had any grading been done when remains buried in 1878? *No.*

To settle the report about 20 men getting away from the battle-field and being killed over toward the Rosebud, Roe took a troop of cavalry and deployed them at a suitable interval and marched them all the way to the mountain and found nothing.

Gen. Roe states very positively that none of the remains of the enlisted men were gathered up and buried on the ridge in the trenches around the monument until after the monument was erected in 1881. He then gathered remains from all around the country. Many or most of the bones were out of the graves and scattered about. There was no reasonable certain way of counting them. (In fact it is known that he did not get them all, because Grover took up some of them on Reno's battlefield on hill years later.) Some hay cutters up from Ft. Custer had disturbed some of the remains a good deal, putting skulls on stakes, etc.

While lying in camp on north side of Yellowstone opposite mouth of Rosebud in August 1876, it was reported in Gibbon's camp that the body of a cavalry soldier and his horse were found on south side of

---

3. Did Mitch Bouyer go with Reno on his scout, and how did he get there? Did he go back with Terry on boat to Powder? Roe says does not think Bouyer went with Reno on scout. In his address he says Bouyer's body was found near the river badly mutilated. Says was found on flat between cemetery and Crow Agency about ¾ mile from battlefield. When disinterments were made, were there any bodies on village hill? Or in village at Ford B? *No, none in either place.* Who personally discovered Custer's dead? Was it Bradley and who with him? How many mounted men of 7th Inf. had he? *Bradley and 12 mounted men discovered Custer's dead.* The night before Roe had seen what he took to be dead buffalo, and at Roe's suggestion next morning Bradley went up there.

(Walter Camp field notes, folder 43, BYU Library.)

Yellowstone, not far from that stream and not far from Rosebud. At the time no one seemed to doubt the story, and it was commonly supposed to have been the remains of a man escaped from the Custer fight. (Try the scale and see what the direct distance. Probably 80 or 85 miles.) The bodies of the two soldiers[4] of Gibbon's[5] killed over there in the spring while hunting for antelope had been recovered by a troop of cavalry at the time.

---

4. Three men from the 2nd Cavalry, privates Stoker and Raymier of Company H, and James Quinn, a civilian, were killed by Indians on May 23, 1876, while hunting.

5. "Report of Colonel John Gibbon To General Terry, October 17, 1876, Ft. Shaw, Montana," is found in the War Department's *Annual Report,* 1876, 471–76 and in Executive Document No. 1, Part 2, House of Rep. 44th Cong. 2nd Session, GPO, Wash., 1877. "Last Summer's Expedition Against the Sioux and Its Great Catastrophe" is found in *The American Catholic Qtrly Review,* April 1877, 2:271–304, and is concluded in October 1877 as "Hunting Sitting Bull," 665–94. This is Colonel Gibbon's story of the march of the Montana column, written from his diary. Reprinted in part as "Red Men" in *Hunter-Trader Trapper* Magazine, June 1933. The message from Colonel Gibbon, June 28, 1876, to Major Daniel Benham at Ft. Ellis appeared in the *Billings Times* (Montana), July 22, 1902, and was reprinted as "Recent Newspaper Items Concerning Custer's Last Battle" in *Contributions* to the Montana Historical Society, 1903, 4:284–86, Independent Publications Co., Helena.

Interview with
Major Sam'l Burkhardt, Jr.
January 16, 1913[1]

Says that when put up markers in 1890 not all of the remains on Custer ridge had been buried. They put up no markers on Reno's battlefield except for McIntosh and DeWolf. They identified some of Lord's remains by distinctive buttons that surgeons wore and placed Lord's marker there. They found a stake marked Mark Kellogg[2] on back side of ridge, where tombstone is now but put up no marker or tombstone at that time, because none had been furnished.

They erected 249 markers on Custer ridge,[3] but does not recall whether any of these were wooden. They put no markers in Crazy

---

1. Camp MSS, field notes, unclassified envelope 64, Lilly Library.

2. A story of Mark Kellogg appeared in the *New York Herald* July 9, 1876, as "The Dead *Herald* Correspondent." A letter by Kellogg dated June 21, 1876, appeared in the *Herald* July 11, 1876, as "Mr. Kellogg's Last Letters," and the July 12 issue of the *Herald* had "Mark Kellogg." His notes were found on the battlefield after the fight, were brought on the steamer *Far West* with the wounded, and were given to J. P. Dunn in Bismarck. The original notes were on scratch paper. The notes from June 9 to 25 were presumably lost. A typescript of the notes is in the Montana State Historical Society Library. "Notes May 17 to June 9, 1876, on the Little Big Horn Expedition under Gen. Custer" appeared in *Contributions* to the Historical Society of Montana 1923, 9:213–25. His diary is also in the *Bismarck Tribune* August 13, 1939, as "His Presumed Diary" and in Jessamine Slaughter Burgum's *Zezula Or Pioneer Days in the Smoky Water Country*, Valley City, N.D., and in John Hixon's *Custer's Mysterious Mr. Kellogg And The Diary of Mark Kellogg*, reprinted from *North Dakota History* Magazine July 1950, 17:3 Hist. Soc., Bismarck, N.D.

3. The following is an excerpt from an attachment to a letter from C. C. Walcutt, War Department, Office of the Quartermaster General, Washington, May 29, 1909, to Walter Camp:

On June 28, 1876, the remains of the killed were buried temporarily where they lay. In what year were these remains disinterred and buried permanently in the trench surrounding the four sides of the plat where the monument now stands? *These remains were reinterred in*

Horse ravine. In identifying graves they went by stakes, excavations, fragments of bones, etc. (as far as I could find they went mainly by guess). They did not find any bodies over cutbank north of Ford B.

Says Brisbin did not come on the ground while they were erecting markers, but he was at Ft. Custer at the time and told them many times about the appearance of the battlefield in June 1876. Brisbin told about finding where a body had been burned in the Cheyenne village, but the body was not seen there June 27, 1876. Major Burkhardt says James A. Campbell died at Ft. Snelling about 1894. Family lives in Brooklyn. Major Brisbin was commonly known in the army as "Grasshopper Jim."

---

the trenches in 1878. In what year were the remains of the officers removed from the battlefield? *In 1877.* In what year or years were the marble markers placed to locate the points where the dead were found after the battle? *In 1886.* In what year was the monument erected? *In 1884.* A photograph taken in 1886 shows the monument mutilated by several large pieces of stone broken from the corners. I am told unofficially that these mutilations were removed by sending stone cutters who dressed down each of the four sides of the monument about three inches in depth and then recut the names and inscriptions on the monument. The monument now appears without any of these mutilations. Is the statement concerning the work of recutting correct, and when was it done? *The statement of mutilation is correct. The monument was recut in 1888.* The monument now stands on a level piece of ground on top of the ridge, said level plat being about 150 feet wide. Veterans who assisted in burying the dead there on June 28, 1876, say that the top of the ridge at that time was much narrower, and that only a small level place then existed. An old-time photograph also shows such to have been the case. Apparently the top or peak of the ridge has been graded down at some time, and the grading operations must have been rather extensive. Do the records of your office show such to have been the case? and when was the work carried out? Are there any data as to the extent of grading at this point? *The records afford no information regarding this grading, but it is probable that it was done at the time the monument was erected or when the trenches were dug around the plot on which the monument stands.*

(In Walter Camp Collection, folder 6, box 4, BYU Library.)

Interview with
Herbert J. Slocum,
January 23, 1920[1]

Col. Slocum told me . . . that the trip to battlefield of Little Bighorn on 10th anniversary, June 1886, was organized by him, and he
had charge of the arrangements all through, including the matter of
taking Gall along. Says he was talking the matter over with Gall all the
previous winter.

When got to Ft. Custer the officers there arranged royal hospi-
tality for them. Capt. Frank D. Baldwin, with a Co. of 5th Inf. went
with them and camped on bottom, under the battlefield, with tents
and everything needed for their convenience and comfort, including
whisky, and Benteen and McDougall and plenty of others got drunk.
They camped there a week and had a royal time. There were several
newspaper correspondents along. Slocum tried to prevent them going,
but they went anyhow, but let Slocum revise their stories which they
reported.

Says that when they got to the battlefield Gall had no idea where
Gen. Custer had been killed. Told them that at time of the battle they
(the Sioux) had no idea they were fighting Long Hair; supposed they
were fighting Crook.

Corporal Foley: Gall showed them where the lone soldier rode
away, pursued by several Indians, and finally shot himself and fell off
the horse. It corroborates my information about Corpl. Foley, as told
me by Turtle Rib. Gall told them this soldier had chevrons on his
sleeve.

---

1. Walter Camp field notes, folder 92, BYU Library. Herbert J. Slocum
graduated from the Military Academy on June 22, 1876, and was transferred to
the 7th Cavalry effective July 28 that year.

★

Terry's
Order

After a conference on June 21
on the supply steamboat,
the *Far West,* at the camp
near the mouth of Rosebud Creek,
General Alfred Terry issued
orders to Colonel John Gibbon
and Lieutenant Colonel George Custer.
In the order given to Custer
(see following letter), Terry imparted
his suggestions regarding Custer's
movement toward the Little Bighorn
in the following days. The order
from Terry to Custer has generated,
and continues to generate, considerable
controversy as to whether Custer
disobeyed either the order or
the spirit of the order.
Following the letter here, Walter Camp
examines the order and brings out a
number of salient arguments
upholding Custer's actions.

Letter from General Terry to Custer

Headquarters Department of Dakota
(In the Field)

Camp at Mouth of Rosebud River
Montana, June 22, 1876

Lieut. Col. G. A. Custer, 7th Cavalry
Colonel:

The Brigadier-General Commanding directs that, as soon as your regiment can be made ready for the march, you proceed up the Rosebud in pursuit of the Indians whose trail was discovered by Major Reno a few days since. It is, of course, impossible to give you any definite instructions in regard to this movement; and were it not impossible to do so, the Department Commander places too much confidence in your zeal, energy and ability to wish to impose upon you precise orders which might hamper your action when nearly in contact with the enemy. He will, however, indicate to you his own views of what your actions should be and he desires that you should conform to them unless you shall see sufficient reason for departing from them. He thinks that you should proceed up the Rosebud until you ascertain definitely the direction in which the trail above spoken of leads. Should it be found (as it appears to be almost certain that it will be found) to turn toward the Little Horn, he thinks that you should still proceed southward, perhaps as far as the headwaters of the Tongue, and then turn toward the Little Horn, feeling constantly, however, to your left, so as to preclude the possibility of the escape of the Indians to the south or southeast by passing around your left flank.

The column of Colonel Gibbon is now in motion for the mouth of the Big Horn. As soon as it reaches that point it will cross the Yellowstone and move up at least as far as the forks of the Big and Little Horns. Of course, its future movements must be controlled by circumstances as they arise: but it is hoped that the Indians, if upon the Little Horn, may be so nearly enclosed by the two columns that their escape will be impossible. The Department Commander desires that on your way up the Rosebud you should thoroughly examine the upper part of Tullock's Creek; and that you should endeavor to send a scout through to Colonel Gibbon's Column with information of the result of your examination. The lower part of this creek will be examined by a detachment from Colonel Gibbon's command.

The supply steamer will be pushed up the Big Horn as far as the forks, if the river is found to be navigable for that distance; and the Department Commander (who will accompany the Column of Colonel Gibbon) desires you to report to him not later than the expiration of the time for which your troops are rationed, unless in the meantime you receive further orders.

Very Respectfully,
Your Obedient Servant
Ed W. Smith, Captain, 18th Infantry
Acting Assistant Adjutant General

Terry's Order[1]

The question as to whether or not Custer disobeyed Terry's order must necessarily be answered on the basis of opinion, and as I have given much study to this particular phase and have discussed it with many men of long military experience, I desire to record my opinion.

Terry's suggestions in the written order were of the nature of advice but not peremptory. Did it say to Custer "You must hold aloof from the Indians until I get up"? No, it was nothing definite on this point. This was only [a] formal part of Custer's instructions, and it did not forbid him to attack the Indians. What may have passed between the two by conversation we do not know. A single remark dropped verbally might have put the written order in an entirely different light with Custer.

Gen. Terry was in a rather different situation, and I regard his order as the most logical one under the circumstances. Terry could not have anticipated what Custer would do if he would get into close proximity to Indians, but when such should occur he (Custer) would be too far from the commander of the expedition to communicate and arrange plans. Terry must then place upon Custer the responsibility for whatever action he would take without consulting his superior officer. Terry's offer to give Custer four more troops of cavalry and the suggestion to take the artillery along I regard as evidence that Terry was forecasting the eventualities. Considering the amount of foresight possible at the time, Gen. Terry undoubtedly did the proper thing, and Custer was no doubt the man of all men to send on such a daring expedition. Terry therefore says, go and do what you think best, but if you find my idea of the campaign impractical you take the responsibility for varying from it.

---

1. Walter Camp field notes, folders 29, 100 and 107, BYU Library.

There is little doubt in my mind but that both Terry and Gibbon expected Custer to attack. I do not think Terry expected anything else than that Custer would attack the Indians before he would get up, else why did he offer him the four troops of 2nd Cavalry, which would have left Gibbon with only a small force and no cavalry. The wording of the order was not inconsistent with this idea, but it was discreet, putting upon Custer the responsibility in case he did attack.

Had Custer gone to the headwaters of the Tongue, as suggested in Terry's order, he would have been delayed three or four days in striking the village, and Terry would have got there first.

Had Custer lain on the divide all day of the 25th he undoubtedly would have found himself surrounded by Indians at daylight the next morning, out of reach of any assistance from Terry. Had he gone around to the south instead of following the trail over the divide, the Indians would undoubtedly have gone up the Little Bighorn 30 or 40 miles to meet him, as they did Crook on the Rosebud the week before, and he would have had the whole encampment to fight, too far away from Terry to get any assistance. The village, being on the alert, with scouts watching the valley to the north, would have taken care of itself and moved out of the way in ample time, as it finally did when Terry approached.

As the Indians had fought Crook and had then withdrawn, they knew he was to the south of them and were undoubtedly alert in that direction. As they knew of the column [Gibbon's] on the Yellowstone, they were watching in that direction. It seems that Custer moved upon them from the direction the least expected and it shows his good judgment in deciding how to find them. He did not intend to lose sight of the trail, whatever investigations he would make to the south. All these things should be borne in mind in keeping with the fact that both Custer and Terry thought Custer had enough men to handle the Indians.

As to investigating the Tullock's Creek region mentioned in the order, Custer no doubt intended to do this on June 25, as his scouts could not very well do so until after crossing the divide. After crossing the divide and finding he was discovered and that he must press on to prevent the escape of the Indians, as he then thought was imminent, he undoubtedly thought there was no time to scout the headwaters of Tullock's fork and wait to learn the result. As no trail led that way he probably thought it his duty to press on as fast as possible.

Up to the time that Custer's presence was discovered by the Sioux I cannot see that he disobeyed either the letter or the intention of

Terry's order; after that point of time I think Custer simply exercised the discretion which the order permitted, with every desire to assume the responsibility. The Indians had discovered Custer's command before he knew definitely where the trail had gone. Let this fact not be overlooked by those who seek to show that Custer disobeyed orders.

Now about continuing on to the south after learning which way the trail went. Was he to do this east or west of the divide? Had he done so east of the divide he would have had to leave sight of the trail entirely and make a long circuit before striking it again on other side of the divide. In keeping to the trail, Custer undoubtedly saw "sufficient reasons for departing from" Terry's views. Had Custer's command come out victorious, it is not likely that his failure to follow Terry's suggestion in every detail would ever have been heard of publicly.

It is clear that Custer intended to keep to the trail himself and do his feeling to the south with a detachment. The complaint which Benteen made of his valley hunting tour was therefore not Custer's personal idea but following out Terry's suggestion. In my way of thinking this suggestion of Terry's was what, more than anything else, was the cause of Custer's fatal mistake in dividing his command too minutely. It is doubtful but for this whether he would have sent Benteen where he did. Had Benteen been up and gone in with Reno there certainly would have been no precipitate flight out of the valley when the Indians appeared in force, and Custer and his five companies would not have had the whole force of warriors to contend with. I regard Terry's suggestions in the order as very unfortunate for Custer, for had he not been hampered with a desire to follow these, he would undoubtedly have had his command better in hand when he found the village.

Now as to the meeting at the mouth of the Little Bighorn at noon of the 26th, there was no written statement about this. The order contains nothing whatever that is definite as to the meeting except that Custer should report to Terry on the Big Horn in 15 days at the latest, which would have been July 7. If anything was said about the two commands meeting on June 26, it was verbal, which implies that other things might have passed verbally.

Had Custer lain concealed near the top of the divide all day, the 25th, as he had intended to do early in the morning, he would have struck the village on the early morning of the 26th. Terry, however, could not have reached them by the 26th. The best his cavalry could do was to get [about 8] miles from there at 9:00 p.m. of the 26th with his cavalry, with the infantry a good ways behind, and they had Indians in their front nearly all the way from the mouth of the Big Horn (showing that the Indians were alert for any approach by way of the valley. They probably did not expect soldiers to approach from the divide toward the Rosebud), showing how impracticable it was to close in upon an Indian camp with two columns.

Custer's justification for attacking when he did was the discovery of his command by two parties of Indians in broad daylight, and the fact that the village was not warned much in advance of Custer's appearance shows that Custer's men traveled nearly as fast toward the village as did the Sioux scouts. . . . It was too much to expect that two widely separated columns could converge on the camp simultaneously. It would hardly occur that they could time themselves closely enough to approach at the same instant, and to attack at the same time, one would have to come within striking distance and wait for the other to come up; this was exactly what Custer did, and saw, or at least, feared, and reasonably so, that the plan would not work. About the best that could have been expected of such a plan would have been for one column to attack as soon as opportunity offered and the other column, as a precaution, would be on hand to head off or disperse the fleeing foe and help take care of the wounded.

It must be considered that the campaign was an Indian hunt, and Custer rightly thought that the best plan was to strike the Indians in their village and break them up. . . . I think his only mistake, considering the knowledge he had of the Indians, was in planning to attack the village in detail instead of in one body with all available men besides those necessary to take care of the pack train. The question as to whether Custer was to attack or not, the order was left to Custer's judgment. Custer used his judgment. How then did he disobey? At the most he could have been charged with nothing more than bad judgment — never with disobedience.

Of course Terry could not give Custer full swing and still take the responsibility, so he worded his order to correspond to that idea. To me the order seems to convey the following instructions: Custer, go ahead, use your best judgment. I think you had better do so and so, but if you think best, you may do differently, and, of course, you take the responsibility.

As the order gave Custer the discretion to attack the Indians, there was at least no technical disobedience of them. As to obeying or disobeying the spirit of the order, I have found no convincing proof either way. Terry, of course, wished to go on record with a written order, and that order did not forbid Custer to attack. It reads to me just as though Terry wished to fix matters so that if Custer attacked before Gibbon's column got up, he must do it upon his own responsibility and merely that. The definite part of the order imposes upon Custer only the responsibility of taking such a route that the Indians must be between Custer and Terry — that is, not to let them escape to the southward. Bearing in mind the fact that both Terry and Custer estimated the number of the Indians at no larger force than Custer alone could handle, and that the elusive character of the Indians was one of the chief considerations on which the success or failure of the expedition depended, Terry very wisely made it optional with Custer as to whether or not he should attack. Suppose Terry had forbidden Custer to attack and that when he found the village, the Indians had started to move and had got away. The responsibility for the escape would then rest upon Terry.

In my mind Terry's orders simply put upon Custer the responsibility for attack in case he would do so. Having given Custer the discretion to attack in case he saw good reason, Custer would have been blamable in case he had found a smaller village than he did and let it get away. Terry was a lawyer as well as a soldier, and this order was so drawn that Custer, in case Indians did escape, would have been charged with responsibility whether he attacked or not. Now, as Custer's relations with the President were strained, he has been accused of rash behavior in an effort to do something big and glittering to retrieve himself. Now let us look at this phase of the matter in another light. Suppose that, Custer being under odium in certain places, the Indians had moved out and got away. What effect, may I ask, would that have had on Custer's standing, under the circumstances? Does not this put the matter in a little different light, and can any fair-minded person blame Custer for some solicitude as to results of the expedition that would not have been in view had the status of Custer before the public been different from what it then was?

In re Custer's obeying the spirit of Terry's order, may not a single verbal remark of Terry's after the promulgation of the written order have assured Custer that he had full discretion etc.? If Custer had defeated the Indians, would he not have received great praise for acting on his own initiative? Oh, if the dead could only speak but once!

Appendixes

White Bull's List of Twenty-six Indians Killed

Medals of Honor Awarded

Muster Rolls of 7th U.S. Cavalry

Detachment of Indian Scouts

Boy Chief's List of Indian Scouts

Beauchamp's Names of Indian Scouts

Detachment of Indian Scouts, 7th Infantry

White Bull's List of 26 Indians Killed in Custer Fight

Long Road: *Chauku Haysha*	Sans Arc	Reno hilltop fight
Dog's Backbone: *Sunku Chan Koha*	Minneconjou	Reno hilltop fight
White Eagle: *Wambli Sha*	Ogalalla	Reno fight up bluffs
Elk Standing High: *Hehcahca Waykal Noziu*	Sans Arc	Reno fight up bluffs
Three Bears: *Mato Yanuni*	Minneconjou	Valley fight
Dog With Horns: *Sunka Heton*	Minneconjou	Valley fight
Flying Charge: *Kinyan Kuwapi*	Silig Sappa	Valley fight
Bear With Horns: *Mato Heton*	Hunkpapa	Valley fight
Swift Bear: *Mato Oheonko*	Hunkpapa	Valley fight
White Bull: *Tatanka Ska*	Hunkpapa	Valley fight
One Dog: *Shunka Wanzila*	Sans Arc	Custer fight
Bear Elk: *Mato Hehcahca*	Sans Arc	Custer fight
Cloud Man: *Mahcpiye Wicharta*	Sans Arc	Custer fight
Killed: *Ktepila*	Sans Arc	Custer fight
Rectum: *Toyzopsake*	Hunkpapa	Custer fight
Young Skunk: *Maka Chin Challa*	Ogalalla	Custer fight
Plenty Lice: *Tahea Ota*	Ogalalla	Custer fight
Bad Yellow Hair: *Pelim Zhi Ghicha*	Ogalalla	Custer fight
Left Hand: *Chatka*	Cheyenne	Custer fight
Has Sorrel Horse: *Snunki Sha Yulia*	Cheyenne	Custer fight
Young Bear: *Mato Chin Challa*	Cheyenne	Custer fight
Flying By: *Kiu Yan Hiyaye*	Cheyenne	Custer fight
Full Beard: *Putiyhi Shina*	Cheyenne	Custer fight
Black Coyote: *Shungomanitu Sopa*	Cheyenne	Custer fight
Swift Cloud: *Mahepiya Oheouka*	Cheyenne	Custer fight
Deed or Act: *Wichoka*	Sans Arc	Killed at a distance from Custer fight.*

About 1892 or before, White Bull went to all tribes and got names of [Indians] killed. Took great pains to get it correct. Wrote it down in a book which I saw.

*Thinks killed by Custer's command as it went along.

Editor's note: This list of Indians killed in the Little Bighorn River fight was compiled by White Bull, a prominent member of the Sioux tribe. In the 1890s and perhaps earlier, White Bull recorded these names that he obtained in conversations with members of other tribes. The number of Indians he listed is less than the usual number given in studies by white men and Indians, but it is the first such list to come to light. In "How Many Indians Were Killed?" in *American West*, July, 1973,X:4, Don Russell uses Stanley Vestal's figure of twenty-six. Major Reno reported that he saw eighteen bodies, but he assumed many more had been killed.

Medals of Honor Awarded in the
Little Bighorn River Fight

Individual	Rank & Co.	Date	Citation
Otto Voit	Pvt. Co. H	10/5/1878	Bravery in Action
Benj. C. Criswell	Sgt. Co. B	10/5/1878	Brought up ammunition
Henry Holden	Pvt. Co. D	10/5/1878	Brought up ammunition
Thomas Murray	Sgt. Co. B	10/5/1878	Brought up pack train
Richard P. Hanley	Sgt. Co. C	10/5/1878	Recaptured pack mule
Chas. Cunningham	Pvt. Co. B	10/5/1878	Continued firing though wounded
Henry W. B. Mechlin	Bks.* Co. H		Sharpshooter for water party
Charles Windolph	Pvt. Co. H	10/5/1878	Sharpshooter for water party
George Geiger	Sgt. Co. H	10/5/1878	Sharpshooter for water party
James Pym	Pvt. Co. B	10/5/1878	Brought water under fire
Neil Bancroft	Pvt. Co. A	10/5/1878	Brought water to wounded
Abram B. Brant	Pvt. Co. D	10/5/1878	Brought water to wounded
Thomas J. Callan	Pvt. Co. B	10/24/1896	Brought water to wounded
Frederick Deetline	Bks.* Co. C	10/5/1878	Brought water to wounded
Theodore W. Goldin	Pvt. Co. G	12/21/1895	Brought water to wounded
David W. Harris	Pvt. Co. A	10/5/1878	Brought water to wounded
William M. Harris	Pvt. Co. D	10/5/1878	Brought water to wounded
Rufus D. Hutchinson	Sgt. Co. B	10/5/1878	Brought water to wounded
Stanislas Roy	Sgt. Co. A	10/5/1878	Brought water to wounded
George D. Scott	Pvt. Co. D	10/5/1878	Brought water to wounded
Thomas W. Stivers	Pvt. Co. D	10/5/1878	Brought water to wounded
Peter Thompson	Pvt. Co. C	10/5/1878	Brought water to wounded
Frank Tolan	Pvt. Co. D	10/5/1878	Brought water to wounded
Charles H. Welch	Pvt. Co. D	10/5/1878	Brought water to wounded

*Blacksmith

Editor's note: The list of those in the Custer battle who received the Medal of Honor award is significant in the number of awards for a single fight. Perhaps no other engagement in American history resulted in a greater number of Medals of Honor. The criteria for award in the Indian wars period, of course, were much less stringent than the criteria used since World War I.

Muster Rolls of 7th U.S. Cavalry, June 25, 1876

Headquarters

Lieutenant Colonel
George A. Custer
Major
Marcus A. Reno
First Lieutenant
William W. Cooke
Quartermaster Sergeant
Thomas Cansby
Saddler Sergeant
John G. Tritten
Commissary Sergeant
Charles Brown
Chief Musician
Felix Vinatieri
Veterinary Surgeon
C. A. Stein
Chief Trumpeter
Henry Voss
Sergeant Major
William H. Sharrow

Band

Privates
Otto Arndt
Conrad Baumbach
Benjamin Beck
Edmond Burlis
Andrew Carter
Joseph Carroll
Peter Eisenberger
Jacob Emerich
Julius Griesner
Julius Jungesbluth
Joseph Kneubuhler
Frank Lombard
George A. Merritt
Bernard O'Neill
George Rudolph
Thomas Sherborn

Guides

Boston Custer
Charles Reynolds
Bloody Knife
Mitchel Bouyer
George Herendeen

Interpreters

F. F. Gerard
Isaiah Dorman

Packers

J. C. Wagner
Chris Loeser
William Lawless
John Fretts
E. L. Moore
William Alexander
H. McBratney
Moses E. Flint
John Lamplough
B. F. Churchill
Frank C. Mann

Editor's note: Rosters of the 7th Cavalry have been published repeatedly in specialized books on the Little Bighorn River fight. Probably no two rosters have been identical. Walter Camp developed his rosters from his interviews and included some of the recruits who joined the regiment after June 1876 and were known as the "Custer Avengers."

Company A

Captain	*Saddler*	Samuel Johnson
Myles Moylan	John Muering	Emil O. Jonson
2nd Lieutenant	*Privates*	Dennis Kerr
Charles A. Varnum	Charles Aller	William McClurg
1st Sergeant	John E. Armstrong	James McDonald
William Heyn	Neil Bancroft	William Moody
Sergeants	Louis Baumgartner	William D. Nugent
Samuel Alcott	Wilbur F. Blair	George W. Proctor
Ferdinand A. Culbertson	Thomas Blake	John S. Ragsdale
John T. Easley	August Bockerman	Francis M. Reeves
Henry Fehler	George A. Bott	Richard Rollins
George M. McDermott	Benjamin F. Burdick	Thomas Seayers
Corporals	Andrew Conner	Anton Siebelder
James Dalious	Cornelius Cowley	Elijah T. Strode
George H. King	Jacob Deihle	John Sullivan
Stanislas Roy	James Drinan	Thomas P. Sweetzer
Trumpeters	Otto Durselew	William O. Taylor
William G. Hardy	Samuel J. Foster	Howard H. Weaver
David McVeigh	John W. Franklin	John Weiss
Farrier	John M. Gilbert	
John Bringes	David W. Harris	
Blacksmith	Frederick Holmstead	
Andrew Hamilton	Stanton Hook	

Company B

Captain
Thomas McDougall
2nd Lieutenant
Benjamin H. Hodgson
1st Sergeant
James Hill
Sergeants
Daniel Carroll
Benjamin C. Criswell
Peter Gannon
Rufus D. Hutchinson
Thomas Murray
Corporals
Charles Cunningham
James Dougherty
William M. Smith
Adam Wetzel
Trumpeters
John Connell
James Kelley
Blacksmith
John Crump
Farrier
James E. Moore
Saddler
John A. Bailey

Privates
James A. Abos
Peter O. Barry
James F. Barsantee
William Boam
Hugh Bonner
Ansgarius Boren
George Brainard
James Brown
Charles Burns
James Callan
Thomas J. Callan
William M. Caldwell
Charles A. Campbell
John J. Carey
Thomas Carmody
Frank Clark
Thomas W. Coleman
Harry Criswell
Michael Crowe
Patrick Crowley
William H. Davenport
Louis De Tourriel
Augustus L. Devoto
Jacob W. Doll
Richard B. Dorn
William Frank
Frederick H. Gerhman
John Gray

John J. Keefe
Ferdinand Klavoistter
David W. Lewis
John L. Littlefield
William Martin
George B. Mask
John McCabe
Bernard McGurn
Terence McLaughlin
William McMasters
William E. Morrow
Thomas O'Brien
James O'Neill
John O'Neill
James Pym
George F. Randall
Stephen L. Ryan
Hiram W. Sager
Patrick Simons
Daniel Shea
Philipp Spinner
Edward Stout
James Thomas
Henry L. Tinkham
William Trumble
Richard A. Wallace
Edwin B. Wight
Aaron Woods

Company C

1st Sergeant	*Blacksmith*	Thomas McCreedy
Edwin Bobo	John King	John McGuire
Sergeants	*Privates*	Ottocar Nitsche
Joseph Boerger	Fred E. Allan	Charles M. Orr
George August Finckle	Herbert Arnold	Edgar Phillips
Jeremiah Finley	James C. Bennett	John Rauter
Richard P. Hanley	John Brennan	Edward Rix
Daniel A. Knipe	John Brightfield	James H. Russell
Edwin Miller	Thomas J. Bucknell	Daniel Ryan
Corporals	John Corcoran	Ludwick St. John
William Brandle	Christopher Criddle	Samuel Shade
Charles A. Crandall	George Eiseman	Jeremiah Shea
Morris Farrar	Frank Ellison	Nathan Short
John Foley	Gustave Engle	Ignatz Stungwitz
Henry E. French	James Farrand	Alpheus Stuart
Trumpeters	Isaac Fowler	John Thadus
William Kramer	Patrick Griffin	Peter Thompson
John Lewis	James Hathersall	Garrett Van Allen
Farrier	John Jordan	Oscar T. Warner
John Fitzgerald	William Kane	James Watson
Wagoner	John Mahoney	Alfred Whittaker
Frank Stark	Frederick Meier	Willis B. Wright
Saddler	August Meyer	Henry Wyman
George Howell	Martin Mullin	

Company D

Captain
Thomas B. Weir
2nd Lieutenant
Winfield S. Edgerly
1st Sergeant
Michael Martin
Sergeants
James Flanagan
Thomas W. Harrison
Thomas Morton
Thomas Russell
Corporals
Albert J. Cunningham
George W. Wylie
Trumpeter
Aloys Bohner
Farrier
Vincent Charley
Saddler
John Myers
Blacksmith
Frederick Deetline
Privates
James H. Alberts
John B. Ascough
Abram B. Brant

Thomas Conlan
Stephen Cowley
Thomas Cox
George Dann
David E. Dawsey
John J. Fay
Harvey A. Fox
John Fox
Patrick Golden
John Green
Joseph H. Green
John Hager
Curtis Hall
Edward Hall
William Hardden
Gustav Harlfinger
James Harris
William M. Harris
Jacob Hetler
Henry Holden
George Horn
Charles H. Houghtaling
Edward Housen
George Hunt
James Hurd
John Kanavagh

John Keller
Fremont Kipp
Joseph Kretchmer
Jesse Kuehl
Uriah S. Lewis
Patrick McDonnell
David Manning
William A. Marshall
John Meadwell
William Mueller
William O'Mann
John Quinn
William J. Randall
Elwyn S. Reid
William Sadler
Charles Sanders
George Scott
John J. Sims
Henry G. Smith
William E. Smith
Thomas W. Stivers
Frank Tolan
Charles H. Welch
James Wynn

Company E

1st Lieutenant
A. E. Smith
2nd Lieutenant
James G. Sturgis
1st Sergeant
Frederick Hohmeyer
Sergeants
William B. James
Lawrence Murphy
John G. Ogden
James Riley
John S. Wells
Corporals
George C. Brown
Thomas Hagan
Henry S. Mason
Albert H. Meyer
Trumpeters
Thomas McElroy
George A. Moonie
Harry Voss
Farrier
Able B. Spencer
Saddler
William Shields

Blacksmith
Henry Miller
Privates
Harry Abbots
David Ackison
William H. Baker
Robert Barth
Frank Berwald
Owen Boyle
James Brogan
Latrobe Bromwell
August Brunns
Edward Conner
John Darris
William Davis
Richard Farrell
Julius Gilbert
John Heim
John Henderson
Sykes Henderson
John S. Hiley
Frank Howard
William Huber
Anton Hutter
John James

John G. Kimm
Andy Knecht
Henry Lang
Herod T. Liddiard
Patrick McCann
John McKenna
Patrick O'Conner
Francis O'Toole
Christopher Pandtle
William H. Rees
William Reese
Edward Rood
Henry Schele
William Smallwood
Albert A. Smith
James Smith
James Smith
Benjamin Stafford
Alexander Stella
William A. Torrey
Cornelius Vansant
George Walker
Jerry Woodruff

274

Company F

Captain
George W. Yates
2nd Lieutenant
William Van Wyck Reily
1st Sergeant
Michael Kenney
Sergeants
William A. Curtis
Henry Drago
Frederick Nursey
John Vickory
John R. Wilkinson
Corporals
Edward Clyde
Charles Coleman
William Teeman
John Briody
Farrier
Benjamin Brandon
Blacksmith
James R. Manning
Saddler
Claus Schleiper
Privates
Thomas Atcheson
William Brady
Benjamin F. Brown

Hiram E. Brown
William Brown
Patrick Bruce
Lucien Burnham
James W. Butler
James Carney
Amantheus D. Cather
Edward Davern
Antoine Dohman
Timothy Donnelly
Alexander Downing
William Eades
Thomas J. Finnegan
William Gardiner
William J. Gregg
George W. Hammon
Leonard Harris
Francis Hegner
Frank Howard
Frank Hunter
John Kelly
Gustav Klein
Nicholas Klein
Herman Knauth
Meig Lefler
William H. Lerock
Werner L. Liemann

William A. Lossee
Dennis Lynch
Bernard Lyons
Christian Madson
Ernest Meniker
Frank Meyers
Francis E. Milton
Joseph Milton
Joseph Monroe
Sebasitan Omling
Edwin H. Pickard
Albert Pitcher
Michael Reiley
James M. Rooney
Patrick Rudden
Richard Sanders
Paul Schleiggorth
Frederick Schutte
Francis W. Sicfous
John W. Sweeney
William Sweeney
Michael Thorp
Thomas Walsh
George Warren
Thomas W. Way

Company G

1st Lieutenant
Donald McIntosh
2nd Lieutenant
George D. Wallace
Sergeants
Alexander Brown
Edward Botzer
Martin Considine
Frank Lloyd
Orland H. Northey
Corporals
Henry Brinkerhoff
Melancthon H. Crissy
Otto Hagemann
John E. Hammon
James A. Kerr
George Loyd
James Martin
John W. Wallace
Trumpeters
Cassius R. Carter
Henry Dose
Farrier
Benjamin Wells
Saddler
Crawford Selby
Blacksmith
Walter O. Taylor

Privates
Charles Barney
James Boyle
Charles Campbell
Edward Dwyer
Phillip Flood
Frank Geist
Theodore W. Goldin
Thomas Graham
William S. Gray
Edward Grayson
John Hackett
George W. Henderson
Benjamin Johnson
Jacob Katzenmaier
Martin Kilfoyle
Joseph Laden
John Lattman
Frank Lauper
James Lawler
Samuel McCormick
John McDonnell
John McEagan
John McGinnis
Hugh McGonigle
Edward J. McKay
John McKee
John McVay

Andrew J. Moore
John Morrison
Thomas F. O'Neill
Henry Petring
John Rapp
John A. Reed
Eldorado J. Robb
Benjamin F. Rogers
Robert Rowland
Henry Seafferman
John Shanahan
John R. Small
Edward Stanley
George W. Stephens
Thomas Stevenson
Daniel Sullivan
Joseph Tulo
Markus Weiss
Pasavan Williamson

Company H

Captain
Frederick W. Benteen
1st Lieutenant
Francis M. Gibson
1st Sergeant
Joseph McCurry
Sergeants
Patrick Conelly
George Geiger
Thomas McLaughlin
Matthew Maroney
John Pahl
Corporals
Alexander B. Bishop
Daniel Nealon
Farrier
John M. Marshall
Blacksmith
Henry W. B. Mecklin
Saddler
Otto Voit
Trumpeters
John Martin
William Ramell

Privates
Jacob Adams
Charles E. Avery
Henry Bishley
Charles H. Bishop
Henry Black
William Channell
John Cooper
John Day
George W. Dewey
Edward Diamond
William Farley
William George
George W. Glease
Henry Haack
Timothy Haley
Charles N. Hood
Thomas Hughes
John Hunt
Julien D. Jones
George Kelly
James Kelly
Frank Lambertin
Thomas Lawhorn

George Lell
Thomas McDermott
James McNamara
David McWilliams
Thomas E. Meador
Jan Moller
John Muller
Elder Nees
Joshua S. Nicholas
William O'Ryan
John Phillips
John S. Pinkston
Francis Pittet
Samuel Severs
Daniel Taply
Michael J. Walsh
Aloyse L. Walter
William C. Williams
Charles Windolph

Company I

Captain
Myles W. Keogh
1st Lieutenant
James E. Porter
1st Sergeant
Frank E. Varden
Sergeants
James Bustard
Michael Caddle
Milton J. De Lacy
George Gaffney
Robert L. Murphy
Corporals
Joseph McCall
George C. Morris
Samuel F. Staples
John Wild
Trumpeters
John E. McGucker
John W. Patten
Saddler
George Haywood
Farrier
John Rivers
Blacksmith
Henry A. Bailey

Privates
John Barry
Joseph F. Broadhurst
Franz C. Brown
Thomas Conners
David Cooney
Thomas P. Downing
Edward Driscoll
Conrad Farber
Frederick Fox
Gabriel Geesbacher
David C. Gillette
Andrew Grimes
George H. Gross
Charles L. Haack
Adam Hetesimer
Edward P. Holcomb
Marion E. Horn
Francis Johnson
Henry P. Jones
Patrick Kelley
Gustav Korn
Mark E. Lee
Frederick Lehman
Henry Lehman
Edward W. Lloyd

Patrick Lynch
John McGinnis
Archibald McIlhargey
James P. McNally
John McShane
William E. Miller
John Mitchell
Fred Myers
Jacob Noshang
John O'Bryan
W. G. Owens
John Parker
Felix J. Pitter
John Porter
George Post
James Quinn
Charles Ramsey
William Reed
John W. Rossbury
William Saas
Darwin L. Symms
Herbert P. Thomas
James Troy
Charles Von Bramer
William B. Whaley

Company K

1st Lieutenant
Edward Godfrey
2nd Lieutenant
Luther R. Hare
1st Sergeant
DeWitt Winney
Sergeants
Jeremiah Campbell
Andrew Frederick
George Hose
Robert Hughes
Michael P. Madden
John Rafter
Louis Rott
Corporals
John J. Callahan
Henry Murray
John Nolan
Trumpeters
Julius Helmer
George B. Penwell
Christian Schlafer
Farrier
John R. Steintker
Blacksmith
Edmund H. Burke
Saddler
Christian Boissen

Wagoner
Albert Whytenfield
Privates
Charles Ackerman
George Anderson
Jacob Bauer
James E. Blair
George Blunt
Cornelius Bresnahan
Joseph Brown
Charles Burgdorf
Charles Burkhardt
Charles Chesterwood
Elihu F. Clear
Patrick Coakley
Patrick Corcoran
William L. Crawford
Michael Delaney
John Donohue
Patrick Dooley
Charles Fisher
John Foley
William Gibbs
Thomas A. Gordon
Thomas Green
Julius Gunther
Walter Hayt
Andrew Holahan

Jacob Horner
Alonzo Jennys
William W. Lasley
Andrew Liebermann
Daniel Lyons
Wilson McConnell
Martin McCue
Max Mielke
Michael Murphy
Thomas Murphy
Michael Ragan
Henry W. Raichel
Michael Reilly
Jonathan Robers
Francis Roth
John Schauer
John Schroerer
August Seifert
Frederick Smith
Emil Taube
William A. Van Pelt
Ernest Wasmus
William Whitlow
George A. Wilson
Henry Witt

Company L

1st Lieutenant
James Calhoun
2nd Lieutenant
J. J. Crittenden
1st Sergeant
James Butler
Sergeants
Henry Bender
William Cashan
Hugo Findeisen
John Mullen
Corporals
William H. Gilbert
William H. Harrison
John Nunan
John Seiler
Trumpeters
Theodore Berman
Frederick Walsh
Farrier
William Heath
Blacksmith
Charles Siemon

Privates
William G. Abrams
George E. Adams
William Andrews
Edson F. Archer
Anthony Assadily
Elmer Babcock
Charles Banks
William Bilson
Nathan T. Brown
John Burke
John Burkham
Ami Cheever
John R. Colwell
Michael Conlon
Edgar B. Cook
William B. Crisfield
John Crowley
Thomas Curtin
Francis Dayton
William Dye
William Etzler
James J. Galvan
Charles Graham
Henry Hamilton
Weston Harrington
Max Hoehn
Francis T. Hughes
Peter Johnson
Thomas G. Kavanagh
Michael Keegan
Samuel S. Knapp
Frederick Lepper

Louis Lobering
William J. Logue
Jasper Marshall
Thomas E. Maxwell
Charles McCarthy
Peter McGue
Philip McHugh
Edward McMath
Alexander McPeak
John Miller
Lansing A. Moore
David J. O'Connell
Charles Perkins
Christian Reibold
Henry Roberts
Walter Rogers
Peter Rose
George Ross
Charles Schmidt
Robert Schutz
Charles Scott
Bernt Simenson
Andrew Snow
Otto Sprague
Henry Stoffel
Byron Tarbox
Edmond D. Tessier
Thomas S. Tweed
Michael Vetter
Amos B. Warren
John Weideman
Joel R. Whitcomb

Company M

Captain	Privates	William W. Rye
Thomas H. French	Joseph Bates	John Seamans
1st Lieutenant	Frank Bowers	Robert Senn
Edward G. Mathey	Frank Braun	James Severs
1st Sergeant	Morris Cain	John Sivertsen
John Ryan	Harrison Davis	William Slaper
Sergeants	John Dolan	George E. Smith
William Capes	Jean B. D. Gallenne	Frank Sniffin
Patrick Carey	Bernard Golden	Walter S. Sterland
John McGlone	Henry Gordon	Frank Stratton
Miles F. O'Hara	George Heid	David Summers
Charles White	Charles Kavanaugh	James J. Tanner
Corporals	Henry Klotzbucher	Rollins L. Thorpe
William Lalor	George Lorentz	Levi Thornberry
Henry M. Scollin	Daniel Mahoney	Henry Turley
Frederick Streing	James McCormick	Thomas B. Varner
Trumpeters	John H. Meier	Henry Voigt
Charles Fisher	William D. Meyer	George Weaver
Henry C. Weaver	Hugh N. Moore	James Weeks
Farrier	William E. Morris	John Whisten
William M. Wood	Frank Neely	Charles T. Wiedman
Saddler	Daniel Newell	James Wilber
John Donahue	Edward Pigford	Charles Williams
Wagoner	William Robinson	Ferdinand Widmayer
Joseph Ricketts	Roman Rutten	John Zametzer
	Hobart Ryder	

Detachment of Indian Scouts*

Official List	Date of Enlistment		Data
Sioux: *Senaru Art*	X	Feb. 3	
Young Hawk: *Achta Wisi Hunne*	+	May 9	
Soldier: *Kanauch*	X	Apr. 26	
Black Calf: *Hunne Catis*	X	Apr. 26	
One Feather: *Ha Cui Tis*	X	May 9	
Forked Horn: *Arri Chitt*	+	Apr. 29	
Bobtail Bull: *Hocus Tarix*	+	Apr. 26	
Little Brave: *Naha Cus Chu Reposch*	+	May 9	
Stab: *Cawars*	X	May 9	
Bull In The Water: *Hocus Ty Arritt*	X	May 9	
Rushing Bull: *Hocus Na Ginn*	X	May 9	
Good Face: *Scari*	X	May 9	
Foolish Bear: *Coonough Sen Gaagh*	+	May 9	
Strike The Lodge: *Tayche - Tay Ree Che*	X	May 9	
Goose: *Cosh*	+	Apr. 26	
Black Fox: *Chilira Two Catis*	X	May 9	
Strikes Two: *Tita Waricho*	X	May 9	
Bull: *Hocus*	X	May 9	
Bush: *Napa Run Ough*	X	Apr. 26	
Good Elk: *Wanee*	X	May 13	
Strike Bear: *Coonough Tacha*	X	May 9	
White Eagle: *Nata Staca*	X	May 9	
Barking Wolf: *Sito Wara*	A	May 9	Carrying dispatches in the field since June 22.
Howling Wolf: *Schiri Wano*	A	Apr. 26	On D.S.** at Yellowstone Depot since June 15.
Wolf Runs: *Schiri to Much*	A	May 9	Carrying dispatches in the field since June 22.
Bear: *Coonough*	A	May 9	Carrying dispatches in the field since June 22.
Bear's Eyes: *Coonough Cherak*	A	Apr. 1	On D.S. at Ft. Lincoln since May 17.

*See following page for a key and information concerning the detachment.
**Detached Service.

282

Official List	Date of Enlistment		Data
Long Bear: *Coonough Tikuchris*	A	May 9	On D.S. at Yellowstone Depot since June 15.
Black Porcupine: *Sami Cotis*	A	May 9	On D.S. at Ft. Lincoln since May 17.
Climbs The Bluff: *Teru Chitt Honochs*	A	May 9	Carrying dispatches in the field since June 1.
Curly Head: *Pichga Ri Ni*	A	Apr. 27	Carrying dispatches in the field since June 22.
Horn In Front: *Arrin Quis Coo*	A	May 9	On D.S. at Yellowstone Depot since June 15.
One Horn: *Achno Arricas*	A	May 9	On D.S. at Ft. Lincoln since May 17.
Laying Down: *Sita Wara*	A	May 9	On D.S. at Ft. Lincoln since May 17.
Owl: *Horr*	A	May 13	On D.S. at Ft. Lincoln since June 17.
Wagon: *Sapararu*	A	May 13	On D.S. at Ft. Lincoln since June 17.
Broken Penis: *Chagoo Hurpa*	D	Nov. 13 '75	D at Ft. Lincoln
Cards	D	Nov. 13 '75	D at Ft. Lincoln
Left Hand: *Quigh Chwi*	D	Dec. 9 '75	D at Ft. Lincoln
Sticking Out: *Bo In E Naga*	D	Dec. 11 '75	D at Ft. Lincoln
The Shield: *Waha Chumka*	D	Dec. 11 '75	D at Ft. Lincoln
Round Wooden Cloud: *Machpa Gachumga*	X	Mar. 31	Sioux
Bear Come Out: *Mato Hinapa*	X	Feb. 3	Sioux
White Cloud: *Machpa A Cha - Mahpia Sha*	X	May 14	Sioux
Bear Running In The Timber: *Matochun Way A Ga Mun*	X	May 11	Sioux
William Cross	X	Apr. 17	Half Sioux
William Jackson	+	June 25	¼ Pikuni
William Baker	+	May 4	Half Ree
Robert Jackson	D	Dec. 25 '75	¼ Pikuni

Information Concerning the
Detachment of Indian Scouts

A   Absent on muster roll of detachment of Indian scouts and did not participate in Little Bighorn River fight.

D   Discharged six months from date of enlistment and did not reenlist.

X   All of these were in the valley fight and ran away to Powder River.

+   Scouts who remained with the command and were reported present in camp at mouth of Little Bighorn River June 30, 1876.

Varnum was assigned to command the scouts on May 3, 1876.

Varnum appended the following note to the muster roll: "I certify that the scouts reported 'missing in action,' on the above muster roll, and who have been paid thereon, have duly returned to duty since muster and before payment and are entitled to pay for themselves and for furnishing their own horse and equipment, to include June 30, 1876." Signed in camp on Yellowstone River July 29, 1876. The price paid scouts for horse and equipment was 40c per day. William Jackson is noted on muster as enlisting June 25, 1876, also "Joined detachment June 25, 1876," also "On Detached Service at Ft. Lincoln Since May 17, 1876." It further appears that Jackson was discharged on the Little Bighorn on June 25, 1876, by reason of expiration of service and reenlisted the same date. Goose is noted as "wounded in action June 25 and sick in hospital." Note that Bloody Knife's name does not appear on the muster. He was employed as a guide, says Varnum. From this it would appear that Bob Jackson may have remained at Ft. Lincoln when sent back with a dispatch from Little Missouri and was discharged there. He may, however, have reenlisted and got back to Powder River, as Fox states, and such fact would not have been known at the camp at Little Bighorn on June 25, 1876. It will be seen that all of these discharged scouts had enlisted in 1875. One of them (Left Hand) was discharged on the expedition. Young Hawk said that when Left Hand's time expired, he joined the Sioux, his own people, and after the battle of the Little Bighorn River his horse was found in the village and his dead body among those left in the village by the Sioux. All the rest, including Bob Jackson, were discharged at Ft. Lincoln.

All of those who accompanied the expedition (except Jackson) enlisted in 1876. William Baker, alias William J. Bailey, reported present at Little Bighorn June 30, 1876. Broken Penis was probably a Sioux. Chagoo (Chagu) Hurpa is not Ree, says Wilde.

(Walter Camp's notes, Lee Library, Brigham Young University, box 6, folder 7.)

Boy Chief's List of Indian Scouts*

Little Sioux: *Sana Piciribust*	Present	*Netach Staca*	Present
Young Hawk: *Nekutawisi Hani*	Present	Spotted Horn Cloud: *Watoksu*	Present
Soldier: *Hunach*	Present	The Whole Buffalo: *Tonheci Tooch*	Present
Boychief: *Wincu Neshanu*	Present	Machpiya Ska: *Nakpieska*	Present
One Feather: *Hach Hetu*	Present	Bear in Timber	Present
Forked Horn: *Ari Cit*	Present	Little Crow: *Kapa Ciripas,*	Present
Bobtailed Bull: *Hugos Tarix*	Present	*Schiri Tirchiwako*	Absent
Little Brave: *Nanugos Ciripas*	Present	Howling Wolf: *Schiri Tiwana*	Absent
Stab: *Kawasach*	Present	Running Wolf: *Schiri Doonch*	Absent
Bull In The Water: *Hugos Tihaart*	Present	Foolish Bear: *Goonuch Sachkunu,*	Absent
Charging Bull: *Hugos Tanawinach*	Present	*Gunuch Chiriku*	Absent
Bear Good Face: *Skaré*	Present	High Bear: *Goonuch Tiwichess,*	Absent
Foolish Red Bear: *Goonch Sanch Waat*	Present	*Sunu Katit,*	Absent
Strike Lodge: *Tekche*	Present	*Terauch Chitt Hunoch*	Absent
Goose: *Gauht,*	Present	Curl Hair: *Pchari Wi*	Absent
Chikawu Katit	Present	Horns Out In Front: *Arrin Quisk,*	Absent
Strikes Two: *Tita Rawici*	Present	*Hckorich Horich,*	Absent
Bellow: *Hugos*	Present	*Ticha*	Absent
Red Wolf: *Sticeri Tipaat Naparanuch*	Present	Owl: *Horu,*	Absent
Red Bear: *Wane, Goonuch Hwat*	Present	*Sapireniwoah*	Absent
Red Star: *Gunuch Tiche,*	Present	Wolf	Absent

*Since the Rees and the Crows had no written language, these names were subject to the interpretation of someone who spoke or understood these Indian languages and could translate them into English. Each interpreter perceived the meaning differently and spelled the Indian pronunciation differently, as is apparent in this and the other lists here.

"Present" and "absent" here indicate whether or not each scout was present for duty with the regiment in the Little Bighorn River fight on June 25. Those marked absent were not in the fight but were somewhere else — at Yellowstone Depot or Fort A. Lincoln or at another location.

Indian Scouts

Tribe	Names Interpreted by Peter Beauchamp	Other Names
Ree	Little Sioux: *Sanana Pichiripasit*	Sioux: *Sananat*
Ree	Young Hawk: *Nikutawiksi Hani*	
Ree	Soldier: *Hcunaytch*	
Ree	Boy Chief: *Winhchu Neshanu*	Black Calf: *Ani Katit*
Ree	One Feather: *Aheu Hitu*	
Ree	Forked Horn: *Ari Chit*	
Ree	Bobtail Bull: *Wkos Tarix*	
Ree	Little Brave: *Nuhukos Chiripaat*	Stub
Ree	Stabbed: *Kawashc*	
Ree	Bull In Water: *Wkos Tihahrt*	
Ree	Rushing Bull: *Wkos Tunawinhc*	Charging Bull
Ree	Good Face: *Skare*	Pretty Face
Ree	Foolish Red Bear: *Gunuhc Sanhcwa*	Crooked Foot
Ree	Strikes The Lodge: *Tekche*	
Ree	Goose: *Goht*	Maga
Ree	Black Fox: *Chiwaku Katit*	
Ree	Strikes Two: *Titara Wiche*	
Ree	Bull: *Wkos*	Bello
Ree	Bush: *Naparanuhc*	Brush; Red Wolf: *Schiri Tipaat*
Ree	Good Elk: *Wau Ne*	Red Bear: *Gunuhc Waht*
		White Calf: *Ani Katit*
Ree	Strike Bear: *Gunuhc Tiche*	Red Star: *Saha Tipaat*

286

Tribe	Names Interpreted by Peter Beauchamp	Other Names
Ree	White Eagle: *Netk Staka*	
Ree	Wolf Standing In The Cold: *Schiri Tipsikahrt*	Barking Wolf: *Schiri Tirchiwako*
Ree	Howling Wolf: *Schiri Tiwana*	
Ree	Running Wolf: *Schiri Dunhc*	Wolf Runs: *Schiri Tomuch*
Ree	Bear: *Gunuhc*	Foolish Bear: *Gunuhc Sakhunu*
Ree	Bear's Eye: *Gunuhc Chiriku*	
Ree	Long Bear: *Gunuhc Tichess*	High Bear: *Gunuhc Tiwichess*
Ree	Black Porcupine: *Sunu Katit*	
Ree	Climbs The Bluff: *Tirowkchit Hunohc*	Charging to the Top of the Bluff
Ree	Curly Head: *Plickariwi*	
Ree	Horns in Front: *Arin Quisk*	
Ree	One Horn: *Hcorik*	Single Horn
Ree	Lying Down: *Tisha*	Laying Down: *Sita Wara*
Ree	Owl: *Whuru*	
Ree	Wagon: *Sapiraniwohc*	
Sioux	Broken Penis: *Kanept*	Growling Bear
Sioux	Cards: *Karu*	Caroo
Sioux	Left Hand: *Qhci*	
Sioux	Sticking Out	
Sioux	Shield	*Waha Chaka*

Detachment of Indian Scouts, 7th Infantry

Commanded by 1st Lieutenant James H. Bradley, 7th Infantry. Enlisted on April 10, 1876, for the campaign of the Yellowstone Expedition. Turned over to the 7th Cavalry June 21, 1876.

One Ahead: *Bah suk ush*		With Custer
Half Yellow Face: *Iss too sah shee dah*		With Reno
White Swan: *Mee nah tsee us*	Wounded June 25	With Reno
White Man Runs Him:		With Custer
Mahr stah shee dah ku roosh		
Hairy Moccasin: *Sah pee wish ush*		With Custer
Curley: *Shuh shee ohsh*	Present at camp at mouth of Little Bighorn.	With Custer

Mitch Bouyer was interpreter for Crow scouts and went with Custer. *Bah suk ush* (One Ahead) was paid $66.98 for April 10 to June 30, 1876 — $35.10 for service and $32.80 for horse, less 92 cents for tobacco. He was paid for 2 months, 21 days at rate of $13.00 per month for service and 40 cents per day for horse and equipment. Curley, White Swan, and Half Yellow Face were the only ones reported present in camp on Little Bighorn June 30, 1876. Altogether there were 25 Crow scouts with Bradley, including the 6 sent with Custer on June 21. This looks as if they had run away from Bradley when they heard the result of the Custer fight from the 3 Crows on a.m. of June 26. Jack Rabbit Bull: *Ees tah tsee dup ish* was reported absent on detached service since May 29. *Eetsee dahkh in dush* (Horse Rider alias Thomas LaForgey) absent sick since June 24 in camp near Ft. Pease. Modern pronunciation of White Man Runs Him is *Batsida Karoosh*.

(Information on detachments of Indian scouts is in folder 7, box 6, Indian Scouts, Walter Camp Collection, Lee Library, Brigham Young University.)

Index

A

"Absaroke," debate over meaning of, 169–70

Account of the Battle of the Little Big Horn by a Scout, Bill Jackson's story in, 193 n

Ackison, David, 145

Adams, Jacob, 6
  Camp's interview with, 121–22

Adobe Walls, battle of, 13

Ainsworth, Fred C., 6

Alcott, Samuel, 6

Allen, Tom, 6

Allison, Edwin H., 6

The American Catholic Qtrly Review, "Last Summer's Expedition Against the Sioux and its Great Catastrophe" in, 251 n

Ammunition mule, escape of, 124–25

Annual Report, "Report of Colonel John Gibbon To General Terry" in, 251 n

Arapahoes
  and General Conner, 15
  resentment of, against buffalo slaughter, 13

Arickaree Sahnish, or Arikara, or Arikaraho, 182

Army and Navy Journal
  "Curley's Narrative" in, 155 n
  Curley's story to Gen. Roe in, 170
  "Custer Battlefield Monument" in, 249
  Herendeen's statement in, 219 n

Ash Creek. *See* Sundance Creek

Ash Hollow, attack of Harney on Sioux at, 14

Ashley, Edward, 6

Assiniboine, 184

B

Bailey, John E., Hodgson's body recovered by, 72

Bailey, William J., 6

Baker, Eugene M., 4–5
  fight of, near Billings, 19

Baker, William H., 187

Baker's Battleground, 19

Baldwin, Captain, and Sitting Bull, 23

Baldwin, Frank D., 4–6

Ball, Edward, horses drowned by, 245

Ball, Major (Captain), dead Indians found by, 73, 139

Bancroft, Neil
  picket duty volunteered by, 113
  in water party, 115

Barnitz, Albert, 6

Barnum, stampede of mule, into Indians, 127

Baronett, John, and Nowlan, 226 n

Barricades, dead horses used as, 68

Bear's Paw, and General Godfrey, 25

Beauchamp, Peter, 187 n

Bell, James M., 6
  wife of, and Reno, 63

Belle Fourche Bee, "The Experience of a Private soldier in the Custer Massacre" in, 128 n

Ben Bear Lies Down, 8

Bennett, Andrew S., death of, 24

Bennett, James C., death of, 241

Benteen, Frederick W.
  assistance to, by French, 120
  brave command of, 72
  bravery of, 62, 67, 96, 114, 136, 225 n
  charge of, 57, 81
  company taken by, 92
  and Custer, 54, 247
  and DeRudio, 82
  drinking of, 254
  fingers grazed by bullet, 68, 81
  and French, 608
  hatred of, for Custer, 63
  heel of boot of, shot off, 122

289

"Notes May 17 to June 9, 1876,
on the Little Big Horn Expedition under Gen. Custer" in,
252 n
"Recent Newspaper Items
Concerning Custer's Last
Battle" in, 251 n
Cooke (Cook), William W.
body of, 58, 95 n
buried by Foley, 147
and Mathey, 78
message to Benteen sent by, 100,
103
and Reno, 55, 55 n, 65
sideburn of, scalped, 68, 87
and Wilber, 148
Corcoran, Patrick, 6
Camp's interview with, 150–51
wounded, 150
Cowley, Cornelius, insane from thirst,
114
Crazy Horse, 208
and Black Hills treaty violation,
20
charge of, 207
fights with, 19
and Foolish Elk, 197
and General Miles, 24
medicine man consulted by,
before battle, 215
and reservations, 19
Crazy Woman Creek, soldiers attacked
· at, 16
Criswell, Harry, Hodgson's body
recovered by, 72
Crittenden
body of, 58, 68
marker for, 158
Crook, George, 4–5
conflict of, with Sioux and
Cheyennes, 21
and Dull Knife, 23
and the Little Bighorn, 21
or Lone Star, 198
and Merritt and Carr, 22
mistaken for enemy, 117
and "starvation march" to the
Black Hills, 22
tactics of, 11–12
or Three Star, or Wicokpi Yammi,
205
Cross, Billy (William), 111, 185, 189,

225
as Ieska, 190
and Little Sioux, 181
met by Weir's troop, 129
Crumb (Crump), John, 6
Curley (Curly), 9, 246
and Camp, 3
Camp's interviews with, 155–173
escape of, 163–64
naked, armed, on Indian pony,
159
released from service, 170
route to steamer of, 168–69
as a scout, 91
as Shi shi'esh, 161
sites identified by, 156
Curtis (Curtiss), William A.
hard bread retrieved by, 91
and hardtack, 74
with pack train, 138
Custard, Amos J., 4–5
death of, and his men, 15
Custer battlefield
dead men and horses on, 102
visited by Adams, 121
Custer Battle Guns, 181 n
Custer, Boston (Boss)
body of, 95 n
burial of, 76
met by Martin, 101, 104
and McDougall, 69
Custer, Elizabeth, Camp's letter to, 3
Custer, George A., 4–5
approach of, to Indian camp, 97
arrested by Terry's order, 123
and Benteen, 247
Black Hills explored by, 20
bodies of men of, stripped and
mutilated, 95
body of, 58, 87, 95 n, 121, 136, 139
bones of, scattered, 226 n
buckskin shirt of, 215
burial of, witnessed by Gerard,
236–37
as "Charge the Camp," 245
companies taken by, 92
defeat of, communicated by
Curley, 164, 169
gambling of, 63
and General Sheridan, 12
and General Stanley, 19
and Gerard, 230

hated by Benteen, 63
hated by Reno, 63
length of battle of, 224
letter to, from General Terry,
257–58
and the Little Bighorn, 26–28
as Long Yellow Hair, 198
moral character of, 140
as Morning Star (Ihcke
Deikdagua), 176
names of men killed with, on
monument, 21
no recognition of, by enemy, 200,
202, 215, 254
as Peoushi, or Pecushi, or Long
Hair, 207 n, 209
poor shooting of men of, 211
remains of command of, found,
169
remains of, identified by
Herendeen, 227
route of, 100, 106, 162
and the Sioux, 19
tactics of, 11
and Varnum, 59 n
wounds of, 102, 110
as "Young Star," 166
The Custer Myth
"Edgerly's Statement Made 18
August 1881 at Fort Yates" in,
58 n
Gerard's story in, 228 n
Herendeen's story in, 219 n
White Man Run Him's story in,
178 n
Custer ridge
grading of, 253 n
markers erected on, 252
*Custer's Last Battle, Narrative of the
Tragedy of the Little Bighorn,*
Gibbon's story in, 249
*Custer's Mysterious Mr. Kellogg And
The Diary of Mark Kellogg,*
Kellogg's diary in, 252 n
Custer's soldiers, buried where found,
140 n
Custer, Tom
advice to scouts from, 159
body of, 58, 68, 110, 121, 248
and Calhoun, 61
company taken by, 92
death of, 77

Indian mistaken for, 86
and party, mistaken for Sioux, 84
wounds of, 102

D

Dale, Alfred W., 6
Daniels, Napoleon H., 4–5
death of, 16
Davis, George B., 6
Deer Creek, engagements from, to
Red Buttes, 15
DeRudio, Charles (Carlo) Camilus,
148
and Benteen, 82
Camp's interview with, 82
drinking of Reno witnessed by,
150 n
and Gerard, 233–34
gold mounted saber presented to,
83
and Hardy, mistaken for Sioux,
84
Indians resisted by, 108–9
and Jackson, in buffalo wallow,
108
and O'Neill, 107
and Reno, 84
and Roy, 116
and settlers of Solomon Valley,
Kansas, 83
and Varnum, 62
saber carried by, in Little Bighorn
expedition, 87
DeWolf, Doctor
death of, 66
hit by Indians, 61
Dirt Kettle, Custer discovered by, 206
Discrepancy in names of creeks and
peaks, 156 n
Dixon, Billy, 4–5
Doane, Captain, wounded transported
by, 226
Donnelly, Timothy
body of, in gully, 139
with pack train, 138
Donovan, body of, 139
Dorman, Isaiah. *See* Isaiah Dorman.
Dorn, Richard B., death of, 71
Dose, Henry C., death of, 99 n, 134
Dough boys, 140
Dry Creek, or Medicine Tail Coulee,

death of, 94
drinking of, 151 n
grave of, 62
hit by Indians, 61
and Mozlan, 107
retreat of, 148
Hohmeyer (Homeyer), Frederick,
body of, buried, 72
Hollow Horn Bear, 9
Horn Cloud, Joseph, 9
and the "Big Foot Massacre," 25
Horn in Front, 182
Horse Creek, Sioux attack on troops at,
14
Howard, Otis, 4–5, 148
and the Nez Perce Indians, 24
Hughes, Francis T., 120
body of, 147
Hughes, Robert H., 120
body of, buried, 72
Hughes, Robert P., dead identified
by, 247
Hump Little Crow, 9
Hunk, village of, seen by Custer, 103
Hunter, Frank ("Yankee"), 139
Hunter-Trader Trapper, "Red Men"
in, 251 n
Hunton, John, 7
Hurst, John 7
Hutchins, Ben. *See* Benjamin
Hodgson

I

Indian battles
and Camp, 2
sites of, visited by Camp, 4–5
Indian Fights and Fighters, Morris's
letter in, 131 n
Indians
interest in, of Camp, 2
number of, killed at Little
Bighorn, 208
ruse of, 144
Inkpaluta (Inkpaduta), 206
*In The Land of Chinook, the Story of
Blaine County,* Herendeen's
biography in, 200 n
Innes, Charles K., 7
*Interview with F. F. Gerard's
Daughter,* Gerard's story in, 228 n
Isaiah Dorman

body of, 122, 135, 136
bravery of, 119
death of, 192, 223, 224
as a scout, 91

J

Jackson, Robert, 111, 193
seen by O'Neill, 107–8
sent back from Rosebud, 135
and Thompson, 125
Jackson, William (Bill)
cowardice of, 193
and DeRudio, in buffalo wallow,
180
and Gerard, 233
found hiding by DeRudio, 86
and Roy, 116
and Thompson, 125
and Varnum, 62
Jenness, John C., death of, 17
Jones, death of, 135
Journal of American History, "A
Survivor's Story of the Custer
Massacre on the American Frontier"
in, 121 n

K

Kanipe. *See* Knipe
Karu. *See* Caroo.
Kearney, Fort Phil., 16
and the Overland trail, 14
Kellogg, Marcus Henry
body of, 136, 248
burial of, 79
with scouts, 231
stake marking grave of, 252
Keogh, Myles W.
body of, 58, 95 n, 121
company taken by, 92
and Custer, 54, 74
gold chain and Agnus Dei
emblem of, secured by Benteen,
102
and picture of McDougall's sister,
72
and Reno, 55 n, 55
watch of, recovered, 72
Keogh, Fort, fights near, 19
Kicking Bear, 208

Rain-in-the-Face, capture of, 2, 128, 138
Rapp, John, death of, 107
Raymier, death of, 251 n
Red Bear, 9, 181, 189, 190
  Camp's interview with, and Young Hawk, 194
  as Good Elk or Handsome Elk, 194 n
Red Buttes, engagements from, to Deer Creek, 15
Red Cloud, 208
  and Black Hills treaty violation, 20
  people of, on reservations, 19
Red Foolish Bear, 183
Red Star, 184, 188, 190, 194
  as Strike Bear, Strikes Bear, or Strikes the Bear, 180 n
  as White Calf, 184
Redwater, Thaddeus
  Tall Bull interpreted by, 212–13
  White Bull interpreted by, 211
Red Wolf, 181, 190
Reno, Fort, 16
Reno, Marcus A.
  and the barricade, 142 n
  and Benteen, 67, 76, 105
  and Cooke, 65
  courtmartials of, 63
  and Custer, 54
  and DeRudio, 84
  hatred of, for Custer, 63
  and Gerard, 236
  intoxication of, 150 n–151 n
  and the Little Bighorn, 26–28, 54–57
  and Lowe, 53
  and Lynch, 138
  messages written by, 63
  route taken by, 92
  sites of battles of, unmarked, 21
  survivors of command of, and Camp, 3
  and Varnum, 61, 63
Reno Creek. See Sundance Creek
Reno Peak (north) and Weir, 56
Reno's battlefield, no markers put on, 252
Report of the Chief of Engineers, "Report of Trip of Steamer Far West Up The Big Horn River" in, 240 n

Reynolds, Charles (Charley), 85, 222 n, 232
  body of, 122
  death of, 223
  fighting of, while wounded, 112
  as a scout, 91
  and Varnum, 60 n
Reynolds, Joseph, 4–5
  and St. Patrick's day incident, 20–21
Riley, James, 128
Rivers, Arickaree names for, 182
Robinson, William W., 8
Roe, Charles F., 8
  Camp's interview with, 249
Roger Mills County, Oklahoma, unmarked battle site in, 12
Romeyn, Henry, 8
Rooney, James M., 146
Rosebud, battle of the, 21
Rott, Louis, water fetched by, 147
Roubideaux, Louis, Foolish Elk interpreted by, 197
Round Wooden Cloud, 9
Rowton, J. G., 8
Roy, Stanislas, 8
  bodies buried by, 116–17
  Camp's interview with, 111–17
  in water party, 115
Running Wolf, 9
Rutten, Roman
  Camp's interview with, 118–122
  horse of, runs away, 148
Ryan, Stephen L., Hodgson's body recovered by, 72
Ryan, John
  and Captain French, 118
  and James Wilber, 148

S

St. Paul Pioneer Press, "The Indian Battlefield" in, 115
Sans Arc, shot, 205
Scabby Wolf, 194
Scollin (Cody), Henry, death of, 119, 131–32
Scott, Hugh L., 8
Server, Frederick E., 8
  Camp's interview with, 242–43
Shangrau, Louis, 8
Share, 190

Sharrow, William H.
  death of, 99 n
  and Hare, 65
Shaw, Foolish Elk interpreted by, 197
Sheridan, General, and Custer, 12
Sherman, General, 226
Short, Nathan, 126
  body of, 137 n, 146
  horse and carbine of, found, 248
  story of, head by Rutten, 120
Sibley, Fred., 4–5
Siebelder, Anton, and Varnum, 62
Siouan Teton family, tribes of, 198 n
Sioux campaign of 1876, Camp's
  interest in, 3
Sipes, James M., Camp's interviews
  with, 240–41
Sitting Bull, 197, 206, 220
  Baldwin's fight with, 2
  and Black Hills treaty violation,
    20
  and Bouyer, 99–100
  camp of, found by Bouyer, 99
  and Captain Baldwin, 23
  death of, 2
  fights with, 19
  and Gerard, 229
  raids by, 24
  and reservations, 19
Sivertsen, John, 8
  Camp's interview with, 141–42
Slim Buttes fight, site of, determined,
  2
Slocum, Herbert J., 8
  Camp's interview with, 254
Smith, A. E.
  body of, 95
  company taken by, 92
  put in command of Company E.,
    83
Smith, Capt. E. W., Curley's story
  corroborated by, 170
Smith, Ed., 247
Smith, Fort C. F., 16
  battle at, 18
Smith, George E., death of, 131
Smith, John, 92, 95, 135
Soldier, 9, 184, 189, 190
  Camp's interview with, 187–191
Soldiers
  mutilation of, 122, 202
  remains of, buried around

monument, 250
Solomon Valley, Kansas, settlers of,
  and DeRudio, 83
"Some of the Indian Battles and
  Battlefields," of Camp, 3
Son of the Star, 187 n, 229
Southern Cheyennes, resentment of,
  against buffalo slaughter, 13
Spotted Tail
  and Black Hills treaty violation,
    20
  people of, on reservations, 19
Squaw pulled by a lariat, and
  Thompson, 126 n
Stabbed (Stab), 184, 188–90
  hat waved by, 180–81
Standing Bear, 9
  buckskin shirt of dead soldier
    taken by, 215
  Camp's interview with, 214–15
Stanley, General, and the Sioux, 19
Stein, C. A., left at Powder river, 68
Sterland, Walter Scott, 8, 145
Sternberg, Sigismund, 4–5
  and the battle at Fort C. F. Smith,
    18
Stoker, death of, 251 n
Stover, George, 8
Streing, Frederick, death of, 118
Strike Bear, as Red Star, 180 n
Strike(s) the Lodge, 181, 184, 189, 190,
  194
Strike(s) Two, 9, 180, 181, 183, 188–90,
  194
  Camp's interview with, 183–86
Strode, Elijah T., and Varnum, 61
Sturgis, Colonel, daughter of, and
  Reno, 63
Sturgis, James G.
  bloody clothes of, found, 248
  death of, 96
  shirt of, with bullet hole, found,
    87
Summers, David, death of, 131
Sundance Creek, other names for, 66 n

T

Tall Bull, 9
  Camp's interview with, 212–13
  destruction of, and his village, 13
Tanner, James J., in water party, 115

301

190
  as Ring Cloud, Spotted Horn
    Cloud, and Round Wooden
    Cloud, 183 n
Watson, James, and Thompson, 125
Weaver, George (Cully), 145
Weaver, Henry C., 145
Weir, Thomas B.
  and communication with Custer,
    129
  company taken by, 92
  and Edgerly, 55
  impatient with Benteen, 75
  retreat covered by, 67
  support of, 62
Wells, Philip, Black Bear interpreted
    by, 203
Welsh, Mrs. H. H., 8
Wessells, Henry, 4–5
Wheelers, 145
Whipple, Jack, 8
White Bull, 9, 212
  Camp's interview with, 211
  as Ice, or Ice Bear, 211
White, Charles, 225
  gun of, taken by DeRudio, 84–85
  and Sivertsen, 141
  wounded, 134
White Bear, Russell
  Curley interpreted by, 161–65
  Goes Ahead interpreted by,
    174–75
White Clay Creek, affair of, 2
White Eagle, 188, 190
White Man (Ba chida crush), 161
  and Bouyer, 167
White Man Runs Him, 9, 246
  as Ba-tsida-crush, 178
  and Bouyer, 155
  Camp's interview with, 178–79
  escape of, 161–62
White Swan (Be da'chish), 161, 185,
    246
  bravery against Sioux, 140
  and Gerard, 155
  and Reno, 166, 172
  and Varnum, 60 n
  wounded, 126, 171, 175, 192, 226
Whitside, and Varnum, at Wounded
    Knee, 63
The Whole Buffalo (Tonhechi Tu),

180, 184, 190
Widmayer, Ferdinand, 8
  Camp's interview with, 145–46
Wiggins, O. H. P., 8
Wilber (Darcy), James W.
  wounded, 115, 120
  in water party, 115
  Camp's interview with, 148–49
William Jackson Indian Scout,
  Jackson's story in, 193 n
Winchester rifles, used by Indians, 20
Winners Of The West, "Curley The
  Crow Scout Once More" in, 155 n
Winney, De Witt, death of, 57, 67
With Custer's Cavalry, Gibson's letter
  to his wife in, 80 n
Wolf Mountain, battle of, 2
Woodruff, Charles A., 8
Woodruff, Jerry, 145
Wounded Knee
  affair of, 2
  battle of, 24
  and General Godfrey, 25
Wounded soldiers, endangered by
  arrows and bullets, 124
Wray, Colorado, battle site near,
  12–13
Wylie, George W., 8
  Camp's interview with, 129–30
  canteen of, shot, 130

Y

Yates, Zachary, 220
  company taken by, 92
  and Custer, 54
  pack train escorted by, 78
Yellow Bull, 9
Yellow Hand, affair of, 2
Young, George S., 8
Young Hawk, 9, 182, 185, 187
  Camp's interview with, 192–93
  as Striped Horn or Crazy Head,
    192 n

Z

*Zezula Or Pioneer Days in the Smoky
  Water Country,* Kellogg's diary in,
  252 n
Zigler, Eli, 8